The Reunification Express

Dedication

To Lorraine- I have no idea why she puts up with me...

ISBN 978-1-84914-258-8

British Library Cataloguing in Publication Data

The right of Mike Millard to be identified as the author of this work has been asserted in accordance with the Copyright, Designs and Patents Act of 1988

Acknowledgements

I'd like to praise the ability of my friends and family to nod in an interesting way every time I mentioned I might write a book. The self control required to avoid bursting into uncontrolled laughter before I'd left the room should be formally acknowledged.

I'd also like to particularly thank Jeffers my tame proof-reader and custodian of the correctly placed comma. His advice on investments may singularly fail but the reports he produces are always grammatically successful.

Day 1

I've always thought that one of the biggest benefits of being English is that we are automatically allowed to distrust the French. My father spent his entire life blaming them for the shrapnel lodged in his neck despite them being allies (of sorts) and him spending all of his war years in Italy. A friend of mine still cites the entire French nation as responsible for his girlfriend dumping him for a chap named Gilbert even though the amorous competitor was, in fact, Belgian. But, as we are all one big European family now, I am disinclined to take a scattergun approach to the allocation of fault. Anyway, I like my retribution to be specific. So, I'm directing my ire on a small, yet bombastic minority: French lorry drivers. In fact if the news bulletins had released his name I would be even more precise with my hatred. My distain would be directed at one particular French lorry driver. The one that decided the best way to mess with my entente cordial was to allow his lorry to catch fire in the Channel Tunnel.

He is the reason why I'm standing under the sagging Victorian canopy suspended over Farnborough station's platform. Weak yellow light from the strip lighting leaks out along its underside and creeps along a deserted stretch of concrete that will be teeming with commuters in an hour or so. But, at 5am the only other customer apart from me is the owner of a raking cough. Each of his rasping hacks sends up plumes of partially frozen germs wrapped in wispy white clouds. It's like standing next to a spluttering kettle.

It was never part of my meticulously laid out plan to be here at this foolishly early hour. My schedule, neatly typed, and tucked away somewhere in my luggage, clearly indicates I should be swathed in a warm duvet, and dreaming of becoming chess champion of a Trans-Manchurian train carriage that is gliding effortlessly across the vast openness of the Siberian Steppes.

Embarking on a train journey from Farnborough to Saigon requires a lot of planning, a modicum of imagination, and a couple of changes after Woking. If I don't get to Brussels by 16.00hrs I miss my train to Cologne. If I miss that I won't get to Moscow in time to catch my train to Beijing. This completely buggers up the leg to Hanoi and turns the timetable to Saigon into a work of fiction. To add an extra layer of complication, the validity of my visas pretty much follows my train schedule. Miss a connection, and my visas are nudged out of kilter. I've read all sorts of worrying things about Russia so I know that trying to get out of it with an expired visa is the quickest route to becoming a Gulag manager's bitch. I want to avoid this at all costs because trust me, I look awful in Cossack chaps and lipstick. I can envisage the complications. By the time I escape I'll be passport-less. The only way back to England will be the illegal immigrant route. That will almost certainly mean hiding in a French lorry and sneaking through the Tunnel. And we all know how safe French lorries are.

I didn't panic immediately I heard the news. I decided to ring Eurostar first. I find panicking to a faceless bureaucratic monolith strangely soothing. Surely all I needed to do was explain my predicament.

'...So you see, if I *don't* get to Brussels by 16.00hrs...'

'Yes, *so you said*,' interrupted a tart voice that bounced around my inner ear like a ricocheting bullet, 'but we cannot, *repeat*, cannot offer you any assurances. There will be limited services, but embarkation for ticket holders will be *strictly* on a first come, first served basis. I suggest you get to St Pancras early. I hope we'll be able to accommodate you.'

'So, what you're saying is that my original booking means nothing. If someone booked on a later train turns up and gets in the queue before me, he gets on *my* train and I don't?'

'Yes.'

'Even though I was originally booked on an earlier train.'

'Yes.'

'Yes, and I hope your arse explodes next time you sit on the toilet.' I said to a dead telephone line.

What did she care? She wasn't to know that I'd been planning this trip for more than a decade. OK, for most of those years my planning involved looking out of train windows, staring into the middle distance and adopting facial expressions more associated with trying to expel trapped wind surreptitiously, but that changed about a year ago. Following a particularly bad commuter day, in which I got home in time for bed instead of dinner, via three previously unknown stations and an expensive taxi ride, I decided it was time to get serious about my rather fuzzy travel plans.

I concluded that the first thing I needed to do was teach South West Trains a lesson so rather cunningly I resigned from my job and cashed in my season ticket. Simultaneously I wrote to their Managing Director, telling him I was fed up with being treated as a faceless commuter and that I would be taking up alternative employment as a normal human being. I ended the letter by telling him he could stick his trains up his Clapham Junction. Needless to say he didn't respond, but I'm pretty certain he was worried, because my PS told him that I would be exacting revenge.

Planning my revenge required that I immediately do lots of unpaid research. The question I wanted to answer was: how far could I get on a train without reverting to other modes of transport? Obviously, Farnborough would be my starting point. It's a town renowned for people trying to leave it. I soon discovered I could get to Japan via Vladivostok but for that I'd need to take a ferry. No good. Then I happened upon a train that runs from Hanoi to Saigon. There is no forward connection after Saigon, if you want to continue your journey on a train the only way is to go back the way you came. I quickly discovered Farnborough to Beijing was feasible and getting to Hanoi from Beijing was a breeze – on paper anyway. Getting to Saigon, I concluded, was about as far as I could go by train. I decided to go to Saigon. This would be my revenge on South West Trains. I'll explain why this might be considered revenge later.

Up to now my planning had moved ahead without incident. Then, as so often happened with my commute, it all started to go pear shaped immediately it was important that it didn't. After the lorry fire a Russian plane was reported to have crashed in Siberia, directly onto the tracks my train was scheduled to chug over on its way from Moscow to Beijing. Do you understand how unlucky that is? Russia has a landmass of 17,075,200 Sq Km. As I write that number, I realise it won't mean anything to you. That many digits are hard to visualise. You need an anchor. Think of one and a half million Wembley stadiums in concentric circles. Still struggling? OK, what about 40 million double-decker buses set out in a giant square? Now, imagine something not much wider than a single stride, threading its way through this vastness, and you'll understand how unlucky a direct hit on the tracks actually is. I've made no enquiries about the crash. If I'm forced to hate a Russian pilot, I'm going to wait until I get nearer to him.

My train pulls in and I climb aboard. Three sleeping bodies are curled up in the carriage. Spluttering kettle slumps into a seat near them and is snoozing by Brookwood. I spend the rest of the journey into Waterloo listening to the 1812 Overture in clogged sinus major, courtesy of the slumbering blocked nose quartet.

Mindful of my need to get to St Pancras quickly, and with absolutely no regard for the expense, or my neatly typed out schedule somewhere in my holdall, I take a cab. I need the cab driver with the steely eyes. The one with white knuckles who is frequently ordered to "follow that car." I get an old man wearing a tie and knitted waistcoat who immediately adopts a butler's approach to other road users. Pedestrian crossings are approached with the sort of caution you might apply to carrying a tray of sherry. Vehicles emerging from side roads are given levels of respect usually reserved for Steven Fry or Michael Parkinson. Amber lights are as good as red.

'Going away are yer?' my butler says, looking at my luggage. I peer into his cab for a glimpse of his deerstalker and magnifying glass.

'Yes, I'm taking the train to Saigon, bit of a rush to get to the Eurostar actually, problem with the connections, if I don't get to Brussels...'

'Not Saigon mate, Ho Chi Minh City now, has been for years.'

'Yes, I know, well, actually, Ho Chi Minh City is a province... I really need to get to St Pancras... fire in the tunnel...' the central district is still referred to as Sai...'

'They showed those bloody Yanks them Vietnamese, same in Iraq. Yanks can start a fight but they don't know how to win a war...'

Thankfully a beautifully renovated St Pancras station is upon us before he can expound further on American military shortcomings.

'Be lucky,' he says, as I haul my bags out onto the pavement unaided and pay an extraordinarily large bill, which needless to say, is not accounted for in my neatly typed budget, probably next to my itinerary, almost certainly somewhere in my holdall.

As I pass through the gothic entrance of St Pancras I draw upon the two most hard earned qualities I'd learned from my commuter days: tolerance and stoicism. I know they'll come in handy for the inevitable queue. When I first commuted into the City the queue I found for the underground train at Bank station was disappointing. Each morning my heart sank at the sight of five hundred rucksacks bobbing up and down on a mass of shuffling pinstripe, in a slow procession towards the platform. But, it didn't take long before I simply acknowledged the queue, joined it, and waited for the first of many rucksacks to sock me in the face.

What's in them? Women are the worst culprits. I frequently see them hauling rucksacks, bulging carrier bags, and the inevitable handbags around with them. I produce less baggage when I move house. Once on my commuter train, and I swear this is true, I witnessed a woman pull a small packet of cereal from one of her bags, a plastic bowl (with matching spoon), and a small Tupperware container filled with milk. After breakfasting she put it all away, pulled out a vanity box that folded out into a small sideboard and proceeded to do her make up. After that, she produced a thermos, had some coffee and re-did her lipstick. Finally, just before we got off, she changed her court shoes over to a pair of trainers. There must be thousands of houses up and down the country that are completely empty after female commuters leave for work.

The two giant suitcases directly in front of me in the queue obliterate my view of their owners, save for the occasional gesticulating arm. By leaning to the side I can clearly see the Eurostar ticket desks. They look tantalisingly close, I can almost touch them, but as the queuing system follows the intestinal model, I am actually over one hundred miles away.

I shuffle past a willowy man several times who is further up the intestine. He has foppish salt and pepper hair that matches a white hanky hanging limply from his breast pocket like a panting dog's tongue. He's wearing a well-fitted, dark grey, three-piece suit. The gleam of his fob watch catches my eye but it's what he's saying that gets my attention. He's with a young lady, Indian complexion, early twenties, large brown eyes, and long, shiny black hair. She's a good foot shorter. They, that is to say he, are having the most extraordinarily loud conversation.

'I think of Botham as so very *un-British*, don't you?'

'In what way Sir David?' She says, in a voice several hundred decibels lower than his.

'This desperate will to win he always displayed: quite unnecessary. After all, cricket *is* only a game.' He adds, after a short pause, 'its not as if he was that fucking good.'

Everyone with a smattering of English, between say, St Pancras and Hammersmith, looks in his direction. He is totally oblivious to his new audience. His friend feigns ignorance also. However, he doesn't entirely get away with his ennobled Tourettes Syndrome. In a great example of the British sense of priority, a lady behind him, who has been queuing for ages without a suggestion of complaining (unlike the French contingent), pipes up.

'Do you mind, my daughter doesn't want to hear that sort of language,' she says, looking down at a four-year old more interested in the content of her nose than the noble Lord's vocabulary.

'Oh, my dear lady, I'm dreadfully sorry.' He, places his arm across his chest and offers a small bow, then turns to his olive skinned friend, and in a stage whisper that could be heard by anyone within the M25 says, 'did I swear? I don't recall.'

Thirty minutes later I'm at the desk handing over my ticket. Within ten minutes I'm seated in a near empty carriage that stays that way as we pull out of the station at the scheduled time. I find it more than ironic that Eurostar stick assiduously to the revised timetable and as a result leave half empty. Meanwhile thousands of people queuing on the other side of the barrier continue shuffling. Still, I make a mental note to phone Eurostar and apologise for willing their operator's backside to explode.

Settling back into my seat I look out of the window at a dank London morning as it gives way to a misty Kent countryside, and then the darkness of the tunnel, before emerging into a rainy French morning. The blurry French countryside offers little distraction so I lean back and give thought to the extra five hours I'll have in Brussels, and how I might fill them. No easy task in a city who's main claim to fame is it's headquartering of a thieving bunch of well-expensed junketeers who make important decisions on the optimum size of a carrot.

I hate anything bureaucratic. Even the word bureaucracy is ludicrously difficult to spell. And I'm ever wary of organisations that keep changing their names. It used to be the Common Market, then the EEC, then at some point they dropped an E, then it became the EU. Why? Dodgy double-glazing firms used to do that. That said I am still feeling well disposed towards Brussels. After all, at five o'clock this morning I was desperate to get there.

Upon arrival I resolve to make the most of it so I dump my gear with a man at left luggage, who surely doubles up as Santa at Christmas, and head into town. My phone informs me rather belatedly that I'm in Belgium, offers to change my clock, and asks me if I want to take advantage of Daylight Saving Time. This is the only service I've ever been offered free by my mobile phone supplier so I accept. I then get a barrage of messages from friends enquiring, well more hoping, to find I'm still in St Pancras. I decide to think of suitably witty ripostes when seated at a picturesque cafe, while being served strong coffee by the future Miss Belgium. She will undoubtedly be modelling her swimwear.

I've always thought that one of the big advantages of train travel over flying is that you arrive in the heart of a city. When you fly you get a birds eye view and then usually sneak up on your destination via a ring road. Brussels Midi station easily challenges my view. Compared to the litter strewn square I make my way across, the ring road might have offered a more attractive vista. But, on the plus side the sun is threatening to shine and the day, like my mood, is warming a little.

Needless to say I don't have a map. Brussels was originally a twenty-minute pit stop on my way to Cologne, as indicated on my meticulously researched timetable. The one safely tucked away in a side pocket of the luggage I left with Father Christmas. I dive into a side road for no other reason than it is there.

I zig zag down streets that have a mildly menacing feel about them. They are chocked with cars that are going nowhere. These are double and triple parked, some partially on pavements, others deposited on small roundabouts. It's like a parking scene you might find if you gave a child three hundred toy cars to play with and then called him in for lunch an hour later. Put my local traffic warden on commission and let him loose here and he could retire before his first tea break. The only thing in more abundance than cars is litter. It's everywhere, dancing about in the mild breeze and finding temporary refuge in the doorways of shops that look like they never open. They are universally shabby. Naked, or partially clothed mannequins stare out at me from their windows with expressions of indifference that seem totally appropriate to the surroundings. This is not an easy area to like. The only person I see is an aged owner of a grocery shop leaning against his doorway. Smoking a cigarette, he occasionally coughs up great hoolies into the road. As I pass, deftly avoiding lake phlegm, I notice the fruit laid out on his shelves is more wrinkled than he is.

I wonder why there are so few people about considering the number of cars. But, the deeper into the streets I travel the more people I see. They look predominantly Arab and African and most of the women are wearing headscarves. Nearly all the men are smoking. Before long I happen upon a wide boulevard, which leads me into a far more affluent looking part of town.

Desperate for a coffee and a sneaky peak at Miss Belgium in her Lycra two-piece, I settle down in a cafe called Grimbergen. Its terrace offers a perfect view of a five-way junction. The narrow roads that meet here do so from outrageously oblique angles. From the sky it would look like a starfish stretching out a yawn. Belgium is not known for road rage, but if it ever catches on it will be at this junction. I sit at a pseudo granite topped table full of anticipation. The early morning cloud has dissipated leaving a gloriously blue sky in its place. I've only travelled a few hundred miles but I can already feel years of commuting torture being scratched from my memory banks. Most people I know can't quite grasp why I'm doing this trip. When I tell them it's all about revenge they display the usual outward signs of interest, nodding, the odd um-hum. Inwardly, I detect the feelings that people often adopt when they talk about the loss of a pet dog.

For years I've suffered at the hands of trains. As a commuter they teased me no end. They'd run on time for weeks, then, whenever it was imperative they run on time, they didn't. They'd either not turn up at all, or arrive late. Or, and this proves just how evil they are, collect me on time and then breakdown on a remote piece of track twenty minutes later. I know what you're thinking. If I hate trains so much, how will travelling 10,000 miles on them exact revenge? But you see that's the point. I worked out that in a commuting year I spent about twenty days travelling to work on trains. That's almost an entire February sitting on a machine taking me to places I didn't want to go. Travelling to Saigon will take me about twenty days. By undertaking a journey I wanted to take I'll have grabbed a February back. Understand now? No, I didn't think you would.

Miss Belgium is about sixty, has a beer gut, and owns a nicotine stained moustache thicker than a Victorian butcher's sideburn. I mark down Belgium's chances of winning the Miss World crown but still think they'll finish above Greece. I order a coffee and while I wait for it's arrival I track a pedestrian who hasn't worked out that five roads converge on the piece of land he's decided is a suitable place to light a cigarette. He avoids a collision with a speeding motorcyclist in the same casual manner the French ignore queues. Being the only incident of any note, I pull out three weeks wages to settle my bill (why is coffee so expensive in European cafes) and make my way over to Le Grand Place for no other reason than anything grand must be worth a gander.

Walking into the cobbled square, the first thing I notice, if we're measuring by scale, is it isn't grand at all. That's not to say it isn't picturesque, enclosed as it is by ancient buildings on every side. The obligatory cafes spread out into the square under deep red canopies and the autumnal sun produces splashes of weak shade but the promise of warmth isn't quite being delivered. Upon entry I bring the average age of the people in the Square down to ninety-eight. The place is packed with American retirees being herded around like cows with Bovine TB. Just like underground trains you hear them before you see them. I latch on to a particularly verbose lot wearing bright yellow baseball caps emblazoned with 'Retirees of Wisconsin' above the peak. Most of them have mauve sweatshirts stretched over whatever they put on that morning, with the legend 'European Tour 2008' in fluorescent green across the chest. American retirees are backpackers on Prozac.

This bunch is circling a man holding a furled umbrella above his head. They are leaning in and hanging on his every word, probably so they can regurgitate it loudly at dinner later. I sidle up a little closer and listen in.

'Zee Archduchess Isabella of Spain, following her visit to the Square in September 1599, wrote "Never have I zeen zomesing zo beautiful and exquisite as zee town square of zee city where zee town hall rises up into zee sky. Zee decoration of the houses is most remarkable".

'Was she the daughter of Filip, the first, or second?' asks a lady balancing a baseball cap on her blue tinged perm. The guide pretends he hasn't heard her and soldiers on with his script. She whispers to the man next to her, who is sucking a mint, 'I don't think this guy knows much Henry.' Henry nods the nod that people employ when being given directions in a foreign language. 'I think it must be the second Filip, because I'm sure he died in 1598, or thereabouts.'

She turns back to the guide. 'How old was Isabella when she visited?' The guide ignores her again. 'See Henry this guy doesn't know a thing.'

I want to stay longer to enjoy her persistence but some of the retirees rumble me as the interloper I am, so I peel off.

I wander off in search of further distraction. A closer inspection of the people in the Square shows significant numbers of craned necks, indicating that all the action is up, which indeed it is. The architecture is regal, with ornate porticoes arching over regimentally lined stained glass windows. Cornices this intricate deserve some attention, unless you are Japanese. Then the dray horses attached to the beer cart get precedence. Don't get me wrong, as examples of dray horses, these are at the top of their game. It just seems strange to me. Why travel thousands of miles to a monumentally historical Square and end up beguiled by an equine scene that is not even historically accurate?

But, perhaps this is not as strange as the man who has placed his camera on a ledge, set it to auto-timer and is sprinting to a pre-determined position to pose in front of it. He makes several dashes, changing the camera position slightly each time. Eventually, after a quick inspection of the camera preview pane he smiles, indicating he's happy with the result. Sad bastard I think, travelling alone, no one to take a picture of him, until I realise I'm travelling alone, with no one to take a picture of me. I leave the Square in search of the companionship of a crusty baguette.

Munching away I wander the streets. What strikes me is the lack of building cranes. This is something the older European cities have in common. They look finished. It seems to me that London is the only European capital to continually shed it skin. Brussels just says, here I am: take it or leave it. I decide on the latter and head back to the station. My train isn't leaving for ages but I like the transient nature of stations. I find a seat in a café and watch the ebb and flow of different nationalities. I don't need knowledge of a foreign tongue: bewilderment translates well into any language.

Not that I need intuition to understand the American in Sam's café. I assume from the volume he is related to one of the Wisconsin Retirees, maybe a son. The eatery is a typical buffet style cafeteria offering pastries and sandwiches that look like they've seen a ghost. Within minutes I know every detail of the latest deal he's trying to pull off.

'Thirty million dollars? What's the point in worrying about ten percent? Geez, the total spend will be more than a hundred mill for christsakes...' he bellows into his phone. I wonder if he's talking to the Lord who nearly broke my eardrums in the queue at St Pancras. A conversation between those two would crack granite.

A group of older travellers shuffle up and settle down around me. The men guard the bags while the women head off to the buffet. English. Only the English divide labour in this way.

'You keep an eye on the bags dear, pickpockets...' a grey haired old lady says to her grey haired old husband. She says pickpockets in a stage whisper, employing every part of her mouth. 'I'll get the tea. Tea all right dear?' She's gone before he can mumble a reply. The men get talking about Thalys trains, which catches my interest. My train to Cologne will be a Thalys.

'Did you travel 1st class?' a tall octogenarian says to a sprightly seventy year old who is looking at some pictures on his digital camera. 'No? Oh dear, you didn't get the ham sandwiches then.'

'Sturdy.' The seventy year old says, taking the lack of ham sandwiches in his stride.

'Oh yes,' the octogenarian says. 'Sturdier than the wife.' He starts laughing, which turns into a coughing fit.

'Excuse me,' I say. 'Are you on your way somewhere, or heading home?'

'Home.' The octogenarian said, 'just waiting for the Eurostar.

Good luck I think. The ladies soon return and I spent an enjoyable twenty minutes discussing their travels and watching them extricate sticky cake from their bottom plates. One of the ladies asks me where I'm going.

'Saigon.' I say.

'Just you?' she says.

'Well, I'm sure there'll be other people there…' I reply.

Brussels station is semi-subterranean, with shops and food outlets living cheek by jowl under the platforms above. The station personnel are dressed for a Hansel and Gretel fairy tale. I have a passing interest in railway uniforms. I like the way they vary from continent to continent. Asia leans towards the militaristic. In mainland Europe they look like Santa's helpers. In the UK they dress in anything that will show up a sweat stain.

I just have time to eat before I board my train to Cologne from platform five. The nearest eatery is called "Wok Away." Walk away would have been a more appropriate name, but I don't know if the Thalys has a buffet car so force down noodles so oily I could have drunk them.

My Thalys pulls out of the station bang on time, the cloud I'd encountered earlier in the day has found me again and is busy covering the blue sky I'd enjoyed in Brussels. I find a young lady in my seat. She's having an animated conversation with two other ladies on the other side of the aisle. She garbles something at me in German. I smile. She repeats it in French. I smile wider and turn my head slightly. Eventually I work out that she wants my seat to be near her friends. I sit near the window. Seconds later she and her friends get up and disappear to the buffet car. She points to her, that is to say, my seat and says in perfect English.

'I'll be back.'

Arnold Schwarzenegger's younger sister? The train began life in Paris so is more lived in than my Eurostar, but otherwise, apart from the livery, which is a deep red, it's remarkably similar. I can hear a few English voices, or more accurately Birmingham accents, but the other passengers are German. Without the benefit of language it's very easy to tell them apart. The Germans have hampers of food and wines spread out on the tables. The Brummies have beer and crisps purchased at the station.

The foreign voices make me feel like I'm really travelling now and things are starting to look different outside the window too. The hideous buildings along the track are thankfully adorned with graffiti to soften the pain on my eyes. I've often noticed that the best graffiti is found on the most appalling buildings, and I can assure you there are some truly wonderful works of art on the way out of Brussels. Most of the buildings are empty commercial units and the tangle of overhead cables simply add to a redundant industrial vista. It's so ugly that when the landscape changes to flat arable farmland I find myself being mesmerised by it. I don't usually get so enchanted by a field full of wheat.

Arnie's sister comes back just before Aachen and is considerably friendlier than when she left.

'Are you OK?' She asks for no apparent reason and slumps down in her, that is to say, my seat.

'Excuse me, ver are you travelling to?'

'Saigon.' I reply.

'Sai...' she giggles and fires off some quick-fire verbal to her friends. They giggle too. 'Vey get off at Aachen.'

I forgive her English pronunciation. After all my German sounds like Herr Flick's from 'Allo 'Allo, but I distinctly catch a slur. This is quickly followed by a whiff of her breath when she asks me if I speak German. She's been drinking. I'd given up my seat to a lush. The seat I could have been luxuriating in while she's been knocking back German lager and Jagermeister shots. All this booze, ironically enough, has given her Dutch courage and she jabbers on for ages in a sort of Eng-man-ish. At no point does she expect me to reply, which is just as well because the sentences falling from her mouth land on my ears in the most abstract form. It is like having a conversation with a Salvador Dali's painting.

Aachen couldn't come quickly enough. Her and her friends gather up their belongings, hitting heads and each other as they pull them from the rack and totter up the aisle. Their sideways motion has nothing to do with the natural movement of the train. As we pull away Arnie's sister waves at me from the platform with the enthusiasm of a drowning swimmer.

Not much later I find myself in a bar at Cologne station. This is another semi-subterranean world. Earlier I'd tried to blag my way into the first class lounge of Deutsche Bahn railways.

'Zis ticket does not allow you access,' the jobsworth said on reception, before dismissing me with a well timed tut.

Never mind Cologne station is full of interesting diversions. I start with the left luggage system, which being German, I assume will be incredibly efficient. It's totally automated, a sort of valet parking for baggage. The machines are dotted all over the station and on the surface are about the size of a medium sized car. Underneath is a sophisticated underground storage depot. I read the instructions carefully and put my money in as instructed, which it efficiently swallows.

The instructions tell me where to place my bag. I do as I'm told. It efficiently swallows it and I wave auf wiedersehen to every pair of pants I own apart from the ones I'm wearing. Now I just have to wait for my code to be allocated so I can retrieve my pants later. Nothing. This is followed by more nothing, which in turn is followed by even more nothing. To be fair, it's the most efficient nothing I have ever experienced but it isn't helping with the concern I now feel for my pants. I press every button available to me and am rewarded with a slight cough and the return of my bag. My money however, refuses to make an appearance, but the fact I have a full compliment of pants puts a spring into my step. I decide to put my bag to good use as a footstool in a bar that is decked out like Germans would expect an English bar to be decked out like, that is to say, Irish.

Earlier, in my travels around the station I hadn't heard a word of English but at least I could make an educated guess on the written language. Soon I'll be in Russia where I won't even recognise the letters. What does a top hat next to a squiggle over a set of parallel lines mean? Once settled at a table I hear the dulcet tones of Jasper Carrot and his relatives. I'm distracted from eavesdropping on why the young female Brummie, with the ponytail and tattooed arms, thinks that cider isn't as gassy as lager, by a woman opposite me. My distraction has long grey hair in no particular form. Her complexion is deep red like the large glass of wine the waitress regularly tops up. Her round face is bereft of makeup and plain, like her clothes. She's wearing black jogging bottoms, white pumps and a green tee shirt under an angler's jacket that has more pockets than a snooker table. The watch on her left wrist has such an oversized dial that the young lady we left in Aachen could probably have made out the time on it.

In front of her is an enormous plate of food. This, I suspect, is where the EU potato mountain ended up. Next to the snow white mashed up tubers is an equally large hill of mince. They are kept apart by a gully that is partially filled with a stream of cabbage and carrots. She is methodically working her way through each pile. First a fork full of potato, then mince, then vegetables. After completing a set of each, she puts her fork down and celebrates with a slug of wine. She then repeats the whole process. Her eyes shrink into her face with every mouthful she shovels in. They then reappear, with a slightly surprised look, just before the next load is stuffed in. It's like watching someone eat the Pennines. I am transfixed and find myself gulping my lager in unison with her shovelling. Each time I think she's going to give up she picks up the fork and carries on. I find the delivery of food to her mouth so metronymic it makes me drowsy.

After she finishes eating she moves to a strange burping phase. There are a series of internal eruptions that make her chest rise up a level each time they occur. Eventually the pressure is so great she lets fly. Some burps resound so deeply they make the wine in her glass ripple. Others come in quick fire coughs, like burps doing hurdles. As a grand finale she lets out a rasping fart and asks for the bill.

I have to admit to feeling a little nervous waiting for the train that will be my home for the next two nights. It's taking me away from the Europe that is familiar and into one that has incomprehensible writing, a penchant for flared trousers, bushy moustaches and the Eurovision Song Contest.

My first encounter with the East is not very encouraging. I track down carriage nine and hand my ticket to a blond lady. She has a bobbed hairstyle and boobs so big she could never do a forward roll. Next to her is a larger and older brunette, and next to the brunette is a man with the sort of belly you used to see on 1970s darts players. They are all dressed in electric blue overcoats with black epaulets and ornate gold buttons. I resist the urge to salute. The blond one scrutinises my ticket and hands it to the man. He looks at it like a solicitor viewing a contract and passes it to the brunette. She scrutinises it further and then scrutinises me. Curling her lip, she reviews the ticket more closely, and then reviews me more closely. After another lip curl she hands the ticket back to the blond.

'Da,' the blond says and they step aside so I can struggle aboard unaided with my luggage.

The carriage corridor is painted green, which makes me feel like I'm walking down the inside of a Gordon's Gin bottle. Picture windows along the right hand side are curtained and the cabins are on the left, unless you're coming from the other direction that is. Numbers are on a small plaque on the wall beside each door. My target is berth twenty-two and I find it half way down. Peeking inside I discover a woman divesting herself of a very large purple rucksack. She is tall and gangly with a cropped haircut that looks like it would give you a nasty cut if you patted her head. She turns to face me and I get my first view of her piggish, black eyes. Slowly, she looks me up and down and after sufficient scanning, adopts the sort of expression you'd find on a llama that's just realised what a vet has to do to check for a breached birth. Her mauve leggings, thicker than chain mail, crinkle just above her knee as she draws herself to full height. Mentally I have already filed her under V for vegan and cross-sectioned the file with my extensive notes on lesbianism.

'Hello,' I say, smiling and placing my bag on the seat opposite her.

'Women don't share with men,' she says directing her eyes to a point over my left shoulder.

I'm not sure if this is a manifesto statement or a reference to our current arrangement. Ever keen to avoid a rape charge I apologise and go back to check with the Provodnitsa, as they like to call them in these parts.

'Excuse me, there is a vegan in berth twenty two, she says they don't share,' I say.

She looks me up and down in the same way a coffin maker might and shoos me away, rattling off some Russian that sounds to my untrained ear like 'fuck off you soft Westerner, can't you see I'm busy standing here doing nothing.' I thank her with all my heart for her unstinting dedication to customer service, which may have sounded to her untrained ear as 'fuck off yourself you cabbage eating, unfeasibly mammaried dwarf.' I traipse back to my cabin sharer. Perhaps if I promise to hang my bollocks outside the cabin overnight she might trust me not to pick the lock of her chastity belt.

When I get back I find my bags outside a firmly shut door. I'm about to tell her through the gap at the bottom of the door that I'd find an alligator in suspenders more sexually alluring, when I realise her cabin houses berths twenty and twenty one. Twenty-two is next door. It is with some relief I pick up my bags and shuffle along to it.

Inside is a man so big he has his own orbit. I pause to consider how he got in. He looks well settled and in no hurry to acknowledge me standing outside. I assume he's been on the train from its original destination somewhere in the German hinterland. Because there is only an inch of free cabin space I remain outside and cough, simultaneously holding up my ticket.

'Twenty two, we're sharing mate.'

He stands up, which to be honest is not a fair description. Try this.

Imagine the construction of a skyscraper being filmed over a year and then replayed so it fits into a thirty second film. The cabin is 8 X 7. He is 8 X 6.5. He can only stand erect by coordinating movement with exhalation. His arms are so thick only one can be accommodated in the cabin at a time. When he turns towards me it's like watching a super-tanker change direction in a duck pond.

Squashing himself against the window he offers me the lower bunk I'd booked and paid for. I squeeze my bags past him and rest them on it. I fleetingly consider the ability of the upper bunk to hold his weight, but I'm knackered, its late, and I need some sleep.

But I'm not going to get any yet though, as before I can follow my bags into the cabin he must make up his bed. He methodically sets about this task using the packet of sheets and blankets provided by the train company. I stand in the corridor eyeing a gigantic carrier bag by the table and wonder what he's got in it. I continue to stand in the carriage and watch the other cabins fill up. There are eighteen, all occupied with Russians apart from the harridan filed under V, cross-sectioned lesbianism. The last person to arrive is a man who looks like Dustin Hoffman's character in Rain Man, sporting a leather jacket, polyester trousers and a rather disconcerting mumble. He opens the vegan's door. She immediately delivers the women don't share spiel. He ups the mumbling and shuffles back down the corridor, coming back a few moments later with the brunette Provodnitsa. She sticks her head into the harridan's cabin and shouts something in Russian. I'm no expert but I think it was along the lines of him looking more feminine than her. She throws Dustin in like a piece of hand luggage. So much for woman not sharing then.

Despite it being a little after midnight my sharer shows no desire to settle down on his bunk. Instead he makes himself comfortable on the stool next to the small table near the window. At least there is now sufficient room for me to sit on my bunk. I sit on my bunk. Silence. Maybe he's shy. I decide to kick things off.

'Hi, I'm Mike.'

Nothing. I point to my chest and up the volume a bit. 'Mike, Mikail, as in Gorbachev.'

His face takes on the look of someone attempting to assemble a piece of flat pack furniture without the instructions.

'Janet,' he says

'Janet.' I repeat. 'Nice… Janet, OK.'

Listen, if a man built like an armoured car wants to be known as Janet that's fine by me. We lapse into another frenzied bout of silence. I think the effort of the last exchange may have taken it out of him. He digs into his unfeasibly large carrier bag and pulls out an unfeasibly large bottle of beer. Swiftly opened, he downs the contents in four gulps. He silently works his way through another five. I make a mental note to sleep with my trousers on and one eye open.

Sneaking a closer look, I'd say he's about 30, which is not far off middle aged for a Russian male. He has dark blond hair, thick enough to knit a jumper with, and a strong jaw line breaking up an otherwise oval shaped head. He's dressed simply in a grey cap-sleeved tee shirt, jogging bottoms and white socks in a pair of plastic sandals. Despite the twenty first century attire it's easy to picture him in the siege of Leningrad killing a German paratrooper with his bottle opener.

After taking his empties to the bin at the end of the corridor he decides he's ready for bed, clambers up onto the top bunk while simultaneously sliding the door shut and locking it. He knocks the cabin light out leaving me bathed in the weak light of my bedside lamp. He's snoring gently when I turn it off. Sleep comes to me quickly.

Day 2

I wake late after a fitful night. The bed was about as comfortable as a sack of spanners. I had to turn every couple of hours to stop the ball joints in my hips from wearing down. We never closed the curtains last night so in my many waking moments I was aware of our passing through stations. The platform lights flashed across the bare wall opposite my bed like the end of a film spool running through a projector. Some stations we stopped at I recognised immediately, Berlin about 5.30 am, Poznan at 7.30 am, but most were just a jumble of letters.

Janet is still growling quietly as I sit up and take a look out of the window. The passing landscape is grey, like the sky, which is leaden and threatening rain. Poland seems to be closed. Perhaps the rumours are true and they are all in Southampton. Very few people are out. The houses, or more commonly apartment blocks, look semi-derelict, many having no discernible roads reaching them. Cars look abandoned on muddy paths and nearly every wall has graffiti on it. Maybe Bankski lives here. I head for the bathroom.

Describing it as a bathroom is being a little generous. There is a toilet, which I make use of. It opens directly onto the track and if you want to recreate the severity of the updraft try sticking your arse out of a plane window at 50,000 feet. Indeed the ferocity of updraft is such that I momentarily worry that the results of my labours may not be sufficiently weighty to make it through. Anything lighter than lead has the potential to come back and pebble dash the toilet walls.

The sink is the size of a mango cut in half and plug-less. It has one of those ridiculous taps that you have to depress at the top to get the water to run out of the bottom. Well, that's the theory. In reality the water disappears long before you can get your hands under the tap. It's like trying to catch air. As a result I wash one handed, using the other to permanently hold down the top of the tap.

I get back to my cabin to find Janet has opened the bar early and is working his way through a breakfast consisting of yoghurt, bread and butter, jam, a whole cucumber, some tomatoes and milk. He drinks the milk in between slugs of beer. I delve into my bag and proudly pull out two bananas. Two bananas later, I'm still hungry so head off in search of the buffet car.

Using Janet's stashed provisions as a benchmark it's easy to understand why there might only be the waiter and me in the buffet car. It's quite pleasantly decked out, with an Italian bistro thing going on and a small bar at one end. I read, while meticulously planning my trip, and am sure I will have notes attached to my schedule to this effect, that buffet cars are always provided by the country through which they travel. So, despite the Italian influence this is Polish. The waiter is too.

I'd passed some luxurious looking cabins to get here and was beginning to think that my first class ticket wasn't first class at all so I collar the waiter.

'I'm in carriage nine, is that first class?' I ask.

'Yrse,' he says in the strangulated way Poles say yes.

'So what are carriages four and five then?'

'Better than first class.'

How can you get better than first class? Why wasn't I offered it? Why is the waiter taking my menu away?

'Breakfast finished.'

'Already?'

'Yrse.'

'What can I have then?'

'Polish breakfast.'

I agree to the Polish breakfast instead of breakfast. Westerners would know it as watery scrambled eggs. When it arrives it sits on my plate like a drunken jellyfish and slides from side to side en masse every time the train takes a bend.

Back at the cabin I find Janet winding down his third beer, the empties regimentally placed in a row on the table.

'Just had breakfast,' I say. He nods and turns back to the table. I sit down and look out of the window. For the last two hours we've been alternating between a sort of muddy Peckham in February and the Yorkshire Dales. It's been like watching a bleak, black and white Scoobie Doo background repeat itself over and over. I sit back on my sack of spanners and make a mental list of the things I know about Poland. It's not much. They were one of the first countries to experience a German Blitzkrieg, which can't have been much fun. Our resulting declaration of war against Germany made Hitler very angry but no matter, the bravery of Polish pilots during the Battle of Britain helped to ensure our sovereignty, and meant their grandchildren could come to England sixty years later and undercut our plumbers. Somewhere in between these events a bloke with a moustache bushier than a fox brush, called Lech, stood up to the country's Soviet puppet leaders. This was way before it was fashionable to disagree with your local communist government. So there is a lot to admire about the nature of the people. Anyone who undercuts UK plumbers is OK by me.

Throughout the morning we've been stopping to let people off. The vegan lost her chap early, but only after he'd spent a full hour watching a loosely connected light bulb flicker in the corridor. This, presumably, constitutes entertainment in Poland, or maybe it's simply more interesting than watching the face of a thousand scowls dress under a pile of blankets. By mid morning there's only the carpet munching vegan, Janet and me left in the entire carriage. That's one Provodnitsa each. Not that we've seen much of them. I spotted them having breakfast together on my way to the bathroom, a veritable feast that put Janet's spread to shame. And I've heard them continuously chatting, clinking glasses and so on. But I've only actually seen them when we stop at a station. As soon as we pull away, the uniforms are replaced with tracksuit bottoms, loose shirts and slippers followed by a retreat back to their cabin for more glass clinking. Occasionally I catch one emerging to keep the samovar topped up with water and enough coal to heat it. This, I suspect is more for their benefit than ours.

The samovar is an interesting contraption. It's a sort of cross between a tea urn and an inter-ballistic missile. It's basically a load of cylinders, of varying sizes, connected by an intricate web of brass piping. Everything eventually feeds to a nozzle with a small black handle. Pull the handle down and you get hot water. Useful if someone needs to give birth unexpectedly. I have an innate ability to break machines simply by touching them, so I've avoided the temptation thus far to use it. I'm worried I might press the wrong button and send us into orbit around Janet.

The scenery outside is changing. Not only is the sky much bluer, the vista is more rural and surprisingly, more prosperous. I spot new BMWs and sports utility vehicles. Houses now outnumber apartments. Some are clearly new builds and others have new extensions or shiny new roofs of bright blue or resplendent red coloured slates. Their shape is much steeper than we would have in the West, presumably to make it easier for snow to fall off. Smoke drifts out of many of the chimneys and the surrounding gardens are given over entirely to the cultivation of vegetables.

Every plot encourages my stereotypical view by growing cabbages. Most are the size of beach balls. I can't really describe these places as towns, more like hamlets. The stations that we pass are a linguists delight. One is called Wschodnia. How do you pronounce that? My inclination is towards something like Skodnia. And if I'm right, why have the W? I ask Janet.

'How do you pronounce that?' I say pointing to the station sign.

'Polska,' he replies, and turns back to his beer. Helpful.

I go back to watching and thinking. I'm enjoying the act of travelling very much. I ponder the thought that metaphorically speaking my whole journey is a sentence and these towns are commas. Saigon is a full stop, but it is so far away it's not on my radar yet. I've probably already travelled around a thousand miles, but that isn't even half way to Moscow. It's only about a tenth of the total mileage I'll cover. The immensity of the distances catches my imagination and I get out my calculator.

I originally planned this trip because it will take the same amount of time I used to lose commuting each year. I'd always thought of this in terms of days. But I hadn't considered the mileage angle. I quickly calculate my weekly commuting mileage in England at about four hundred miles. So in pure mileage terms I've already got back about two and a half weeks of commuting mileage. This is good news. I make another calculation. The total mileage for the trip, excluding my flight home, is about ten thousand miles. Under my mileage formula that's twenty five weeks of wasted commuting time retrieved and equates to almost six years worth of actual commuting.

My brief reconnection with maths, like the train, comes to an abrupt halt. I can't work out why. We are not at a station as such, more a siding. There are a few muddy paths leading away from it but that's it. I spot Mr Fat Belly Provodnik scurrying down one of them. Fifteen minutes later he comes scurrying back up with two heavy carrier bags. Fifteen minutes after that I smell cooking coming from their den. I suspect we stopped so he could go shopping for provisions. Cooked cabbage smells waft along the corridor causing Janet to sniff the air like a sommelier and me to think of school. His nostrils decide its time for lunch and his brain quickly follows. Pulling his large bag towards him he digs out a large, half eaten garlic sausage, a packet of ham, some fresh black bread (where did he get that?), another whole cucumber, which he demolishes in four bites, a selection of pastries, and a packet of biscuits that look like brown paving slabs. I pull out a banana, and then, feeling inadequate, pull out another. He washes down his repast with a couple of large beers, burps, and climbs on to his bunk for a siesta. I gently dab the corner of my mouth with a napkin, take the banana skins to the bin, and settle back on my bunk for a think. We will soon be at the border crossing into Belarus. I've heard all sorts of scare stories. Most involve heavily armed, vodka-fuelled veterans of Russia's Afghanistan adventure and a latex glove. My UK travel agent offered me some sage advice on this regions border crossings before I left.

'Mike, customs officials are always right.' She said, before suggesting I might benefit from a little preparation when it came to the currency declaration that both Belarus and Russia ask for. Naturally, they need to know what money I arrive with and how much I'm leaving with. In between these two administrative events, I can do what I like with it, so long as I keep all the receipts and can account for every penny. I asked her for a little clarification.

'Would a nicely formatted Excel spreadsheet do, or should I invest in a full Sage accounting package?

'Oh, no Mike, in practise you just need to jot down an approximation on the declaration form.' Then, in whispered tones that only served to add menace, she said, 'but don't count your money out in front of them. You have to remember the cash you're likely to be carrying may not mean much to you, but it will be a fortune to them.'

My mild paranoia of ex communist states is not helped by the fact that I grew up in the 1970s. The Cold War was at its height and scare stories were in The Sun most weeks. One such article mapped out what effect a nuclear explosion would have. Greenham Common, a base for American nuclear missiles, was used as the central target point and concentric circles were drawn at distances of twenty mile radii. According to The Sun I would have survived a blast in Farnborough but spent the rest of my life skinless.

Of course, times have changed. Poland is part of the Common, EEC, EC, EU Market now. My local town even has a Polish cafe. Poland is, in the International sense, a neighbour. But anything East of Poland makes me nervous. Which is why my heart beats a little faster when we pull up at a siding at a Terespol. The weather has turned drizzly, the sky is blanketed with grey clouds, and the straggly grass growing through the tracks to the side of the train all add up to put me on edge.

A gang of storm troopers steam through the carriages wearing full battle dress, belts full of guns, phones. Walkie-talkies crackle static. They take a look in each cabin and then disappear. It wakes Janet from his gentle snooze and he dismounts from his bunk and pulls out his passport from his jacket hanging by the door. It must be customs, but I'm not sure whose customs. I've been travelling through Poland for most of the day.

They're part of the EU and the train has come from another EU country. Presumably, I think, we don't need to clear Polish customs. Then there is a burst of activity from the Provodnitsas. They scurry between cabins, offloading bags of clinking contraband in occupied cabins. The brunette bungs one in ours and rattles off some Russian to Janet, who simply nods and opens a beer. She then asks me something. I can't understand her, so she asks Janet something and nods at me, looks back at him, tuts and leaves. Before I can apologise for not learning to speak Russian fluently overnight I am interrupted by the arrival of a far more sinister looking delegation.

These men are in more formal uniforms, still armed to the teeth, and unsmiling. One of them stands in the doorway and barks out an order that I don't understand. I assume he wants my passport and I hand it over. He scrutinises the cover and looks at me. I look back and smile. He doesn't. He turns to his compatriot.

'Grit Britin en Norturn Earland?' His partner nods. He repeats the last bit with more stress, 'Norturn Earland? His friend nods again, impatiently, and takes it from him. They take Janet's also and disappear with both. I watch him disembark and walk off to an office with my passport in a transparent document sleeve under his armpit. I think about latex gloves and whether I've got clean pants on.

'Russian?' I say to Janet nodding in their direction. He shakes his head.

'Byelorussian?' He shakes his head again.

'Polska,' he says, finally, to avoid my working my way through all the other nations of the former USSR.

I can't really get to grips with this. Why are we going through Polish immigration? I want to ask someone, but the vegan has her door shut again and no one else speaks English. So I wait with sweaty palms and try to think positive thoughts. Then the train pulls off. I still don't have my passport. Inwardly I panic like mad, but outwardly I offer an air of mild curiosity and do what the British always do when facing catastrophe. I apologise. Knocking on the Provodnitsa's door, which is already open, I address the Blond Bob.

'I'm really sorry to bother you but we appear to be moving off and I don't have my passport.' She looks me up and down contemptuously, throws her head back and tuts at the same time.

'My passport you see, they still have it...'

The carpet-munching lesbian pops her head out of her cabin.

'You'll get it back at the station.'

'Oh, really, what station?'

'The one were pulling into now,' she says before shutting her door again.

I turn to apologise again for having the temerity to speak to a fucking carriage attendant who has probably not seen her feet in twenty years, but she's already opening the carriage door and stepping on to the platform. Within minutes the man with the fascination for Northern Ireland hands me my passport back and we pull away. Shortly afterwards the brunette comes to my cabin. I think she wants her contraband and I point to the bag she gave us earlier. She waves my gesture away and shouts something at me. I'm about to tell her that I'm sorry for being rude to her mate due to my being worried about my passport and the orifice I shit out of, when she garbles off another lot of nonsense.

'Look,' I say in a slow, deliberate voice, 'there is no point you shouting at me, I still won't understand you. I am English...'

'An - glee skee?' An - glee - skee?' Its like a big penny dropping, that induces her to rattle off something like 'rabbit, fart, pumpkin, mince, angle-poise lamp,' and scamper off. She comes back with a customs entry form for Belarus - in Russian.

'No, I'm English - An - glee - skee.'

She looks at the declaration, tuts, like I'm the idiot who bought the wrong form, and waddles off again. A few minutes later I've completed my English declaration, no questions left unanswered, crosses and not ticks, in appropriate boxes, and a signature that fits neatly into the space provided. It's all done in duplicate, as ordered. My money declaration is complete, although I haven't told them about the Chinese currency, English Pounds or American Dollars currently decaying in the money belt that's chafing my groin.

When the train stops again I am aware of a hairy and vicious looking Alsatian, before the Navy Seals become visible. They have dark blue military caps, matching tops and trousers tucked into heavy black combat boots. They all carry the expression of people who've sat on a hot iron but are hell bent on not letting you know they have. My passport disappears for the second time in ten minutes along with my incredibly neat customs and money declaration forms. They now have more paperwork to review than the average Child Support Agency officer, so I settle back and expect a long wait. I'm not even surprised when the train sets off again, although, watching Janet change hurriedly into a pair of jeans is mildly interesting. In a purely biblical sense, you understand. He adds a couple of sweaters, then steps into the corridor and pulls on his heavy jacket. If he'd put it on inside he'd have had to be hoisted out of the roof.

It takes a while to dawn on me, but this must be where the bogies are changed. I also read about this when planning the trip. Apparently, so the story goes, Russia was so paranoid of being invaded when building their rail network they built different rail gauges to the rest of the planet. Belarus, as part of the old USSR does too. This will be no simple task. Every carriage must be lifted and their wheels replaced. Obviously we will be here for some time and I wonder whether I should take advantage and get off the train and explore the station and surrounding area.

But I find myself reluctant to get off. I think its because part of me will relish having the cabin to myself. And for some reason, that I can't totally form, I feel I'm being unfaithful to the train. This is home, and I don't feel like I can leave. That and I don't trust the Provodnitsas. They'd steal your eyes if you weren't looking. Not to mention stashing tons of contraband under my bed to avoid paying the excise duty. No, I'll stay on the train and experience my carriage levitating. Janet offers a nod, which is a lengthy chat for him, and leaves. He may have even been smiling.

Shortly after, while luxuriating in the solitude, I catch a glimpse of a shape moving at pace in the corridor. It's just a blur across my open doorway, but enough to grab my attention. I'm sure its human so sit up for a better look. It runs past again in the opposite direction and I catch sight of a brightly coloured scarf billowing behind it like a pennant in the wind. Its footsteps stop suddenly on the third pass and track back a little more slowly. Then the scarf pops itself round my door. I'm pleased to see there's a head attached. It's a woman, I'd say about seventy, but it is hard to tell. There is another scarf wrapped loosely around the lower half of her face. The only features I can see are her eyes, a little bit of cheek, and some forehead. Its this bit I consider to be seventy. Her body offers no clues, being wrapped in more layers of clothing than a tramp settling down on a cold February night in London. She is carrying two bags. Pulling down her lower scarf she reveals a mouth that undoubtedly housed a full set of teeth at some time in her life. Now I can only count three and one of them looks like it might topple at any moment.

'Claff, flaff, igtaff, sleef?' At the end of each word her eyebrows raise like Grouch Marks's delivering a punch-line.

I shrug, 'An - glee - skee.'

She sprints towards me, grabs my hand and shoves it in one of her bags. It's full of hot newspaper parcels. She then makes a chewing motion with her mouth that makes her look like she's warming up for a gurnying competition. I deduce it's food and ask how much. We spend a little time negotiating with my calculator and settle on one hundred and fifty roubles, about £3.50. Money and goods exchanged she scampers out of the cabin. Thirty seconds later she returns with a tall willowy young lady, immaculately made up, large oval, hazel eyes, and owner of a full mouth under a nicely shaped button nose. Her hands are manicured and painted a rusty red. I wonder what I've actually purchased, and stand up to straighten my imaginary tie. I can't believe the beauty before me is related to the scarf lady, but they are working in unison. The young girl digs into her bag and hands me another parcel. Before I can ask how much they disappear. Clearly my not inconsiderable outlay was for two parcels.

I open the first parcel as my carriage is shunted into the sheds for their wheel change. Its a half a roasted chicken, a little oily, but tasty. In the next one I discover waxy potatoes, still warm from the paper insulation. They taste delicious, and every mouthful exports me back to the potatoes I had as a child: earthy and fresh out of the ground. Not like the bland supermarkets ones whose only quality is they meet EU shape requirements. By the time I've devoured the last one I'm five feet higher.

Essentially the carriage is positioned between four lifting devices, one at each corner of the carriage. They look like static forklifts. The hydraulic power they exert when lifting the carriage causes them puff like a deep sea diver breathing through a scuba mouthpiece. A gang of railwaymen, all in high visibility jackets flecked with grime and oil, set to work on uncoupling the old wheels and running in and attaching the new ones. There is another carriage running parallel to mine going through the same process. At least I assume its one of ours as the livery looks similar. Presumably we get reassembled at the end of the process. As wheel changes go its not quite as exciting as Formula 1 but interesting nevertheless. I soon find myself back in the station where I am reunited with my passport and all my currency paperwork seemingly untouched. Should I keep it or take the paperwork back?

Janet returns, in what is for him, a cheery mood and opens a beer to celebrate. I think he's drunk, or certainly on his way. It's getting late, but instead of going through his usual bedtime routine that starts with drinking beer, he begins packing stuff away. Men don't pack like women, what they actually do is move things about a bit. I spend an enjoyable fifteen minutes watching Janet pack one bag, only to unpack it and remove some of the contents to another. And then back again. Eventually he finishes, sits at the table and has a beer. He takes the empties, and all the rubbish he found while packing to the bin and returns to sit at the window. At ten o'clock we pull into Minsk, the capital of Belarus, and he gets up, offers a small bow, says 'das-veh-dhan-ya' and leaves. My offer of good luck and good-bye easily makes this the longest conversation we've had. I follow his gigantic silhouette as it crosses over the railway line and down a track that presumably leads to a wood where he will fight bears all night. I shut and lock my cabin door quickly, before the hags can squirrel in half a dozen Byelorussians. I'd like to admit to missing Janet but the truth is I have almost erased him from my memory by the time I switch off my light and settle down to sleep. As travelling companions go he made a good goldfish.

Day 3

I wake up to find the train gliding through an infantry of silver birches. Autumnal gold has been wantonly dabbed across the landscape and the cloudless sky is as blue as a Faberge egg. The occasional husks of long abandoned log cabins serve to remind me that the human race has an uncanny knack of spoiling an otherwise jaw dropping vista. They put the heating on in the night. I know this because I woke at three o'clock with a core body temperature of a pottery kiln. I spent a surreal ten minutes feeling round my cabin in the dark searching for a temperature switch, before I realised Janet didn't live with me anymore, and switched on a light. In the process of searching for the switch I head-butted the window so hard I nearly fell over. It's sore even now and I can feel an angry bump forming.

I really am ill equipped for this part of my journey. My extensive planning notes, tidily packed away in my luggage, with my pristine travel schedule, is clearly to be found wanting. Most of my research starts at Moscow. I didn't really give the leg from the UK to Moscow a second thought. I simply assumed it a quick commuter hop prior to the real journey starting. In the same way I forgot to think about Poland, I've totally ignored Belarus and I'm feeling a bit guilty about it. By the time I get to its Russian border I'll have spent the best part of twenty-four hours in it. It deserves more. After all, it is costing me a fortune to pass through it. Belarus was easily the most expensive visa in my collection, made all the more galling when you consider I won't even step on its soil. I have another guilty secret about Belarus. I didn't really know it existed until it was drawn in England's World Cup qualifying group. Oh, come on, most of you didn't either. The truth is I'm still struggling with all the name changes in Africa, and Belarus isn't exactly famous for much.

The national pastime is being annexed by Russia. In the thirties it briefly declared itself a republic and established its own borders. World War 2 broke out and Russia immediately annexed it again. Following the Soviet collapse it reformed as a republic again, but in name only, because in reality it's a dictatorship. And guess what is the top of this dictatorship's agenda? Yep, that's right: it's currently negotiating to become part of Russia again. So, now that I've spent best part of a day chugging across Belarus I think I'm in a good position to offer plenty of insight. So, what is my conclusion? The potatoes are good.

The hamlets outside the window are getting more frequent and the shacks are sliding down the design ladder a few rungs. Most have concrete bases. Roofs are predominantly corrugated iron with almost vertical sides that only begin to pitch half way up. The bit in the middle is primarily wooden and painted in yellows, creams or lusty reds. As in Poland the gardens are given over to vegetable cultivation, or to be more accurate, cabbage cultivation. There are some fruit trees but they are skeletal and have long since been stripped of their cabbages. Logs, covered with tarpaulin or under open sided lean-tos, line the sides of the houses, in preparation for the hard winter that will not be long in coming. Houses nearest the train track make use of the strips of land separating them from the train line to grow more vegetables. They are close enough for me to discover there are more than just cabbages. I can see potatoes, turnips and sprouts. Old fashioned, hardy vegetables that will make their way into winter stews. Access roads are still strangely absent. Muddy tracks are the only visible means of entry and exit and many of them cross the rail tracks and disappear into thick coniferous woodland beyond.

The station names are now totally impossible for me to read. They follow the Russian Cyrillic script. To my eyes its part script and part pictures. Some letters are vaguely recognisable, albeit they are often the wrong way around, and then you get others that are totally alien. These are interspersed with the ubiquitous pictures of houses on stilts, and top hats with legs.

It's the sort of written language you'd get if you asked a class of pre-school children to invent one. In fact, the station nameplates appear to have been written by five year olds, perhaps they did invent it.

As well a nameplate each station has a small glass covered shelter over a row of plastic seats. These shelters are very popular with suicidal men drinking from oversized beer cans. Maybe they're employed by the railway to add atmosphere, or perhaps this line is where depressed train spotters meet to discuss suicide options.

Before very long the train is pulling us through the outskirts of Moscow and I feel a tinge of excitement. In the middle distance I can see Soviet era apartment blocks mingling with new builds. They may sit cheek by jowl but architecturally they are a hundred years apart. It's like looking at a mouthful of decaying teeth slowly being replaced with gleaming white new ones. The scene nearer the track is more industrial and as we cross the Moskva River, via a thick iron riveted bridge, I see crane barges lying idle with their mechanical limbs bowing forlornly like a depressed octopus. The fat Brunette comes in and hands me back my train ticket. I can't think why I should need it.

'Do I need a customs form?' I ask, with little hope of getting an answer. I'm not disappointed. She ignores me and walks out. I haven't encountered Russian customs despite crossing into Russia some hours ago but I give it little thought. Moscow is home for the next two nights and I can't wait to explore.

The train slows to a halt in Moscow's Belorusskaja station, which is painted a rather un-communist turquoise. I've arranged a transfer to my hotel. My beautifully laid out itinerary reminds me a Russian agent will be meeting me. I scan the platform for someone furtive. Nothing. After a bit of hanging about I'm approached by a small grey haired man who looks like an emaciated blackbird wearing a C&A coat. His beak of a nose is the only part of his face that doesn't move. His eyes dart, never once resting on mine directly, and he mutters under his breath continuously. He offers me a handshake so weak our hands hardly touch. With a little flourish he pulls a piece of white cardboard from behind his back with my name on it. How did he know I was me?

'Mr, Mulliard I presume?'

Close enough, 'yes, how did you know?'

'Your carriage number is on my itinerary, and you are the only man to leave it.' He passes me an envelope.

'Your ticket to Peking,' he says, 'I will explain to you by car, come.' He takes the envelope back and heads off towards the exit at a lively pace. I struggle on behind with my bags, just managing to keep close enough to him to avoid being picked off by the taxi touts who all look like they got C&A coats for Christmas too.

Our car is sandwiched between the station and a socking great building site around which millions of cars slowly circle. It looks like a ballistic missile has recently exploded and the ensuing traffic chaos is producing a cacophony of beeping horns that combine to create a wall of noise several million decibels louder than the pile hammers pounding the foundations of the building site. My avian agent produces the envelope again and shows me the ticket to Beijing. He bellows some instructions that are totally lost in the noise and introduces me to another man and ratchets up the volume.

'He will take you to hotel, not tip,' he says wagging a finger at me, ' included in price,' he shouts this into my ear. They both watch me manhandle my bags into the boot and I jump into the back seat. No sooner has my arse hit the seat than I'm treated to a throbbing techno disco racket from the radio. The driver cranks it up even louder once he is seated. It's marginally quieter if I open the window. In between the incessant electronic drumbeats there is a break for the presenters to shout. I have no option but to listen.

She: Dog pig cat water toilet.

He: Cow udder dinner fishing rod.

She (with stress): WOMANISER!

He (with more stress): WOMANISER?

She: Da! WO - MAN - IS - ER

He: Dog Fart Bronski Beat Reggae

Then it's back to more bum-hole loosening Euro crap. The permanent damage this is doing to my ears is academic as there is no way I am going to survive the taxi man's driving.

We enter the roundabout surrounding the building site from the outside lane by executing a handbrake turn into the inner lane. This necessitates six emergency stops none of which are executed by my driver. Once in the inside lane he displays the sort of brinksmanship normally associated with Russian roulette. It doesn't get us very far. Thirty minutes later we've travelled about twenty yards but are, at least, directly opposite the exit he wants. He executes another handbrake turn towards the outer circle of traffic. Some cars brake so hard the drivers are standing. Eventually, like being squeezed from a circular tube, we escape down a tree-lined boulevard of such serenity I think we've actually turned into another country. My heart rate, however, is running at the same speed as a chicken's and banging away as loudly as the techno shit thumping at me from the driver's radio.

The three or so miles to my hotel are taken up with trying to kill pedestrians. Some foolishly attempt to negotiate pedestrian crossings. My driver treats these naive idiots with the sort of contempt Eric Cantona used to offer to Crystal Palace supporters. One hapless individual had to dive for cover in between two parked cars.

Despite my being tossed from one side of the back seat to the other, I think about what I'll do when I get to the hotel. Top of the list has got to be a shower. It's Wednesday and I haven't showered since Sunday. I smell of diced carrot, which might be my money belt, or worse, it might just be me. I soon find myself dumped outside the hotel reception with my bags. Needless to say I get them out of the boot unaided.

The Hotel Tourist isn't actually one hotel: it's seven hotels. Combined they once formed part of the athletes village for the 1980 Moscow Olympics. The buildings sprawl out from a central square. There are some shared facilities, a restaurant, small business centre, and somewhere, although it is not currently apparent to me, a casino. Birch trees line the inner road, all painted white from the base up to about hip height. There is no lighting so I assume this is to stop cars crashing into them but it might be to make them easier to crash into. After 30 minutes in the car with that nutcase, I favour the latter. Like everything else in Russia this complex was state owned, but since the fall of communism it's been in private hands. When my travel agent suggested it I looked it up on the Internet to get some background. It offered a list of reasons why I should choose it and in between "luxurious rooms" and "fine cuisine" it curiously described itself as "functioning" for over fifty years. Anything that considers "functioning" to be an asset deserved an investigation, so I agreed to take a reservation. Eager to experience it functioning in person I push open the door into a small lobby and approach the desk.

'Passport,' says an attractive but unsmiling blond girl, aged about twenty. She's sitting next to an older lady who could be her mother. My passport gets handed to mother. She scrutinises every page and hands it back to the blond who places it next to a computer monitor. She taps out some keys.

'Block seven.'

'Pardon?'

'Block seven.' She hands me back my passport.

'What is block seven?' I ask, being careful to smile at both of them. She tuts, slaps down a piece of green card outlining the complex on the counter, and draws a cross and an arrow. Beside the cross she writes 1. Next to the arrow she writes 7. She slides it across to me with my passport and resumes functioning with her mother.

'Thank you,' I say, 'sorry to have disturbed your busy day.' I struggle back out with my bags.

Although its early afternoon I can feel a chill in the air. Never mind, I soon warm up lugging my kit to the block next to her arrow. Block seven has a very small reception area with a reception desk that is unusually high. I stand in front of it like a first year in the head teacher's office. At least this receptionist is smiling, and she does so all the way through check in. I ask her what the weather's been like. She smiles. I ask her for a non-smoking room. She smiles. I ask her if she will be registering my visa, as is required by Russian law. She smiles. I soon work out that smiling is the only English she knows, apart from pointing to the lift, which she also manages in perfect English.

The room is, well, functional, with a retro-seventies feel

about it. The only thing it's missing is a lava lamp. I strip off, head for the bathroom and shower off a few days of grimy train journey and watch my dirt struggle past the plughole at the bottom of the shower tray. After drying myself off I apply a fresh pair of pants and kick the old ones towards my bag. They make a cracking noise, like a leg breaking. Ensconced in my clean pants my nuts celebrate by humming 'The Yellow Rose Of Texas' and I head down to the restaurant for lunch. OK, I know nuts can't hum, but if mine could they would have.

It's not what you'd call a posh eatery. The tables are lined up in uniform rows, like you might expect when sitting an exam. There is a small bar at the front with a clear view through to the kitchen beyond. The floor to ceiling windows sucks in a lot of light, but rather than bringing warmth they simply add to the clinical feel of the place. The waitress is blousy, about thirty and wearing a cream diaphanous shirt that strains across a set of ample bosoms, encased in a mauve bra. They look like a couple of giant aubergines trying to escape a dense fog. The black pencil skirt that she is wearing might have fitted her when she was a teenager. A phone is strapped to her ear and held there with hands that have fingernails bitten to the quick.

'Table for one please.'

'Bis-in-nus lunch - fush.' She continues her conversation into the phone.

'Pardon? Can I have a menu please?'

She gabbles something into the mouthpiece, rests it on her voluminous boobs and looks me in the eye. 'FUSH - BIS-IN-NUS LUNCH, FUSH.'

Clearly she assumes inverting the sentence, and shouting it at me will aid my understanding. It doesn't but she looks like she's sizing me up for a right hook so I sit down. She huffs off into the kitchen still talking into the phone.

By watching other people coming into the restaurant I work out its a set lunch and what the form is. They enter, pick up a plate of shredded cabbage from the bar counter. By the time they sit blousy delivers the Borsch. This is a beetroot soup, which is almost florescent purple – the sort of colour Dracula's curtains used to be. By the second mouthful of Borsch the main course arrives, which is, in fact, fish, not fush. It is accompanied with a massive pile of mashed potatoes, more shredded cabbage, and peas the size of gob-stoppers. No one talks, food at this pace requires total concentration and anyway they wouldn't be heard over the noise of the television. It's showing a gangster film of the sort that involves regular killings, all accomplished by emptying the magazines of at least five Kalashnikovs into cars that crash into something explosive, like an oil refinery. Needless to say it's at a volume that cracks teeth.

Wine is free with the meal but it a similar shade to the soup so I order beer, then another, and then another. Its nice stuff but just to make sure I like it I order another. I'm about to order a fifth when she hands me my bill. Apparently I've finished. Just as well, I pay, cheap at a little over a tenner, and head out for some fresh air.

Fresh air is not difficult to find, it's everywhere and the weather is decidedly nippy. I am ill prepared. Russia is my only cold stop, and I'll be spending much of it on a train. After here, it's much warmer Asia, so I head back in for an extra tee shirt and dig out the only long-sleeved jumper I have with me. Before leaving my room I take another look at my Moscow map to try and orientate myself. I am North of the Moskva, so if I head east I should, in theory, bump into a park. It will either be the Ishmaylovskaya, or the Sokolniki, or the Botanical Gardens, or somewhere else. I would get my bearings from a road name, but they are in a language only decipherable to a Clingon. I decide on the left, right, left right method of navigation that has served me so well in the past. As systems go it may seem a little haphazard but it's still better than following an English guidebook in a land with no English.

There is another purpose to my journey. I want to check out the Metro system. My guidebook made it sound like a breeze, but nevertheless, I'd like to observe it in action before I use it. Tourist guidebooks are always out of date by the time they're published. This anomaly is of scant consolation if you walk into the "quaint family run restaurant," to find a chapter of Hells Angels initiating an unsuspecting tourist by hanging him by his genitals from the fan. It pays to eyeball stuff yourself sometimes.

I'm a hardened London commuter and the Moscow underground map looks simple to follow. The map itself is nowhere near as complicated as London - on paper it looks easy. But then, I imagine, so did the battle plans to invade Russia, when Hitler was giving them the once over.

My hotel is not far from Botanichesky Sad Metro station, but there is another station named an impenetrable Vdnkh by the park, so my aim is to do my observing there and then stroll around the park before coming back to my hotel for a snooze. The bed of spanners I spent two nights on ensured a real lack of sleep and it's catching up with me. I feel decidedly sluggish, and no, it has nothing to do with the strong Russian ale I sampled at lunch.

I find the station quite easily, across the road from the park entrance. Which park I couldn't say, there is no English signage of any sort. In fact, there is no signage at all, but the entrance is spectacularly grand, with huge white portico gates. It looks promising and I make note to pop in there after I've reconnoitred the station.

The underground entrance is circular and rises out of the pavement like a dirty cream tiled organ stop. There is an entrance and exit. I memorise the Russian Cyrillic for each by inventing an English equivalent to associate with them. In my mind entrance is Bxoa, exit is Blixoa and exit to street level is

Blixoa B Ropo. It doesn't take me long to work out you pay at a booth and get a plastic card. I know from my in depth research, in which there will, I am sure, be notes to this effect, that you can charge the card for any number of journeys. A journey is one entrance and one exit and each journey is the same price, about 15 Roubles. The equivalent expenditure on the London Underground wouldn't get me past the ticket barriers.

I emerge from the ticket hall feeling confident and a little colder. The temperature is dropping fast so I decide to look for a short cut back to my hotel through the park. There are a few people about as I enter through the gates, some roller-skaters and a short line of old people queuing to get on a coach. They are dressed for winter: heads covered in furry ushankas, which for the uninformed are hairy hats with earflaps, not cockney rhyming slang for gentlemen that like their own company. When the hats are in situ they give the impression that a beaver is eating the wearer's head. Their coats are thick with fur collars. Lord knows what they wear when it's really cold.

Once through the gates I'm confronted by a grandiose monument gleaming white through the gathering gloom. It's at the end of a long boulevard and from this distance resembles a posh wedding cake decoration. I'm tempted to take a closer look but am distracted by a Ferris wheel to my right. This has the benefit of being in the general direction of home so I head towards it. I soon find myself in an amusement park. I detect little by way of amusement – more a bemusement park. The desolation and emptiness could be because it's a week day and late in the afternoon, but I suspect that it's always like this. The wheel isn't in action, or any of the other amusements come to that, but some food stalls are open. They look startlingly similar so I select the first one I come to. I'm not hungry but it's been over an hour since my last beer and underground reconnoitring is thirsty work.

A man is stationed at the front smoking chunks of meat over a barbecue pit. He is also smoking a cigarette that hangs precariously from the side of his mouth. The pit is made from an elongated steel drum cut in half and the coals are grey hot. He warms his hands over them, occasionally turning the meat. Fag ash drops in periodically for added flavour. I get a burst of warmth as I walk past him to the seating area and bar. Behind the bar is a woman in her early thirties swathed in clothing and hiding her face behind a big woolly scarf. She has dark, untidy hair and is texting.

'Beer?' I enquire.

Not looking up from her phone, she nods towards a cabinet at the side of the bar. This constitutes a conversation in Russia. I collect my beer and place it in front of her. She ignores me.

'Glass?'

She tuts, puts down her phone and looks at me like I've

just asked her to extinguish the barbecue by pissing on it. She fumbles about in her tabard for a bottle opener and nods towards the barbeque pit full of fag ash and the owner's broken dreams.

'Chicken? Fish?'

'No thanks, just a beer.'

I am rewarded with a large harrumph while she knocks out the price on her calculator. She slides it across to me. I pay and pick up my goods: at least the beer is cold. She is back texting before I sit down. As I work my way down my beer I contemplate my experience of Russian service. I'm no expert but I think it needs some work. So far it's been service with a snarl, which can get a little wearing when there is nothing else to contrast it with.

Twenty minutes later I'm back in my room, which I'm pleased to say is far warmer than the reception desk welcome. Pleasant social discourse was probably hindered by the administration involved in getting my key back. "It is forbidden," and I am quoting directly from the sign in my room here, "to take your room key outside of the building." No, this is Russia, when you want to go out you must leave your key at reception. In return you are given a receipt, duplicated, confirming the key is now in the possession of the hotel. To get it back, you produce the receipt. If this can be matched to the duplicate copy at reception, the key is returned. Naturally the receptionist couldn't locate my duplicate receipt.

'But you know I'm a guest here, you checked me in earlier.'

I watched my obvious logic float hopelessly over her head. I am certain she doesn't understand one word of English, except possibly, the word "Beckham." As she rummaged about for her copy of the receipt I tried another tack.

'OK, give me the key, and if someone else tries to get in the room later I promise I'll move out.' She waves away my suggestion on the basis that answering it would require a crash course in Janet and John English. This is the type of conversation I imagine nurses have with dementia patients.

No nearer finding my errant duplicated receipt, she calls over blousy from the restaurant. Blousy points to a drawer where the duplicate receipts are kept. The receptionist then spends an age rummaging through them and a further five minutes checking that her copy matches with mine. Finally, accepting I am the man she checked in only a few hours ago she hands me, rather ungraciously I feel, my key. Back in my room with a sheaf of papers to file I fall on my bed exhausted and immediately fall asleep.

I wake in a darkened room, slightly disorientated and if I'm honest, a little light-headed. Must have been the fresh air. Lights twinkle from an apartment block outside my window, but they are the only illuminations by which I can orientate myself. There is no street lighting pushing through the curtains and nothing lit in my room. I am, consciously and practically, in the dark. I get up and immediately stub my toe fumbling for the light switch by my bedside table. I can't find one. Maybe I haven't got a bedside light? I feel along the wall, hoping to find the main light, trip over my bag and end up in a heap on the floor. I decide to stay low and crawl to the bathroom in search of illumination. I discover the shaving mirror light and it works. Heading back into the main room I spy the faint outline of a light switch by the door and flick it on. Nothing. I find some more switches and turn all of them on. Nothing. Great, the only light that works in my room is the one in the bathroom above the sink.

Undaunted I take a shower in the dark, which is like being washed by a stranger. I blindly drag my bag of clothes over from the bed and dress in the hall by the light of the bathroom shaving mirror. Putting on my socks I lose balance yet again and reach out to the wall in an attempt to avoid another descent to the crusty carpet. In the course of doing so I slap another switch and the whole room lights up. It's a master switch. I spend ten minutes turning off lights I'd spent twenty minutes turning on, then head downstairs in search of dinner.

Walking past the steely glare of the blousy waitress I skip past the reception and head out into a freezing cold night, ignoring the rule about keys. If I want to get involved with that much paperwork again I'll take up tax accountancy.

Block three has a restaurant, which I now run to, not because I'm hungry, but to stop the early onset of hypothermia. It is bloody freezing. I crash through the door whilst simultaneously pulling up my flies, which rather belatedly I realise are undone. I also notice I'm wearing a patterned blue sock and a white one.

Due to a well-oiled hinge, and the velocity I'm travelling at, the door collides into the wall with the explosive force of a hurricane hitting a landmass. It's the sort of entry that normally precedes a shooting spree so understandably the thirty or so diners all look in my direction with more than a little concern. Once they realise I'm unarmed they go back to what they were doing, which, in the main, is not eating but drinking. A waitress takes me to a table and points to a seat. I sit.

Directly in front of me are four women, early thirties, neatly made up, universally slim, all sporting immaculately painted nails. They look like anorexic peahens. Their clothing is expensive, and collectively there is enough gold dripping from them to re-decorate the Golden Temple at Amritsar. Each have a meal in front of them and occasionally one spikes a morsel with a fork, but I never actually see any food make its way to a mouth. Two empty bottles of champagne line the other end of the table and it's not long before two more join them. They are not really talking much but there is plenty of texting.

To my right are another group of women, with a single man at the head of the table. The man is eating, but the women are not. One of them is on her mobile another is texting. I wonder whether I've blundered into a mobile phone shop by mistake.

I'm presented with a menu. The waitress waits beside me gently tapping her foot. I'm pleased to see my menu has an English translation and I order a spicy mutton soup to start and "special" Black Sea fish as my main. It doesn't take me long to discover that special Black Sea fish means sardines. And the reason it doesn't take me long is the seemingly universal need in Russia to dispose of the eating part of a meal as quickly as possible. My main course arrives a millisecond after putting down my soupspoon. Fine dining in Russia is really an eating relay race in which the diner is on each end of the baton. I'm finished within twenty minutes, and that includes the coffee, and settling the bill. The only reason others are still in the dining room is that they had the foresight to order a couple of bottles of Vodka for their starters, and are slowly toasting their way through them. Never mind. An early night will do me good. After all, tomorrow I have a date with a dead man.

Day 4

I arrive in Red Square early, and apart from Lenin, who is almost certainly still asleep, I'm pretty much the only person here. Earlier, after a breakfast served at a speed that melted the jam, I'd headed for the dreaded Metro. It was quite a relief to emerge from the station nearest to Red Square into a beautifully clear blue sky I am now standing under. But, the journey hadn't quite been the breeze I was expecting.

Last night I'd worked out a cunning plan. My route, on paper, was simple: I had to travel from my local station, Botanichesky Sad, on the orange line, for four stops to Prospect Mira, an interchange station for both the orange line and the brown line. Taking the brown line for two stops I needed to get out at Kurskaya, another interchange station for the brown, blue and green lines. From there I simply needed to travel one stop to Red Square using the blue line. My neatly worked out assault relied on my checking my progress by matching the Cyrillic station names on my map with the station nameplates at each station. It didn't take me long this morning to discover a flaw in my meticulous planning: there are no station nameplates on the Metro's station walls. A set back, no doubt, but I am a hardened London commuter and as such always have a contingency plan. I decided I could use a combination of counting stops and colours. And so we come to the problem with contingency plans: if they were any good you'd have made them your primary plan. Although I am endowed with a superbly analytical brain and counting for me is as easy as, well, one two three, I am colour blind. Green, blue, and brown all look the same to me.

I think I took the green line, but when changing platforms I became disoriented and appeared to have doubled back to the brown line. Every time I tried to correct my error I ended up back at the brown line, or it might have been the green line, or possibly blue... What quickly became apparent was that I was lost. Right, time to unfurl the contingency, contingency plan. Eez-vee-**nee**-tyeh is the Russian for 'excuse me.' I'd memorised it specifically for my underground adventure, and I started using it liberally, in combination with showing my fellow travellers where I wanted to be by pointing at stations on my Metro map. The reception I got was frostier than a Siberian winter. Not one person offered any help. They were so indifferent that they didn't even tell me to fuck off. Those I cornered in a carriage darted off into the crowd like scolded babushkas as soon as the door opened and others simply turned their backs. I was truly flabbergasted: this was ignorance on a national scale.

Undaunted I decided to double back on the lines I'd previously double backed on. My only minor success was to find Prospect Mira several times. By the time I'd whistled through it for the fourth time I'd developed the sweats. I was genuinely worried I might not be able to cope with direct sunlight should I ever escape this subterranean hell. Commuters continued to take advantage of the wide, slatted floor carriages by dropping their shoulder and making for the space behind me every time I approached them. It must have looked like some form of demented country dancing routine to anyone looking in from the platforms. Some tried other methods to avoid me. Pretending to read or hiding behind others were quite popular. I was close to losing my temper as Prospect Mira flashed past me for a fifth time but then a young school girl asked me, in excellent English, if she could help. She was about thirteen, boyish in shape, quite tall, with a face that looked like it had been sneezed out of shape. But, to me she was a beautiful angel.

'Thank you very much,' I said, 'I'm trying to get to Red Square.'

'Ah, yerse, you have lost, I will show.'

'That's very kind,' I said, then quickly thinking how odd this might look, 'but if you could just show me on the map, that will be fine. Really, thank you.'

'No, map shit, I show, can practice my English same time.'

She grabbed my sleeve so as not to lose me in the crowd, all the while asking me important questions she had about England: did I support Manchester United or know David

Beckham? Was the Queen old? Was Hercules Poirot English? Her mild questioning continued for a bit and then she upped the ante, 'you like Russia?'

'Oh, um, yes, very… interesting.'

'Russian people very friendly, you like Russian people?'

I didn't think it appropriate to say every Russian I'd met so far was about as approachable as a sunburned pit viper, so I settled for, 'I haven't met many, but if they are all as helpful as you, I'm sure I will.'

'Ah, here, your stop.' She guided me from the train by my clammy hand and took me to the base of the escalators. Once at the top I waved to her before walking out of the wrong exit. However, I could see the minarets of St Basil's peeking out between the buildings and headed towards them, all thoughts of killing Russians removed from my mind.

Red Square is of course iconic and instantly recognisable and I felt a mixture of excitement and anticipation with every step I took nearer to it. Now, standing in its centre, the first thing that comes to mind is how considerably smaller it looks in the flesh, a bit like when you meet someone off the television. Behind me is St Basil's, the sunlight behind it accentuating its beauty and casting onion shaped shadows towards the imposing walls of the Kremlin. Half way along the outer Kremlin wall is Lenin's Mausoleum, a pyramid of dark brown and black marble. I have a date with him later. If he were capable of sitting up, he'd be looking directly at the world famous GUM department store. At the far end of the square is the terracotta coloured State History museum. Looking around I realise I'm standing on about the same spot Russia's Communists leaders used to stand to watch the military parades goose step past after the waves of nuclear missile batteries. It sends a shiver down my mildly Cold War paranoid spine.

The parades stopped soon after the breaking down of the Berlin Wall and the collapse of communism. Everyone got swept away in the post communist euphoria. In this period Russians adopted an optimistic frame of mind and decided wearing Levi jeans or listening to the BBC was no longer a capitalist threat. The nation was tired of sixty years of central planning, of state before individual, of mindless bureaucracy. This was a country looking towards a new exciting capitalist nirvana. But like so many big ideas fed to the Russian people this utopian dream turned into another battle for survival. By 1998 Russia was essentially bankrupt. Inflation was so rampant prices went up between joining the queue and getting to the front of it. The ordinary man in the street had to sell his Levis just to put food on the table.

When you think about it Russians have had some shit leaders. Communism, as Lenin might have described it before they encased him in his Mausoleum, was about bringing equality to the masses. It failed. Prior to that cock up the Czars subjugated the populace for hundreds of years. And before that Ivan the Terrible brutalised them by way of entertainment (which is what happens when there's no television).

Communism must have seemed like a relief when it arrived. Even if the populace had to put up with being ruled by inky grey cadaverous Politburo chiefs with grand houses in Moscow, Dachas in the country, and a penchant for caviar baths. Russian capitalism turned out to be rather ugly too. To be fair the Russian elite had to work hard to balls it up. Russia has the largest reserves of natural gas in the world, as well as substantial deposits of oil, coal, iron ore, manganese, asbestos, lead, gold, silver and copper. All of which will continue to be extracted long after most other countries supplies are exhausted. Oh, yes, and its forested regions cover an area nearly four times larger than the Amazon basin. So as natural resources go, the country is literally sitting on a gold mine.

The Russian people, quite rightly, expected the torchlight of capitalism to shine a path out of the perpetual communist gloom but unfortunately they selected Yeltsin as the torchbearer. His vodka-fuelled strategy was simple. He decided the best way to manage all this untapped wealth was to hand it over to a clique, forever described in the Western press thereafter as Oligarchs. In less than a decade he contrived to put control of the nation's wealth into the hands of a small elite. So, total subjugation under the Czars gave way to communist poverty, which in turn gave way to a new form of Russian capitalism: one that saw the elite became modern day Czars. No wonder the average Russian commuter can't identify my getting lost on the Metro as much of an issue.

Walking up the gentle slope towards the State History museum I draw on a lifetime of watching Inspector Morse, and notice that Red Square isn't red at all. The cobbles I'm walking over are definitely grey. It matches my mood. I've been in Moscow less than twenty-four hours but it's wearing me down. Russia to date has been a pain in the arse. My visa to get here was a bureaucratic nightmare, involving my being "invited" by my hotel (a service for which they charge by the way). I have to register my presence, now I'm here, despite being invited. Eating is more to do with conveyor belt processes than taste, and leaving my hotel for the day involves more paperwork than buying a house. Getting around on the Metro necessitates that I memorise words made up of letters that look like they're been written by a late stage Alzheimer sufferer. Travelling by road is not an option either. It involves negotiating a taxi fare with men who cut their fingers off to demonstrate just how tough they are to their fellow inmates, and being taken out to some murky grey piece of wasteland to be buggered. There are no duel-language maps, no tourist information booths. I've been grimaced at, tutted at, shouted at, ignored, and on the whole made to feel thoroughly unwelcome in a country that Lonely Planet describes as being inhabited by "extraordinarily hospitable people."

So here I am in Red Square and frankly I'm not in the mood to do anything more than go back to my functioning hotel room and quietly function there until my train is ready to depart to Beijing.

The dulcet tones of an Imam stop me from acting on this impulse: Islam in Red Square? I can't see a minaret so set off in the general direction of the wail to investigate. Walking through the arches to the right of the museum I find the Imam. Its a little old lady bundled in numerous layers of clothes carrying a raft of folded newspapers over her arm. She uses her other arm to hold up a battered megaphone to her mouth into which she needlessly shouts. It's the London equivalent of "stanar, e-nin stanar." She employs Joseph Stalin to collect the money for her so she can concentrate on shouting and doling out the papers to a doleful public. He is one of about a dozen Uncle Joes ambling about in uniform and renting themselves out to tourists by posing for photographs. I'm tempted because I've never had a photo taken with a man responsible for the death of at least forty million people but a line of port-a-loos distract me.

Of the type you'd find on an average UK building site, they are arranged in a block of five. The block I'm fascinated with has only four available cabins. There is a fifth, but it has been converted to make the block manager's life a little more comfortable. A bucket and mop rests on the outside wall like a thin spiv waiting for a punter. She is about sixty-five and wearing a patterned headscarf drawn tightly and knotted under her chin. A slightly stained blue tabard hangs over a thick woollen jumper with a tatty hem that rests on her dark trousers. Her spectacles are delicately balanced on the end of her less than delicate nose. Her convenience has been decked out with all the accoutrements of a person who has spent a lifetime living in a toilet. There is a blue plastic chair and small table, upon which sits a small primus stove. A steaming hot mug of tea rests next to a bowl of fruit and a checked blue curtain is draped where the toilet would have been prior to the conversion. She looks remarkably cosy, intently reading the newspaper that she presumably paid the murderous dictator Joe Stalin for. If you lifted her little home and dropped it in Much Deeping you'd be looking at Miss Marple's housekeeper.

Every now and again someone walks up and drops some money on the table. After methodically collecting each coin and depositing it in the front of her tabard she leads them to a vacant cabin and unlocks the door for them. When they finish their business, she gets up again, cleans the cabin using the spiv and bucket, locks it and goes back to her reading. Positioned just outside one of the most iconic Squares in the world seems an odd site for a bog franchise but this is Russia don't forget, a country that takes shit seriously. But what is really vexing me is the logistics of this enterprise. How does she get her toilets home at the end of the day: the Metro? This distraction into Moscow's bog franchise system lifts my spirits sufficiently enough for me to keep my date with Lenin.

Some might consider being mummified in your own mausoleum as a little elitist for the founder of communism. But, in keeping with his doctrine of equality, the Centre for Biological Research, the organisation responsible for mummifying him and keeping him from looking like a month old pepperoni pizza, offer a full mummification service to the masses. Prices start at $300,000, depending on the exchange rate.

When Lenin died a report of the autopsy was published in Pravda. This scrupulously independent research by eminent doctors declared that Lenin's brain was extremely large. This is obvious when you think about it, he did, after all, think a lot. His fellow communists hailed this as proof that the communist system was superior to any other and immediately founded the Institute of Lenin's Brain. Yet more eminent scientists set to work to discover the secret of his greatness. Incentives for discovering something positive about Lenin's brain were compelling. They included not being poisoned by the end of an umbrella or being burned to death and having your remains made into an ashtray. Despite these enticing inducements the Institute never did get round to publishing its findings and, forty years later, it quietly closed.

Naturally there are certain rules that have to be observed when having an audience with a dead icon and I am busy reading them when I'm approached by a man so American looking I think he's going to sing to me that his wife has left him with four hungry children and crops in a field. The squeak from his new crocodile boots reaches a pitch that could fell a dog.

'You won't get in without a guide now my friend.' He is Russian and says 'my friend' in the same way James Bond's cat stroking enemies do.

'No thank you, I think I'll get in. There's plenty of time.'

Slowly scanning me, he spits out 'fool, pah!' turns on his heels and squeaks off down the line at a much faster pace than his arrival. Close your eyes and you'd swear you were listening to a trolley that needed oiling.

I go back to the list. No drink, no food, no cameras, no phones, no shorts, no sleeveless shirts, no blacks, no Irish, and no pets. No getting into Russia without an invite, no getting into your room without an affidavit signed by a magistrate, etc. etc.

The queue takes no time and as I pass the first entrance area I hand in my offending phone and camera to a hand sticking out of a hole in the wall at about knee height. I can collect it later providing I have the right sheaf of paperwork signed off by three justices of the peace and Felicity Kendall. I will also need to stoop at knee height for twenty minutes without collapsing. Walking along the immaculately manicured garden area towards the mausoleum entrance I pass a long row of sculptured busts, some of whom I recognise. That is to say Brezhnev and Andropov who were active in my era of paranoia. Undoubtedly different, the busts do have a common denominator: they are all incredible ugly and the marble they are made from simply amplifies it. The marbled Brezhnev looks significantly more alive than he did when he used to breathe. The pyramid housing Lenin is immaculate, constructed entirely from brown marble with black inlays and I am very quickly at the entrance. The general hubbub is mainly American with a smattering of French. If there are any Russians here they are keeping a low profile: just like they we forced to when he was alive I suppose. Attendance wise its similar to what you might expect for Dumbarton Vs Stenhousemuir in a mid January evening fixture.

The darkness inside is in sharp contrast to the bright day unfolding outside and the further I venture in the darker it gets. Before I realise it I'm standing so close to a guard we could kiss. Rather than pucker up he points me in the direction of a display case. Slowly my eyes become accustomed to the darkness and I make out a plinth with steps leading up to it. On the third step I catch my first side on glimpse of the great man. It doesn't take long for me to make it around to the feet end so I can look up his nose. No bats in the cave. Like Red Square he is smaller than I expected. The musty yellow lighting shines off his slightly protruding forehead giving him a ghostly pallor similar to the colour of undercooked Chinese dumplings. His hands are tiny but immaculately manicured. There is a hint of a welcoming smile: perhaps he's on a percentage of the admission take. It's a remarkable sight but surreal in the extreme. I mean, come on, I've queued up to look at a corpse. Not only a corpse, but one that's been artificially preserved to look like he might get up and chat with you if you could only find the slot to drop the penny into. They've set his face to look studious and a thought strikes me; do they set it to match the time of the day. Obviously gravitas is required for the masses filing past, but what about when they close, does he get a relaxed face then, perhaps a cigar?

This train of thought continues to amuse me as I stand there gazing at this dead icon that should, in all honesty, be bone dust by now. A guard taps me quite hard on the hand. Is he a mind reader? Does he realise I'm having a titter at his country's iconic statesman's expense? He taps it again and I realise he wants me to take my hands out of my pocket. Why? What does he think I'm up to? Has he read the smile on my face for something other than my ghoulish sense of humour? Perhaps he's mistaken me for a communist with necrophilia tendencies. I leave to retrieve my camera and phone before the collection point closes, which is not for another hour, but, you know how it is, paperwork, paperwork, paperwork.

Lenin doesn't know it but he forms one of the points in my mummified leaders' triangle. Chairman Mao awaits me in Beijing and Ho Chi Minh in Hanoi. I can't think of three more worthy candidates for mummification. Pity they waited until they died though.

I think about what to do next while watching the changing of the guard at the tomb of the Unknown Soldier. The march is a combination of marching and kung fu. Surely the original point of marching was to get to a battle quickly. I fail to see how this can be achieved by copying the Ministry Of Funny Walks sketch.

I could go into the Kremlin itself. It means queuing, depositing all my belongings in a holding area again and all the resultant paperwork that involves. Also no food is allowed, so I will have to adopt the afternoon eating habits of a Buddhist Monk. I wrestle with the thought that I've travelled a long way to get here, and the entrance is less than fifty yards away, but eventually decide I can't be arsed. What I really want to do it find the Phlegmatic Dog Internet cafe, which according to my Lonely Planet guide is very close to where I am now. I decide on a compromise. I promise my conscience I will take some pictures of St Basils, and have a quick gander in GUM, and then I'll look for the Phlegmatic Dog.

St Basil's looks like a very ornate cake decoration. Ivan

the Terrible commissioned it and was so pleased with the result he had the architect's eyes pulled out so he wouldn't build anything to equal or surpass it. Well, come on, what did you expect? He wasn't called Ivan the Architect Lover was he? I'd like to say how interesting it is, but to be honest it just doesn't float my boat. In my mind cathedrals are gigantic like the one in Salisbury. This one is like an ornate Swiss clock. If I wait until the top of the hour I'm sure a farmer with the cow will come out of the side to chat with the shepherdess with a crook entering from the other. Disgusted with myself for being such a philistine I wander over to GUM, walk in the side entrance, and walk out of the central one. Department stores are an anathema to me, and whilst GUM may be architecturally very pleasing on the eye, and incidentally, I believe the architect died with both of his, it is, after all is said and done, only a department store.

The Phlegmatic Dog proves impossible to find with my very English map, so I spend an irritating hour or so walking up and down roads that lead to nowhere in particular and have nothing diversionary on them. I decide to head back to my hotel. I've missed the charming wit and repartee of the receptionist and decide the futile twenty minutes of charades that precedes my getting my key back is just what I need to lift my spirits.

I only get lost once on my way home. I work it out for myself, as I can't find a schoolchild to help me. Mulling over things on the train I can't shake off my curmudgeonly perspective so I decide to tell the receptionist I've lost my key chitty to see what happens.

'I've lost my chitty… sorry.'

She offers me her usual bewildered look.

'My key chitty, I've lost it,' I say patting my pockets for effect.

She looks at me, shrugs, and hands me my key.

'But I haven't got a chitty.'

She walks off. What is the point?

Later in the restaurant I'm ready when the waitress brings the menu. I'm not going to be fooled this time, so I order a bottle of sparkling wine called Rossiskoe. This time lady I'm here for the long haul. She doesn't look particularly impressed so I order a veal soup called Khaslama, and grilled sturgeon to follow. I'm tempted by a page on the menu I hadn't noticed the night before headed "Farinaceous" food, but this section is all in Russian. Still, what is "Farinaceous" food, and why tempt me with a heading in English? I contemplate this while casting my eye around. They alight on a couple of Russian men or as you would recognise them: two neatly turned out Littlewood's window models. They both have slicked back hair and sport wobbly beer guts that droop over their trousers like giant's teardrops.

The waitress has bought them a bottle of Stolichnaya vodka and a couple of cartons of tomato juice. The next half hour follows the same pattern; the tomato juice is poured into tall glasses, the vodka into shot glasses. One or other of the men offers a toast and they both down the vodka, then immediately lug down a good measure of juice. This is repeated until the vodka is gone. The ratio, I calculate, is three cartons of juice to one bottle of vodka. Neither seemed to enjoy the vodka, each pulling the sort of face you might see on someone who has just swallowed an oyster for the first time.

The ordering of my sparkling wine has done nothing to slow down the delivery of my meal, so yet again I finish eating fifteen minutes after I sit down. I still have two thirds of a bottle of wine left so I turn my attention to that and the table to my left which houses five people, all totally pissed. There are three women, one of which is in charge of vodka replenishment, and two men. The older man is very fat, and has already worked his way through one large soup and is attacking another bowl with chunks of black bread. He joins in the toasts only when they coincide with a break in his soup shovelling. The younger, thinner man, seems to be top dog, he is the one ordering all the vodka. The women don't appear to be eating at all, just drinking. Collectively their heads are getting nearer to the table with each toast. Either that or the glasses are getting heavier and they can't lift them.

I'm disturbed from my nosiness by my waitress who taps

my table to get my attention.

'Caffe?'

'Yes please,' I say, rather shocked she has shown an inclination towards customer service

'Double - 2?' she sticks two fingers up.

'Da,' I say, confidently having no idea what she's on about.

'Sahne?'

'Sahne? Sorry, I don't understand.'

She shrugs and walks off and I realise this was probably the longest conversation I've had with anyone in Moscow since I got off the train and stepped onto the station platform to meet birdman.

She brings me back a coffee with a packet of creamer, points to it and says, 'Sahne,' whilst looking at me like I'm some sort of simpleton. The coffee tastes like boiled carpet underlay. In desperation I sprinkle some pepper in. It now tastes like peppered underlay. The bill arrives even though I haven't asked for it. I can take a hint so I pay it and leave. The pissed table are now so low in their chairs their hands are touching the floor.

Day 5

I wake after a fitful sleep. I'm worried about my visa registration. The next time I encounter Russian customs officials I'll be six thousand miles from Moscow on the Chinese border. I figure this is not the best place to try and win an argument on the correctness of my paperwork. I have good reason to worry. Before I left home I read the results of a study on Russian border guards undertaken by the TASS news agency. They found that sixty percent were considered so unstable they shouldn't be allowed to carry guns. By macabre coincidence, and usefully underlining the horror of this statistic, a border guard stationed at my Chinese border crossing went on a rampage with his sidearm two days after the study was released. Five of his colleagues will never guzzle vodka again.

Getting my paperwork sorted is my first priority today so I resolve to put aside other plans and seek out my travel agent, who, according to my paperwork, is based in the Hotel Cosmos, conveniently located "next to Prospect Mira Metro station." I have to check out of my hotel by noon but I won't be back by then, so I cart my stuff down to reception to ask if they can store it until later. The usual receptionist is on scowling duty this morning. We've gone through the key/chitty process together many times before, using the often under rated power of mime to conclude the transaction, but we've never actually spoken to each other. That is about to change. Her eyebrows lift when she spots my bags and I detect the hint of a smile.

'Check out?' she says confidently.

'No… well yes, but I'd like to store my luggage.'

'Check out?' she repeats, a little less confidently. Moving from her well drilled check out script is like dipping her toe into a pool of unwelcoming cold water. The request to stow my luggage produces a series of facial expressions more associated with accidentally sitting on barbed wire. Why does a hotel that names itself "Tourist" staff its reception with people who can only speak Russian? Do they only expect to attract tourists from the local neighbourhood? I persevere, but her glazed eyes tell me I'm flogging a dead receptionist.

'Yes, I am checking out, but I want to store my luggage.' I point to my luggage, and enunciate my words like an opera singer loosening up his facial muscles in preparation for a performance. 'My luggage, I'd like to store it.'

She gulps, looks down at her desk, looks up, holds up her hand, looks down again, puts her hand down, looks up, then shouts at the man who sits on the desk near the entrance. I've walked past him most days but I've never actually seen him move. I just assumed he was an ex-communist leader, that is to say dead but still at his post.

The cadaver manages to scrape his chair back and shuffle over. I repeat the whole charade again, but in a slightly higher octave. Exasperation drips from my every word, but sadly, like my words, it fails to translate. He offers me a smile more usually associated with an unexpected encounter with the mentally disabled and picks up the phone. He holds his hand up to me to indicate I no longer need to talk. A few moments later he hands me the receiver. The disembodied voice speaks English, so I repeat my request to her, pass the phone back to the man, he listens, then puts the phone down and repeats my request to the receptionist. Twenty minutes later, my account is settled, my bags are stowed and I leave with a pile of paperwork two inches thick. If I stay in Russia much longer, I'll need to invest in a filing cabinet.

I zip around the Metro like a local, that is to say I look at the floor a lot. I ascend at Prospect Mira like the hardened commuter that I am. Obviously there isn't a hotel in sight, let alone next to the station. Nevertheless I spend a fruitless forty minutes looking, and about five pounds ringing a missed call from the UK. It's a garage asking me if I've heard how versatile the Nissan Qashqui is.

'Will it help me find the Hotel Cosmos in Moscow?' I ask in an attempt to stop the car salesman talking.

'Well, satnav is extra but...'

I cut him off to avoid bankruptcy and, on impulse, walk into an Italian restaurant. I don't know about you but wandering around aimlessly in a strange city, whilst having an expensive conversation with a persistent car salesman, always makes me hungry.

The first thing that strikes me is that it doesn't look like a feeding station in which the seats are leased out on twenty-minute time slots. There is no florescent lighting. It looks like a proper restaurant. A Trattoria in fact, red gingham table cloths, old Chianti bottles with melted wax down the necks and lighting that kisses my bald patch rather than peeling off a layer of skin. The waitresses are all young, wearing crisp white shirts and black skirts that fit. They look like slender glasses of Guinness and, rather disconcertingly, they're smiling. Proper smiling, with their eyes, not smiling that involves stapling the corners of a mouth to each ear lob. Its almost like they're pleased to see me.

'Good afternoon Sir, table for one?' asks a long necked Goddess with blond hair like liquid gold.

English, she speaks English. This isn't real. I resist an overwhelming desire to pinch her as she gently leads me to a table. She hands me a menu, which is also in English, and I order a spicy pizza and salad quickly, before I burst into tears. The food is delicious, there isn't a cabbage in sight, and to top it all the coffee doesn't need pepper to make it drinkable. I'm in a daze when I walk to the door, but manage to snap out of it long enough to ask the waitress if she knows where The Cosmos Hotel is. She does, and in perfect English explains its one stop down from where I originally got on. Perplexed I show her the headed paper showing the Hotel's address as Prospect Mira. She smiles.

'I can see what it says Sir, but, it's not right.'

'Well, thank you for your help,' I say, and wander back to the metro station in a state of delirium.

The Cosmos Hotel is gigantic and not far from the station I used to check out the Metro the previous day. However, upon surfacing from the Metro I immediately get my bearings wrong and end up back in the park with the non-turning Ferris wheel. Realising my folly I do an about turn and head back. Its late afternoon and I'm feeling cold and keen to search out some heating. Turning into the long drive leading up to the hotel entrance I'm confronted by Charles De Gaulle, or rather an eighty foot brass facsimile. He looks as arrogant as ever so I ignore him and hurry through to the reception. It's a rather grand affair housing shops, Bureau de Change, some eateries and my travel agent. It's also very, very warm. In contrast to my hotel the desk is staffed with people who don't look like they will cack themselves if I speak something other than mediaeval Russian. A rather helpful gentleman directs me to an office upstairs. I decide I need to divert to a loo first so ask a security guard by the bottom of the stairs where I might find them.

'Could you tell me where the toilet is please?'

He offers me the look of a man who's just been told his mother was his father, and his father was the family pet. He points vaguely in the direction of somewhere else. I know a hotel that he would be perfect for. Ablutions complete I present myself at the travel agent. They are efficiency personified and allocate me Katiya. She is petite, about twenty five, neatly dressed and has long dark hair.

'So, Mr Millyard, they have not registered visa?' This is not good. You leave tonight. This is not good.' The registration office closes soon. This is not good.'

Katiya has many qualities. Engendering confidence is not one of them. She smiles a lot, which, having been starved of any form of human kindness, I find endearing. Her diagnosis, however, does nothing to ally my fears. I feel the deep pang of agony I get in my stomach every time I see Simon Cowell on the box. Sensing my precarious condition she comes up with a solution.

'I will get desk here to register passport for you. Passport please.'

'Its at my hotel reception, they won't give it back to me until I completely check out.'

'This is not good.' Can you get it?'

'Well, it is my passport but trust me Katiya, they don't speak any English, its quite possible I could die in the process.

Can I have you're telephone number and if I get stuck I'll ring you and you can explain to them in Russian why I need it?'

'OK, and I'll ring them too, to explain why you need it.'

'That's what I just... oh, never mind, OK.'

Armed with this cunning plan I set off taking a short cut across the park towards my hotel. I want to avoid the Metro as rush hour is now in full swing. The area around VNKDh station is teeming with people. Viewed under a microscope it would look like the unfriendly bacteria in your stomach. Despite my need for speed, I notice, for the first time, that there are lots of kiosks in this area. Most are selling beer and snack foods others are dedicated to CDs. They are all about the same size, around eight feet by six feet. There are no customer doors. Instead they have an aperture about the size of a large letterbox which is used to converse with the sales assistant hiding inside. The really odd thing about them is that the aperture is placed at about 4' 5" from the ground. The net result is everyone over the age of about ten has to stoop like a heavily laden peasant to make a transaction.

My distraction extends to a long line of old ladies spaced out at regular intervals along a fence. Well dressed for the dropping temperature they stand holding a single item, presumably in which they specialise. Respectively they are holding, a hat, a boot, a top, a belt, and a flower. It would be possible to kit yourself out down one side of your body within the space of one hundred metres. Occasionally the line is broken up with a stall selling bags or fruit and vegetables. Business is not brisk with the exception of one stall that is surrounded by short, fat ladies. I have to elbow my way in to see what's so popular. I swear this is not a lie. It's a cabbage shredder, and it's flying off the stallholder's shelves so fast he has two assistants working flat out bagging up and collecting the money.

My phone rings, its Katiya.

'Mr Mulliyard, I have spoken Hotel Tourist. They register your visa electronically so everything OK. That is good.'

'But, it needs to be stamped Katiya, you said so yourself, why can't they stamp it?'

'No need for electronic registration, everything good.'

I start to tell her I'm still worried but she cuts me off mid sentence.

'Electronic good, no need stamp, don't argue with Hotel Tourist Mr Mulyard, not good.' I'm inclined to agree. Arguing with Hotel Tourist would be like arguing with a radio.

I get back into my hotel reception at about 8.30 pm after a yomp through the park in which I didn't feel entirely safe. More than once I wished I'd stuck to the main road. There's something about Moscow, I don't know what it is, some undercurrent that makes me feel edgy. Or it might just be the jaundiced view I've developed while I've been here.

The receptionist and dead man are still on duty. He gets my bags and I only have to sign twice, in triplicate. I turn to the receptionist.

'My taxi to take me to the station doesn't arrive until 10 pm. would you mind if I waited in your lobby?

'Eh?'

'Lobby, can I wait in the lobby for my taxi?'

The bag man walks back over to the reception from his desk by the door.

'Tax? He looks at the receptionist and smiles. 'Tax.'

'Ah, Tax.' She smiles and reaches for the phone.

'No, I don't need a taxi. I have tax.'

'Eh?' she says. 'Eh?' he says.

'Airport? She asks.

'No, no, I don't need a tax. I have a tax. I just want to sit in your lobby for an hour.'

And believe me if it wasn't minus two degrees outside I wouldn't be having this conversation at all. I'd be sitting on my bags on the pavement. Blank faces don't do justice to the activity behind their eyes. I suspect back there its pandemonium. I pull out a piece of paper and write on it "tax 21.45." I point to it.

'Not tax, wait in lobby,' I point to the couch opposite the television, do a driving charade, and repeat 'niet, niet, niet.'

'Ah!' She says and picks up the phone again.

'Fuck me, what is the point,' I say, reaching over to stop her phoning a taxi. The bag man grabs my wrist and smiles. I assume a Russian Rouble is dropping. This assumption is based entirely on his eyebrows no longer being knitted together. He reaches for the phone.

'Fuck me sideways,' I say, grabbing his arm. I am ready to fight if this conversation goes on any longer. He calmly removes my hand and smiles, dials a number and hands me the phone. It's the woman I spoke to earlier.

'Can I help you?' she says.

'Yes,' I say, trying to get my voice back from the falsetto its been operating at. I have a taxi booked to collect me at 21.45 and all I want to do is wait in the lobby until it comes.'

'What time tax?' she asks.

'21.45,' I repeat.

'OK, pass me to administrator I will tell her book tax.'

'No listen. Please listen. I don't want a taxi. I already

have one booked.'

'Ah… you book tax already?'

'Yes! And if we keep this conversation going any longer, waiting in the lobby will be irrelevant.'

'OK, understand now, give administrator please.' I hand the phone back to bag man. His face lights up like a jackpot on a fruit machine and he puts the phone down, waffles off something to the receptionist, probably in a dialect only understood by her and his cousins, and shows me to the couch that I'd pointed to a lifetime ago.

There is a Russian variety show on the television being presented by a buxom wench in a red dress and overflowing boobs. She's watching a guest who's performing a song in English. When he finishes she walks across the stage to greet him, her bosoms are about three paces behind her so when she stops they take a while to catch up. There is a brief hiatus while both wait for them to become stationary.

'Fuck you!'

'Fuck me?' He says back, 'you want to fuck me?'

'Fucking beautiful,' she responds, and they fade out to a commercial break.

OK, as interviews go its not in the David Frost mould, but you have to admit its different. I spend an enjoyable hour watching her guests murder rock and pop classics, dressed in jumpers knitted by babushkas in the Urals. Each song is preceded with a short film showing the singers relaxing at home. You're probably thinking cocktails by the pool, or flopped out in the private cinema with a wife with unfeasibly large, plastic bosoms. You'd be wrong. Think of the shack in Deliverance, furnished from redundant MFI stock with Nora Batty cooking soup in a kitchen.

My taxi driver arrives and I bid farewell to the receptionist and the dead man. They, together with the taxi driver, watch me struggle with my luggage to his car. I take one last look at the Hotel Tourist and decide that the description of functional so proudly highlighted on their website is the most accurate piece of English I've encountered while staying there.

There is some more English on the taxi dashboard. A sign reads, "a few dollars are better than big thanks." The brass neck of it hammers another nail in the coffin that is my Moscow experience. The driver picks up his mobile and makes a call.

"Millud! Millud! Then after a brief silence, "dugrub, gallows, turdy, deng bottle, MILLUD, MILLUD!"

This continues for some minutes until he throws the mobile onto the front passenger seat in disgust, and says to his rear view mirror, 'Intourist - shit.'

Intourist are my agents in Russia and the ones

responsible for my transfer from the hotel to the train station. He is an employee.

To my surprise the agent meets me at the station as agreed, he is a non-descript man with grey hair, and looks like a composite grandfather. He watches me wrestle my bags out of the boot, and then asks me to follow him into the Yaroslavsky train station. Externally the station is quiet a gothic affair made all the more atmospheric by the mist swirling around it. The inside, however, is like my hotel: functional. My agent gives me a quick lesson on how to decipher the electronic train timetable, wishes me good luck and he's off. Five minutes later he's back to explain where the platforms are in relation to the electronic timetable.

'But don't go outside until it's near your boarding time at 23.55, its very cold.'

I discover he could have also added its full of drunks as I head out there immediately he goes. Don't get me wrong, electronic timetables can be riveting but I'm travelling again, and I want to get going. Sitting still is not easy.

I find the platforms swathed with a pearlescent light that is fighting a losing battle with a thickening mist. I take in a scene that could easily have been plucked from an Agatha Christie thriller. Despite my need to deflect the odd drunk, I'm filled with anticipation. This is the part of my trip I've been looking forward to the most. I'll be travelling on the second longest continuous train journey on the planet. The numbers are mind boggling, 5623 miles and seven nights. My longest train journey prior to this was getting to Moscow from the UK, prior to that it was Paris, and prior to that it was Farnborough to Waterloo. This journey is going to blow a hole in my revenge numbers.

I think about this as I watch the red numbers of the electronic clock click over. I now have two methods of measuring the progress I'm making towards reclaiming a February back. Purely in day terms this is a winner. It's roughly a third of a year's worth of commuting. And in mileage terms it has no equal, re-crediting me years of commuting hell.

Finally the platform gate opens and I head up the platform looking for my carriage. The train is long, and the mist is now so thick I can't see the engine that will pull us. While struggling with my luggage in search of carriage nine I think about bribing the Provodnitsa to put me in a cabin without a sharer. I'm travelling first class, but that only entitles me to a two-berth cabin. I want to avoid another Russian at all costs. I'm worried the non-stop chatter and jovial atmosphere will kill me.

I try, without success, to persuade the gaggle of four carriage attendants I should have a cabin to myself. This is primarily because they don't understand me, but also due to a level of ignorance that makes the Hotel Tourist receptionist look like a fawning butler.

Five minutes after I arrive a large man enters, I smile, and he ignores it. He's looks about thirty, but could easily be younger or miles older, and has thick, light brown hair, glasses obscuring dark brown eyes and a full set of lips. That's to say his lips are full, not that he has two of them, which of course he does. He drops a holdall on to the seat that will soon convert into his bed. His other bag is so large it won't fit through the door: it's about the size of a small saloon car. Eventually he manhandles it through and sits on his seat. The bag is between us and effectively filling all the space that isn't furniture or human. He looks around and scans the cabin several times, studiously avoiding eye contact with me. I wait for him to acknowledge me: he continues to scan, as if looking for a way out.

Eventually I give in and introduce myself. He tells me his name is Janet. Fuck, another one, I think.

'Do you speak English?'

'A little,' he says, standing up.

He manoeuvres his giant bag back into the corridor and follows it. He's now blocking the route to most of the other cabins, and people start moaning. He pushes it back in so they can pass and then sets about trying to push it under his seat. It's like trying to park a lorry into a domestic garage. He tries it from every angle until eventually he gives up and disappears for a smoke at the end of the carriage. I take advantage of the gap to head out into the corridor. The train has just pulled away and I want to catch my last glimpse of Moscow, just to make sure we're definitely leaving it behind.

I can recommend Moscow at night. If you can't spare the time to go and witness it for yourself, look out of any train at midnight, you'll get the idea. By the time I get back Janet is sitting down looking at his oversized bag with a furrowed brow. He pulls out a can of beer from one of its many compartments, takes half a dozen large slugs that empties it, pats his shirt pocket for his fags, stands up, pushes the bag back into the corridor and heads off for another contemplative smoke.

While he's gone, I move his holdall to his bed, convert my seat into a bed, make it up, stow my luggage, and run the vacuum round whilst whistling the "shake n Vac" song. OK, I'm not doing the last bits, but I am looking smug. He stands looking at his bag suspiciously, like it's grown since he last saw it. He scratches his head. I head for the loo, they're open again, which must mean we've left the Moscow municipality.

By the time I return he's found a solution to the bag problem and stowed it. He's been forced to empty most of it onto the open ledge above the door and hang other bits of clothing from suitable protuberances on his side of the cabin.

Since I moved his holdall he has been careful not to encroach on my side of the cabin. By 1 am we are both in bed, he dressed in the clothes he arrived in (minus his two coats and hat) and me in a pair of shorts. It's not long before I drift into a deep sleep. At 3 am I wake to the pssst of a can opening, followed by half a dozen large glugs, then silence.

Day 6

Its good to be back on the train and I can feel a subtle change about me. Maybe I've become the train equivalent of a salty mariner. If I'm not in continual motion I don't feel comfortable. Perhaps that's why I didn't like Moscow: I never acquired my city legs.

I wake later than usual, mainly because my bed is far more comfortable than the bag of spanners I had to endure on the last train. My first impulse is to check out the bathroom. But, before I set off I manage to slide my hand down the side of my razor, while rummaging through my wash bag. The result is a neatly sliced fingertip that is gushing blood. The expletives that fall from my mouth do nothing to stem the flow, or wake Janet, who slumbers on. I try a plaster but the cut is too awkwardly situated for it to gain purchase. I am dripping copious amounts of red liquid over the floor so in desperation I swathe the offending digit with a couple of paper tissues. They immediately blush red and anchor themselves to my finger like singeing nylon.

Standing in the bathroom I wonder how I might replace the tissues. Tentative teasing gets me nowhere so I decide that yanking it off is my only option. This angers my finger greatly and it starts to gush again. I opt to swathe it with the toilet roll hanging from some wire on the back of the door. I know what you're thinking: this will simply repeat the problem I had with the tissues. Ordinarily I would agree, but the toilet roll on this train has the consistency of Ryvita. With a little effort I mould it into a one-fingered glove and fit it tightly over my throbbing digit. It's not perfect but the blood is struggling to dampen the corrugated cardboard texture of the bog roll. The downside is my hand is virtually useless for any tasks able-bodied hand owners take for granted.

I take in the austerity of the bathroom to take my mind off the pain. The floor and walls are burnished steel. Even the mirror is in a burnished frame. It's like being inside a tin can. The window is fixed open with screws and the ensuing draught allows Siberia to creep in with all the dignity of a flatulent aunt. I make my now customary inspection of the facilities. Once again the toilet flushes directly onto the track. Ordinarily it wouldn't take such a direct route. There is a flapper that is supposed to catch your business. This seems to me to be a rather dubious design feature because it only acts as a temporary resting place. Once the foot pedal at the side of the loo is depressed the flush kicks in, the flapper drops, and last night's cabbage based dinner is deposited all over the track. Why I'm bothering to spend time thinking about this is a moot point because the flapper on this toilet is hanging there like a broken limb. I push the seat down to reduce the whooshing noise, which is like continuous mortar fire when the seat is in the upright position.

Shaving is an interesting experience with a critical digit

bandaged to the size of a farmhouse sausage. The train ramming into the points like David Hemery clearing hurdles exacerbates my problems with coordination. Life is not made any easier by the futile size of the sink and a tap system that refuses to give up more than a small cup of water at a time. I bought a universal plug with me, which I quickly discover is not universal. It's about an inch wider than the hole in the sink. The fault probably lies with Russia. My experiences so far would indicate that universal is not a description into which it fits very comfortably. I conduct my ablutions as best I can and I wrap some fresh Ryvita around my digit, which continues to pump out blood with the efficiency of an oil derrick.

When I return to my cabin I find Janet hidden under his blankets making gentle gurgling noises. I stow my wash bag as quietly as I can and head off in search of the restaurant car and breakfast. On the way through my carriage I detect movement. There is an older couple next door, and two ladies, early to mid fifties I would say, three or four cabins up. The Provodnitsas though, are conspicuous by their absence.

I don't have far to travel, as the restaurant car is the next carriage down from ours. First impressions are that it has promise. To my right there is a small, semi-circular bar area, then on either side of the central aisle, four cubicles that can seat four diners each. Pink curtains are draped at each window, tied back with lace ties, turning the rectangular picture windows into triangles. There is a large no smoking sign under which two Russians are smoking like steam trains. I miss the entrance to the galley on the way in but the smell catches in my throat. It's a sort of musty cabbage, not unlike geriatric homes at dinnertime.

The waiter pops up from behind the bar. He looks like Charles Bronson from the Death Wish films, except his features aren't symmetrical. The left side is out of kilter with the right, like someone jogged God's elbow in the design phase. He's wearing a black suit, black shirt buttoned to the collar, and a pair of blue furry slippers. It's the sort of garb I imagine Johnny Cash's mother might have worn when relaxing at home. When he smiles it makes him look ill and me feel ill.

'Menu An - glee skee?' I say with a phrase learned this very morning from the back of my guidebook.

'Da - breakfast?' he says. I detect mild incredulity.

'OK.'

'Eggs, cheese, butter?'

This seems an odd combination, and I'm not sure if he's offering me breakfast or a recipe.

'No cheese, please.'

'No cheese?' He says this like I've just informed him Putin is a lesbian, but nevertheless shuffles off, presumably to meter out some vigilante justice on the chef.

I look out of the window: it's my first proper view of Siberia. While I slept I missed about 300 miles of it, but I'm not worried, there is still another 4400 miles to go before I reach its eastern border with China, and yet another 900 miles before I jump off in Beijing. This thought catches my imagination.

As I mentioned before, Moscow to Beijing covers 5623 miles of track. Not that I believe it. Who decides where to start measuring in Moscow, and where to stop in Beijing? Have you ever seen, in any city in the world, a marker post heralding it as the centre of the city? The mileage signs showing distance to London used to be marked out from Charing Cross. There's nothing in Charing Cross to indicate this but it is supposed to be the central measurement point for London. Or was until they moved it to Whitehall, but I bet they never changed all the signs.

I start to think of more reliable ways to measure my progress. What about books? I have four books with me so Moscow to Beijing could be measured as four books long. The benefit of this measuring system is that I can adjust my reading to meet my estimated arrival time. For example, I've already started a Bill Bryson book that I know I will read slower than a fast-paced thriller. A little bit of careful planning in this respect and reckon I'm onto a winner. I warm to the idea and decide it's the only form of measurement flexible enough, so I decide to adopt it throughout my trip.

However I'm not sure it adequately solves the time issue. I'll be passing through 7 time zones. Keeping track of this is made all the more complex by the train insisting on retaining Moscow time throughout the journey. This means just before I get off the train at Beijing it'll be 11 pm in the corridor but 6 am on the platform. That may be one small step for me but it's one giant leap for confusion.

But a solution comes to me. What if I wear seven watches? Set at hourly differences I could use the watch nearest my elbow from today and as I get nearer to Beijing I can progressively work down my arm, until I am using the watch on my wrist. All I need to put this plan into action is another six watches...

We passed Nizhny Novgorad, better known as Gorky very early this morning and the next town of any significance is Vyata, which, not that long ago it's citizens called Kirov. Despite my internal machinations I'm becoming quite blasé about the distances. That might be why my mind turns back to the subject of ablutions. More specifically: toileting. The regimented forest decked out in its early autumnal uniform marches past me outside my window, but fails to deflect me from this train of thought.

What's vexing me is this. There are eighteen people staying in my carriage, two Provodniks and one Provodnitsa. That adds up to twenty one arses. Times that by the eighteen carriages and you get 378 rear-ends when the train is full. Then there are the train drivers who supply a pair of buttocks each on strict rotation. Assume, on average, people do their business four times on this journey, a fair average for a week I think. That adds up to an almighty 1512 dumps. OK, the toilets are shut just before, and just after stations, but that still leaves an awful lot of shit on the tracks. From the air it must look like someone's trailed a thick brown felt tip from the back of the train.

I'm driven from my diversion by the arrival of breakfast. Bronson coughs over it as he places it in front of me. He also places down some black bread that he doesn't cough over, but it does have his thumb print in it.

'Beer?'

It's early but I look at the meal and think it might be a good idea.

'Da.' I say fluently, using a rare Russian dialect I picked up from my hotel receptionist in Moscow.

The breakfast has been delivered in a sort of miniature frying pan without a handle. It's not immediately clear whether this is because the chef couldn't transfer it to a plate, or if it's his flamboyant take on a breakfast classic. I rather think it's the former. The contents look like a large fried egg with a big knob of butter melting in the yellow yolk. The whole is specked with light brown droppings, which I promise my stomach is ham. I dig in. I can't tell you what the bottom half tastes like because it is impossible to peel away from it's casing, but the top half tastes OK.

Despite Bronson handing me the bill as he collects the remains of my breakfast, I linger in the restaurant car drinking coffee, which is awful but improves with my clever remedy of sprinkling pepper in it. The Russian smokers left some time ago and nobody has replaced them. No one has even walked through. The chef came out of the kitchen once, which did nothing for my appetite. He looked like the reflection a praying mantis might get in a Hall of Mirrors. His baggy shorts offered me an unrestricted view of his legs that, like the ends of his fingers, were the colour of nicotine.

I'm expecting to see Janet up and about by the time I get back to my cabin but he's still in bed, asleep. Encouragingly, there are signs he may have had some breakfast as a large tin mug the size of a potty has appeared on the table, together with some packets of plain brown biscuits. This can mean only one thing: he's not dead.

The rest of the carriage is as quiet as Janet and everyone is hiding behind cabin doors. In fact ours is the only one open. I sit on my bed with my head resting at the window end and watch the Siberian vastness unfold through the large picture windows in the corridor. Thirty minutes later I swap ends and watch Siberia pass by out of the cabin widow. If I were a betting man I'd say the corridor side is passing by quicker than the cabin side. There's not a lot happening. Occasionally we huff our way through a hamlet or small village. They are all deserted. Indeed I only see one person, a glimpse of a hunter in full camouflage kit with a rifle slung over his shoulder. At least I assumed he was a hunter, he may have just run rampage through a village. I'd be surprised if he found anyone to shoot.

I settle down to Bill Bryson's Notes From A Small Island. I read it some years ago, but bought it along as I thought it might remind me of home. It does, a little, but mostly it reminds me of a past that no one would recognise if they travelled there today. It's amusing nonetheless. He captures quirky nuances perfectly and with great brevity. It's a trait of his writing that makes him so readable. In fact, before I know it I've read about 100 pages. This will make a mockery of my four book measuring system. I only have three other recreational books with me. At this rate I'll run out. I resolve to ration Bryson to four chapters a day.

There's been some activity while I've been reading, light traffic back and forth to the samovar. This one is much shinier than the one on the previous train and it gets lots of use. The Nordic ladies, I now think they are Icelandic, pass by regularly with flasks. Others have wandered by with Pot Noodle cartons to be filled, and the couple occupying next door have sashayed past regularly holding a teapot like a dance partner. I must say they make quite an elegant pairing, excellent deportment, and very neatly turned out with matching sweaters.

I've made the acquaintance of all of our carriage attendants. That is to say they have taken it in turns to grunt at me. One is short and blond, not as busty as Blond Bob from the last train but certainly top heavy. She is pretty in an odd sort of way and reasonably young: late twenties. Her brown eyes are slightly on the squinty side. She has a small nose above a very small mouth that I have yet to see break out of a glum pout. The Provodnik doesn't look Russian at all. He his trim, with a military bearing and a healthy outdoors complexion, like he exercises regularly. His slightly flared nostrils bring to mind an angry horse. The third I have yet to see in a uniform and I rather think he is some sort of handy man. He has permanently greasy black hair, brushed back in a Count Dracula style, piggy brown eyes and a beer gut he must have worked on for some years. He lollops about in tracksuit bottoms, slippers, and a baggy black tee shirt that doesn't quite cover his gut. He continually sniffs and wipes his nose with the back of his hand.

By one o'clock the carriage is again quiet. Janet purring gently in his bed is the only noise I can hear. I've never known anyone sleep so much as him, other than Lenin maybe. Outside the landscape gradually becomes more urban until eventually it is a mass of concrete and graffiti. We arrive at Kirov. The train shudders to a halt and immediately the carriage bursts into life. The attendants take up station by the door, decked out in their livery of electric blue and gold braided coats with matching hats. The Nordics amble past, offering an almost indiscernible nod. My elegant neighbours follow them, wrapped up in thick jackets and matching scarves. I have now christened them Howard and Hilda. Three sets of people struggle by with their luggage that I vaguely recognise from embarkation in Moscow. They offer a curt smile as they pass my cabin on their way to the exit. I let the commotion die down and go to look out of the corridor window. I can see people from my carriage milling about on the platform, sticking close to the carriage entrance, in fear of the train pulling away without warning.

It's a drab scene, grey concrete, hard, unwelcoming bench seats. There are plenty of people about, all well dressed against the cold. A few food stalls are open offering packets of plain biscuits, crisps and other packets of food that look alien to me and probably unappetising to aliens. I contemplate going to buy some stuff but am put off by the need to put on a sweater and shoes. I'm comfortable and warm, and can't be bothered.

The train pulls out fifteen minutes later and I realise that we are now in another time zone: this is Moscow plus one. Nevertheless, the clock in the carriage continues to tick resolutely to Moscow time. It will for the whole journey, because as far as the train is concerned we never left Moscow. I've resolved to keep local time, so on my side of my cabin it's an hour later than it is on Janet's side and in the corridor. I will be another hour ahead of the corridor later this evening.

Confused? Good. How do you think I feel? Janet slumbers on to the gentle clicking of the Moscow clock.

Shortly after Kirov we pass through Bum, an unfortunately named town but appropriate, as this is where Janet gets up to go to the toilet: his first of the trip to my knowledge. He comes back a couple of minutes later, and studiously avoiding eye contact, proceeds to make some food, clearly unaware that it is heading for mid afternoon in our cabin. If he eats it in the corridor he might get away with calling it high tea. His preparation makes for a diverting interlude though.

Firstly he ladles in four tablespoons of a porridge mix from a box he pulls out from his luggage. He is meticulous in ensuring they are level spoonfuls. Then he adds some cold water from a water bottle by his bed. After that he mixes in some purple liquid that looks like the stuff dentists ask you to sloosh with. The whole lot is vigorously amalgamated with the back of his ceramic spoon. Once he is satisfied with the texture he ambles down to the samovar and fills it with hot water. Back in the cabin he covers it with some silver foil, and leaves it to stand. There follows another brief interlude that he fills by scanning the cabin without looking directly at me. Ten minutes later he eats it with the dry biscuits that look like bars of carbolic soap. The going ratio of biscuits to each mouthful of gruel is two to one. Once he's finished he repeats the whole process except he doesn't eat it. Instead he covers the mixture with foil, slinks back under his covers and resumes sleeping like a hibernating Grizzly.

After a little more window gazing I decide on an early supper and make my way to the restaurant car. Charles Bronson seems surprised to see me again. Maybe its because in his world its mid afternoon, but the truth is I don't think they get much repeat business. I sit at my now regular table, and ask for the "menu An-glee-skee."

He slouches off and rummages about behind the bar, returning with a proud look on his face and a dusty menu that he hands to me with a flourish.

'Menu An-glee-skee,' he says, offering a crooked smile. It's the only type of smile his jagged face can manage.

The menu is actually a mixture of Russian and German and the words on the pages look like they've exploded and been stuck back together by a three year old. Nevertheless the list of options runs to four pages and I am suitably impressed. I point to an item with the most English looking letters in it. This is the culinary equivalent of Russian roulette.

'Niet. He says confidently.

I point to another.

'Niet,' he says without looking at where I'm pointing.

After five or so points, followed by a corresponding

number of niets, I look up at him and shrug. He points to something.

'Da,' I say, and he shuffles off. I notice his slippers have been replaced with a pair of scuffed brogues without laces.

There are no customers in, but there is a new face and I suspect he's the boss. He's about as wide as a bull elephant and as bald as a newborn baby. I'd need three hands to strangle him. He's been tapping away on a calculator since I arrived, whilst simultaneously watching cartoons on the TV above his head. The volume distorts the sound sufficiently to make the Ninja Turtles sound like Daleks.

As I have come to expect in Russia, it's not long before some soup arrives. I would say it has its origins in Borsch, but there are bits of ham floating about in it. This solves the mystery of the light brown flecks in the frying pan breakfast this morning but does nothing to help me identify this as a foodstuff known to man. I have a go at it regardless and to my surprise it's not bad. I'm only half a dozen spoonfuls in when the main course arrives. This isn't a restaurant: it's a pit stop.

'Meat,' Bronson says, as if he's passing me state secrets. It might be stroganoff, it might be stew, or might be the remains of the dead cat I saw on the side of the rails earlier this afternoon. All I can say for sure is that it's hot. I order beer to cool me down. Beer is a word that truly is universal and he understands immediately.

Outside the window I very occasionally catch a glimpse of twinkling lights, like diamonds in a black velvet pouch, but mostly all is darkness. The stew thing is stringier than a cat's cradle but edible. The beer is delicious so I concentrate on that. I order another and wave away my bill when he tries to serve it on me like a writ. I decide to toast my first full day on the Trans-Manchurian Express and have another. Then I toast the window with another, and the table with yet another. I toast myself for being such an energetic toastmaster and then by way of a nightcap I have a beer. No one has come into the car in all the time I've been here, so I toast my solitude. I slip into another time zone and toast that, and realise it must now be time for bed. I take a bar of chocolate with me from the off sales as all this toasting has made me hungry.

Janet, naturally enough, is asleep when I get back. I ready myself for bed, which is no mean feat on a wobbly train with a wobbly belly. I lock the cabin door, fall on the bed, literally, and I'm asleep before my head hits the pillow.

At about three in the morning (on my side of the cabin) I become vaguely aware of a pssst, followed by four or five gulps, but it might have been a dream.

Day 7

It's raining when I wake. Rivulets of water cascade down the window like an army of sperm in an urgent quest for an egg. Outside the window the vista is industrial. There are rusty brown freight cars in sidings, snaking trains of oil containers fifty or sixty cars long, all blocking my view of the countryside beyond the tracks. Cables lattice the sky above me and grey stanchions bridge the line every 20 yards or so. We're pulling out of Tyumen some 1300 miles east of Moscow. My head is thumping to the beat of freighters hitting points and Janet is nowhere to be seen. Tyumen is Siberia's oldest town and was once a major staging post for convicts and exiles on their way to gulags. They used to be route marched there until the railway arrived in 1887. Then they were taken in cattle cars so crowded you had to get the person next to you to pick your nose for you. Luxury. At some point in the night we stopped at Yekaterinburg to change engines. Or so my guidebook reliably informs me this morning. I slept through it. I also missed the Europe - Asia obelisk. This narrow pyramid of concrete officially marks the end of Europe and the start of Asia, if you're travelling east like I am. If you're travelling in the opposite direction you'll find the Asia – Europe obelisk. It's the world's only schizophrenic obelisk.

I head off for a wash in the tin can with my wash bag and a packet of nappy wipes. Yes, you heard, nappy wipes. My logic is simple. The Trans-Manchurian train doesn't provide showers, although I've heard rumours that some do, so avoiding a build up of grime can be tricky. Especially when, like today, you discover there is a device on the tap that stops water coming out. This is why I undertake a full body wash with slithers of moist tissues. It's like washing Hampshire with a dishcloth. My ablutions fall into the rhythm of the train. Pull from container, four swipes – dispose – pull from container – four swipes – dispose. I would like to say that my rub down was refreshing but to be honest it just made my thickening film of dirt and grime smell of Johnson's baby shampoo. On my way back to the cabin I pass Blondy. She's drying her hair down with a towel and looks suspiciously like she's had a shower. I do a charade of taking a shower and ask where I can get one. "Niet" is all I get from her, but the subject of showers vexes me while I change into my daywear, which is my nightwear with the addition of socks.

On some Trans-Siberian trains there are showers, and I read in my guidebook that, often, the Provodnitsas keep them shut, only opening them for their exclusive use, or for passengers willing to pay. Now I come to think about it, Howard and Hilda next door always seem well turned out, and the Nordics. Its no good asking Janet, he remains comatose in his bed, and anyway, he has almost certainly not bothered with washing since before he got on in Moscow. I resolve to investigate potential showers later.

Before I know it, its midday. That's to say it's midday on my bunk. It's only ten o'clock in the corridor and God only knows what time it is on Janet's side of the cabin. Probably 1980. In an hour or so we will pass another time zone and it will be Moscow plus three hours. I wonder what the restaurant car is serving, Breakfast or lunch? This amuses me greatly so I head off for lunch, or brunch, or possibly breakfast. Blondy fires up the vacuum as I pass by her in the corridor. I do another shower charade. She scowls at me but she knows I'm on to her.

Bronson, calculator man, and the praying mantis chef are sitting at a table playing dominoes. Bronson has the same suit and shirt on as yesterday. None of them acknowledge me as I wander past them unaided to my usual seat. I look out of the window. Drizzle is falling out of a slate grey sky and turning into flaky snow that evaporates upon contact with the earth. The forests have disappeared and been replaced with mile after mile of reed beds. Occasionally I see a heron soaring above them before it swoops away out of sight.

The mystery of which mealtime I should expect is soon resolved. He hands me the same menu he offered me yesterday. The simple answer is, the menu is the menu. We go through the pointing game until he finally gets bored of saying niet and points to two things on the menu. I try to check mate him by only selecting one. Don't want to spoil my taste buds too much do I? What comes out is yesterday's soup but with a twist. It has a chicken thigh in it. This may be to compensate me for the lack of bread as the tasty black bread has been replaced with a stale white variety. Or it might be black bread with alopecia.

As usual he brings the bill before I've swallowed the last mouthful of soup, and as usual I ask for coffee. This confounds him again and he looks at the bill forlornly. I've buggered up his paperwork. The coffee today surpasses itself. It is truly vile. Even with a good sprinkling of pepper it is undrinkable. I pile in a ton of sugar, which I hate, but it makes no difference. If you want an idea of what it tastes like wear a pair of pants for two weeks then liquefy the crutch. I push it away.

Janet is out on a fag break when I return to the cabin, its good to see him so active, however when he returns he climbs back into bed for a nap. Smoking not only kills it really takes it out of you. Having now spent a little time with him I have noticed there is a difference between his napping and his sleeping. He keeps his glasses on when napping.

There is plenty of movement in the carriage from the Nordics and Howard and Hilda but everywhere else is as quiet as the grave. This is unsurprising considering all the other passengers have left. I briefly consider bribing Blondy to open a cabin for my exclusive use, but I can't be bothered. I'm settled in here and its not as if Janet is a demanding sharer.

I've done very little today but the time has flown by. That's the thing about taking a train journey this long. There is no point in doing anything quickly. Why get up early, or eat at normal times? What indeed are normal times for eating? Why not eat when you feel hungry? There is nothing I can do to influence the speed that this train travels at, nothing at all that will get me to Beijing quicker. And why get there quicker anyway. I am, without a doubt, more relaxed than I think I've ever been. If you exclude that foot massage in Bangkok in 1997...

I'm still in awe of the distances. We're averaging 1100 miles a day. That's like travelling to Glasgow, remembering you've left the iron on, travelling back to Farnborough, turning it off, then returning to Glasgow, every single day. Between going to bed last night and waking this morning I'd travelled the equivalent of Manchester to Land's End.

We stop, very briefly, at Nazyvayevskaya, which is worth about ten million scrabble points. It's also famous for being at the centre of Khruschev's Virgin Land campaign of the 1950s. In an effort to address the chronic shortages Russia suffered after WW II he ordered 25 million hectares to be cultivated for grain. Now, 25 million hectares may not mean much to you, but if I tell you the whole of the UK, not just the green bits, the entire UK is 13 million hectares you might get the picture. Like all Russian initiatives it went wrong. By the 1960s this over-intensive farming turned a fifth of the land into desert. The area is famous for other things: mosquitoes. Clouds of them plague the area in the summer. Most are the size of eagles and can turn a human into a dried prune with one suck.

Late in the afternoon we approach Omsk from a rather ugly bridge that crosses the Irtysh River. When we stop at the station I discover that the bridge is actually the jewel in Omsk's particularly dreary crown. Omsk is Siberia's second largest city with over 1.2 million people living there. The line between Omsk and Novosibirsk, 400 miles to the East of us, has the greatest freight traffic density of any railway line in the world. There are freighters everywhere. Some are longer than an Alan Bennett monologue.

The Nordics and Howard and Hilda get off to stretch their legs. I decide to join them, it's been 1700 miles since my feet touched solid ground and I want to see if they still work. I nearly knock over a girl walking past the carriage door as I alight. I have never seen anyone so skinny in my life. Ranging up to about six feet her legs can't have been any wider than my wrists. She is entirely out of keeping with the rest of the platform traffic. They are Mongolian in appearance, stocky, like their cattle, and despite it not being that cold, well wrapped up.

The railway line around Omsk was laid down in the early to mid 1890s, under hostile conditions. It runs through the Barbara Steppes, which is a vast expanse of greenish plains, dotted with shallow lakes and peat bogs. Firm ground here is more rare than a bilingual Russian hotel receptionist, and the mosquitoes in summer make the ones in Nazyvayevskaya look like blue tits.

In keeping with Russia's propensity to ignore a commercial opportunity all the food stalls on the platform are closed. With no opportunity to shop I satisfy myself that my legs still work and get back on the train, kick off my shoes and settle back down onto my bunk. Just before we pull away some new passengers pass through from another carriage: two Russian girls and a couple of Mongolians. They're heading for the restaurant car. If Janet had been awake I would have placed a bet with him on them never going in that direction again.

At about midnight my time, but only 9pm on Janet's side of the cabin I realise I haven't had any supper. I can't be bothered to eat a full meal now so I traipse down to the restaurant car for a snack. Much to my surprise there's a queue and Bronson is looking flustered. I fall into conversation with a man behind me who speaks perfect English. He's Dutch. Obviously.

'This is the first time in a week I've had a conversation with someone in English,' I say sounding a little more desperate that I intend.

'Me too, you've been staying in Moscow then?' he says, knowingly.

'Yes, what about you?'

'I'm with my wife.'

'At least you have someone to talk to,' I say.

He looks up at the ceiling. 'We had a fight in Moscow, she is speaking to me less than the Russians.'

Before he can out morose me I make a purchase of some Russian chocolate and pistachio nuts. The chocolate is delicious and I can still taste it as I drop off to sleep. This has been a good mileage day.

Day 8

The militaristic delivery favoured by the station announcer in Mariinsk is an effective alarm clock, unless you are Janet who doesn't stir. He could sleep soundly inside a freshly ignited rocket. The announcer keeps me interested by moving up a few octaves. I picture him delivering his well-rehearsed lines while simultaneously feeding his gonads through a mangle.

As is becoming my custom, before I contemplate getting out of bed, I reach for my guidebook to get a handle on what I've missed in the night. Most notably I slumbered over the Great Ob River Bridge: all seven spans of it. At 500 yards long it needs every one of them. The Ob River is one of the longest in the continent of Europe, flowing over 250 miles across Siberia from the Altai Mountains to the Gulf of Ob below the Arctic Ocean. The word Ob makes me chuckle for some reason. I think it may be the fact it rhymes with knob. Before you write me off as nuts you try spending most of your life in a box with a narcoleptic Russian, named after a 1970 Maggie Thatcher impressionist. I calculate I'm about 2300 miles east of Moscow. I reach for my calculator. That's nearly 6 weeks of commuting revenge on the MMS (Millard Mileage Scale). This is excellent news. I check what else passed me by while trying to work out why I dreamt of pork chops all night.

I notice I've also missed Novosibirsk, to the east of the

Ob River. This city's only exists at all because of some short-sighted councillors from Tomsk. You see, the railway was never supposed to pass through Novosibirsk. The original plan in 1893 was for this section of the railway line to follow the route of the Great Siberian Post Road. This was the Russian equivalent of the Pony Express, but without daily scalping incidents and Doris Day. The Post Road route would have taken the railway through Tomsk. The city administrators at Tomsk convened a meeting and did some serious drinking. Then they did some thinking: and some more drinking. The net result was a refusal to grant the railway permission because they feared it would break their monopolies and bring down prices. This decision turned out to be about as clever as Stalin's decision to enter into a pact with Hitler.

The railway authorities had no choice but to take an alternative route, forcing them to hack their way through some of the most inhospitable terrain in Siberia. The taiga regions were then, as indeed they are now, vast swampy forests. Most remain frozen until mid-July each year. Not much of a building season, especially considering the sheer extra effort involved in diverting onto the new route. In fairness things were made a little easier by the lax labour laws in operation then. Thousands of convicts were drafted in and paid well below the minimum wage. The holidays were crap too. The fifty-mile detour took over a year to build.

Tomsk's elders looked on in what can only be described

as smug satisfaction, as the engineers, with only unlimited convict labour, and the fear of failure to fortify them, struggled through terrain more unwelcoming that the inside of the carpet munching lesbian's purple tights. They tittered at these foolish railway workers follies, drank hearty toasts to the Post Road and the enduring star quality of Doris Day.

Of course, the net result is Tomsk became a member of the cast: never to recover its once exalted star billing. Meanwhile, the tiny inter-bred village of Novosibirsk became Western Siberia's capital and now has the largest train station in the whole of Siberia. It manages to sustain a bustling population of 1.4 million. Residents would reserve their smirkiest smirks for anyone visiting from Tomsk but that doesn't happen very often these days due to a radioactive waste disposal plant blowing it up in the sixties and contaminating an area the size of Dorset.

While comatose I also missed another time zone. It's now Moscow plus four, or as we say on my bed 10am. Only two hours till lunch. But what time is it in the restaurant car? If I go there at noon my time it will be 8am their time. Will I get breakfast or stroganoff? I decide to have a quick grime loosening session with the nappy wipes and find out.

On my way to the bathroom I see Blondy in her attendants cabin, she's making a stew concoction. It smells like dinnertimes at my junior school. I do my shower charade, smile, and watch her withering look disappear behind a sliding door. Once inside the bathroom I strip down to my money belt. It has been hanging there since I left Moscow and I've decide it's high time to break with my guidebook's advice and take it off. Its not so much the fact I look like I have a colostomy bag on when I wear it, it's more to do with decay. The smell emanating from it might seem like crushed orchids on a bed of lavender to a sewage loving cockroach but its beginning to make my eyes water. I'm worried the stench might permeate into the currency it carries. I've read the Chinese are notoriously fickle about the quality of the currency you offer. If it's not pristine they reject it. If it smells like Charles Bronson's socks I've got no chance.

Today there's a contraption fitted to the tap's outlet nozzle. I turn on the hot tap. Nothing. I turn on the cold tap. Nothing. No water. I'm naked, and looking for help to solve this riddle will involve my dressing again. I can't be bothered. The nappy wipes are losing their novelty value but smelling like a freshly cleaned baby's arse is still preferable to being followed around by Pepe Le Pew.

On my way back to the cabin I notice Blondy has re-opened her door.

'No, water,' I say, 'in the bathroom, no water.'

She thinks I'm doing a variation of my shower charade and tries to close the door again. I stop her and repeat, this time pointing towards the bathroom, 'no water, IN - THE - BATHROOM, no water.'

She tuts, puts down her stirring spoon and follows me. I twist each tap in turn.

'See, no water.'

She looks at me as if I've just smeared myself in donkey shit in some sort of foolhardy attempt at an Amazonian mating ritual. Tutting loudly and shaking her head, she pushes the nozzle upwards with the palm of her hand. This releases a trickle of water, which she shakes off onto my training shoe before walking back to her witches brew. How was I supposed to know that the fucking taps would operate entirely differently to the day I arrived? Fuck me, I'm always on these trains. And it wasn't in my guidebook, despite it talking affectionately about how friendly and helpful the train attendants are. This thought sets off a train of guidebook related rants in my head. Because, in a nutshell, my tap situation highlights what is so frustrating about guidebooks. In many ways my Trans-Siberian guidebook is excellent. It is full of indisputable facts. It lists destinations along my route. They are undoubtedly there. It gives me all sorts of other facts, how far a town is from Moscow, what the population is. I've been anally following this aspect of my guidebook and enjoying it immensely.

But it also dresses up opinion as fact. According to my book, "Russian people are renowned for their hospitality, they are inquisitive, friendly and welcoming to strangers." No they're not. If I counted every word Janet has said to me since he got on this train it wouldn't make a sentence. If I counted the number of different words he's used I would only need to employ half a hand. Russians don't even acknowledge you if you move out of their path in the corridor. They look down at their shoes and power past. I've never been so close to another human being and not had my existence acknowledged. My guidebook told me to bring photographs of my family. "Russians love seeing photos of your family." Janet hasn't even asked if I have one. In fact Janet hasn't asked me one question. Not one.

"You won't find time to get bored on the train, you'll be playing chess with a Russian, discussing politics with a Chinese intellectual, or haggling with a Mongolian trader." I'm the most loyal customer in the restaurant car and they won't even let me join in their domino games. The nearest thing I've got to intellectualism is nodding towards Howard and Hilda. It's all bollocks.

Back in my cabin I calm down by looking out of the window. The nothingness has given way to more homesteads and villages. Mainly of wooden construction, the smoke spiralling from their chimneys offers the only evidence of life. The homes are surrounded by dirt tracks. Needless to say the tracks don't seem to lead anywhere at first sight, but on closer inspection they converge at something like a petrol station, or a shop. Most traverse the railway line and invariably melt into the forest. Ladas are scattered about like confetti at a giant's wedding.

About an hour later we pull into a small town called Achinsk and Janet sits up. His thick reedy hair, which has been in almost constant contact with his pillows, looks like a field of hay that has been haphazardly harvested. By the time we leave, no more than three minutes later, he's returned to the horizontal and gone back to sleep. We are nearly at the halfway point across Siberia. This is marked with a white obelisk that is unfortunately not visible from the train. By my reckoning Janet has only got out of his bed for fags and the toilet. His toiletry bag hangs unloved on the coat hanger by his bed and he is still dressed exactly how he was when he got on the train in Moscow. By rights he should smell like a stoker's armpit, but, apart from the pungent fag smell when he returns from a smoke break, I'm not picking anything up. This is worrying. Maybe I smell the same and our respective hums are cancelling each other out. It might explain why Blondy always misses out our cabin when she runs the vacuum around the carriage every morning.

I continue to soak up outside. It feels like we've been passing freight trains for hours. They're sagging with coal and lignite. There are gas containers and oil. Some of the names on the side of the freight containers are familiar to me, Goldstar, Hapag Lloyd. Others have English lettering, Moscow Freight,

Byelorussia. Train after train of logs go by, its like every owner of a log cabin, east of here is moving, log by log, to the west.

Janet musters, studiously ignoring me, to take his vitamin tablets. This is a daily ritual I have come to look forward to. Well, there's not much to do on here, except play chess with gregarious Russians, or pick a fight on Confucianism with Chairman Mao's nephew. First he gets all the packets out of his bag. Deliberately, he takes out the blister sleeves from each and pops a couple of pills from one, a single from another. These are laid out in a line on the table. The motion of the train makes them shiver. I count twelve in total. Each one is taken individually, in a specific order, washed down with a slug of water. He then puts the sleeves back into the wrong boxes, corrects himself, puts the boxes back in his bag and then goes back to sleep. It's like watching a drug addict with obsessive-compulsive disorder.

At Krasnoyarsk, on the Yenisey River I get out to stretch my legs. I have to say, despite their lack of use, I find walking surprisingly easy, like riding a bike. Well, not like riding a bike, but you know what I mean. It's the usual platform scene, except I find a food stall that is open. I buy some doughy things, and some oranges. Fruit. I haven't eaten fruit since I left Farnborough. Sod the restaurant car, its a fruit and doughy thing lunch for me. I turn to find the carpet munching lesbian from my train to Moscow behind me. Before I tell her I don't share queues with homogeneous plankton, I decide I'll offer a smile. Not just any old smile. If she cares to study it closely enough she will see this smile is conveying the sort of contempt I reserve for politicians. Before I can fully form it she trumps me with a sucked lemon look and walks off. I watch her still purple clad legs climb up the steps to a train that is heading to Irkutsk. I suspect she's on her way to Lake Baikal in search of the elixir of eternal happiness. Miserable cow.

Just prior to my arrival at Krasnoyarsk the scenery changed from open plain to small valleys that the train had to zig zag through like a slithering snake. I spotted lots of villages nestled into the hillsides. Many of the houses were brightly coloured, some new, or under construction, others that looked like they'd been sticking out of the tree line forever. Every bit of spare land within their boundaries was given up for cultivation. Some even spilled over into railway land. Cabbages, the size of beach balls, were everywhere and most of the plots were being worked by old ladies bundled in so many layers of clothing they looked like the cabbages, only with legs.

Despite the lack of roads these villages had a real permanence about them, in complete contrast to most of the towns I'd passed previously that simply looked like they'd been napalmed with cement. They had block after block of high rises that cast shadows over derelict garages. Old cars littered the roads. The people I have seen have been as grey as the landscape and have either been lighting a fag, smoking one, or flicking one away. The Siberian uniform of anoraks with hoods pulled up over woolly hats, garish puffa jackets and gloves have been ubiquitous.

Once past Krasnoyarsk I notice a marked difference in my vista. It's dominated by mile after mile of lumber mills. The wooded hillsides have butchered bald patches where the loggers have been most active. Open cast mining adds to the violent vista. It's like the hills have been attacked by a giant axe-man. It's a saddening sight so I turn away and watch the corridor traffic. Howard and Hilda pass by regularly, he now offers a nod, the Nordics continue their relay race to fill flasks and I also catch sight of the healthy looking Provodnik, who passes by with Fatty. I haven't seen those two for a day or so. I've heard them mind. Every mealtime they congregate at Blondy's house. It's the only time I hear laughter, or conversation above a whisper. I doze off.

I wake around 7pm, famished and head for the restaurant car. Surely they must be worried about me, they haven't seen me all day. Much to my surprise there are customers. Four men, who I mark down as Belgians simply because they have bushy moustaches, are sitting at a table finishing off their meal. They look like accountants on a jolly. They acknowledge my existence, get up, and leave. What is the collective noun for accountants? A spreadsheet? They say goodbye to Bronson in English, but its heavily accented. Bronson nods, which looks only lightly accented.

We go through our usual pointy game. Point, niet, point, niet, until eventually he says, 'pork chop.'

'Pork chop? I repeat. I've been dreaming of pork chops.

'Da, pork chop.'

Pork chop? Blimey, I haven't had pork chop in ages, what a great idea, pork chop. I decide to have one. Can't wait. Pork chop, if there's one thing I could eat right now, at this point in time, it's a pork chop. Mmmm... pork chop. Lovely.

It's a meatball with an egg on top, accompanied with fried tomatoes, shredded cabbage and some cucumber.

'Pork chop?' I say looking down at the plate like a child who's just got a book on equations for Christmas.

'Pork chop, niet,' he says shaking his finger for emphasis.

Not only do I not get a pork chop it takes over an hour to arrive. OK, passing through another time zone has a lot to do with it, but I mean, no pork chop? I take my mind off the lack of pork chop by thinking about tomorrow. In mileage terms it's a long slog, although it's followed by a relatively short day when we cross the border into China. Most of the time will be taken up with bureaucracy rather than miles travelled and I'm not looking forward to it at all. They invented red tape in this part of the world. Here, paperwork means a job, not repetitive strain injury. The last thing I want is an unhinged Russian border guard rummaging about in my festering pants. The rotting smell might just re-ignite memories of his burning flesh in a Chechen torture chamber.

The predicament I have to face when I get back to my cabin is: should I read my Bill Bryson book? I haven't kept to my four chapter rule and there's no way its going to last all the way to Beijing. I consider swotting up with my Beijing guidebook but can muster little enthusiasm for it. The trouble is I'm enjoying the train journey so much the city stops are bordering on a hindrance in my head. The only enthusiasm I can marshal for China's capital is the thought of a shower and change of pants.

I turn out the light and turn over. It's nearly midnight in my bed. Janet takes lights out as a cue to get up for dinner. He prepares and eats his porridge entirely in the dark. A shaft of light troubles me when he opens the door on the way to his post porridge fag, but I don't remember him returning.

Day 9

The immensity of this train journey is really starting to affect me. Every morning the view from my window changes so markedly. I had become aware of a lot of Provodnitsa activity outside my cabin at about 8 o'clock, bought on, I think, by our arrival at Irkusk. This town has a bit of a wild past, in no small part due to the discovery of gold in the nineteenth century. According to my guidebook it was a veritable den of iniquity, although personally I don't believe it. Russians don't like being happy. It was probably just full of places that allowed you to sit about smoking and training your face muscles to adopt the shape of a Blood Hound. Apparently it was once known as the "Paris of the North," which is incentive enough for anyone to sleep though it, which I pretty much did.

A couple of hours later I wake properly to find the train threading its way through a thick forest of cedar and beech trees. The track is sufficiently snaking for me to catch glimpses of the engine powering us across the vastness. A stiff breeze is searching out the weakest leaves and plucking them from the skeletal branches, sending them on a slow descent to the forest floor. Almost immediately the updraft of the train blows them skywards again. I watch them skit back into the air on a spiralling trajectory before re-settling on the damp ground. At window level I am treated to a crow, sleek and black like liquid tarmac, flying furiously in the opposite direction to the train, before giving up and wheeling away on an invisible thermal. The scenery is mesmerizing and I'm transfixed until I remember we will be passing lake Baikal pretty soon. I rush to the bathroom for my daily smearing ritual.

I've given up on ever extracting water from the contraption on the tap, so I strip off sufficiently for easy nappy wipe access. I'm doffing a cap to the world of hygiene but it's more like being grouted than washed: at least I'm trying.

Surprisingly my digestive transit, which has been pretty much a non-existent bodily function since embarkation in Moscow, indicates that a train of my own is heading for the end of a tunnel. As a precautionary measure I sit on the rocket launcher toilet. If you want an idea of what it's like try sticking your arse out of the cockpit of a Red Arrow mid display. To my pleasant surprise I'm shaping up for my first proper poo since I left Cologne. This uncomfortable state of affairs is entirely due to Russian food. It's harder to break down than James Bond. I can only wonder at the panic my stomach enzymes have endured each time I've send down another brick of indigestible matter. They must feel like nineteenth century tin miners on a straight seven-day shift.

The Siberian wind funnelled directly up my rectum is worryingly, quite pleasant, but I don't tarry as there is a real danger my arse will catch pneumonia. Reaching out for the container that holds the Ryvita paper, I discover the post-box like aperture has been taped up. No matter I have a solution to hand and my nappy wipes are dragooned into action for a more traditional purpose. They follow the results of my labours onto the track as the waste bin is taped up too.

Back in the cabin I'm shocked to find Janet both awake and sitting up. These are two actions I have rarely seen him undertake simultaneously. He then does something quite worrying: he speaks.

'Morning, Mike, soon Lake Baikal.'

Just as I think we might be shaping up for a conversation we enter a tunnel and everything goes black. When we emerge I get my first glimpse of the Lake. Despite the heavy grey sky the water's reflection is deep blue. It's easy to see why it's called the "Blue Eyes, of Siberia." And like 'ole blue eyes,' when he made his last film, its 50 million years old, making it the oldest lake in the world, by some millions. On a distant shore, in total contrast, I can see the sandy coloured Primorsky Mountains, bathed in sunlight.

Whichever way you want to measure it Lake Baikal is truly impressive. It's the deepest lake in the world at nearly 5,400 feet, which means nothing to you unless you're at the bottom of it and struggling to get to the surface before you run out of breath. However, here's a sobering thought if you fancy some perspective. Lets say you are on a boat in the middle and have an overriding urge to step off it and not get wet. Here's what you do. Firstly, throw Ben Nevis overboard. Balance the Gherkin building in London on top of that and then quickly pile on 26 London buses. Finally, place the latest edition of the Health & Safety Executive rulebook on top of all that. That should break the surface sufficiently for you to remain as dry as a bone. But, the impressiveness doesn't stop at depth. It's also four hundred miles long and forty miles wide at its portliest. We will only be skirting its southern shores. As the train descends from its high vantage point we pass through some tatty farmsteads and an ugly mining village at Slyudyanka. The buildings are mainly constructed of untreated grey wood and are in total contrast to the beauty that surrounds them. Ahead in the distance I can just make out the red striped storage tanks of a gas facility. It sits there like a bleeding gash on a model's face.

'It's very beautiful,' Janet says, startling me. I'm pretty certain he means the lake. 'Yes, it is,' I reply. 'Will we pass it for long?'

'I don't know,' he says, laying back on his bed and closing his eyes. He has his glasses on still so I know he's only planning a nap.

We pull into the station at Slyudyanka, which is only a short stop so the attendants won't let us off. This is a pity because the lake is very close, and it would make a great place to take some pictures. I've had to take mine through the glare of the window in the cabin, so I know the majesty of the landscape will look like its been wrapped in cling-film when I download them to my computer. I stand looking at the platform from the warmth of the corridor. There are quite a few women congregating by our carriage door trying to get in but the attendants stop them. The ladies are dressed for the sharp freezing wind whipping across the platform from the lake. Swathed in layers of scarves, and bundled in coats, they hold up smoked fish skewered onto spikes. It's Omul, a fish only found in the lake. I'd love to tell you what it tastes like but fatty keeps the train passengers and fish sellers apart. He will no doubt be savouring them later though, as he purchased half a dozen before we pulled away. Fat bastard.

We skirt the lake for over a hundred miles, fording small tributaries that feed into it under rusty red bridges. Freight trains stacked with logs regularly block my view on their journey west. Nevertheless, I sit at the window transfixed at the sheer majesty of my surroundings. Sometimes we come so close to the lake the spray from its waves flecks our cabin window. In whichever direction I look I see untainted nature, raw and virgin. Except for the odd dirty village, or run down factory belching out shit. Irritating blemishes yes, but despite their concerted efforts they fail to spoil the munificence of their surroundings. Why Janet would prefer to sleep through it is beyond me. At some point he dispensed with the glasses, and is gently snoring when the line turns east through what remains of the ancient volcanoes of the Khamar-Daban foothills, towards Boyarsky.

The day is becoming murkier as we trundle through more homesteads and small towns that are uniformly ugly. Rubbish is everywhere, literally piles of it. I've never seen such disregard for an environment. It bleeds into the beauty surrounding it. The nicest thing I see that is man made is a graveyard, or more accurately a grave wood. Brightly coloured tombstones are interspersed between the trees that are remarkably well maintained. Pity the locals couldn't put as much effort into their towns.

I'm sorry to be leaving the lake. It's been remarkably relaxing. My mind has wandered all over the place. Not like the daydreaming I'm used to on my commuter train. I could only classify that as a slight amble. Here my daydreaming has laced on stout walking boots and strode out into the blue yonder. A friend asked me before I left, what I might do all day on the train.

'Oh, I don't know,' I replied, 'bit of reading, some thinking.'

'Thinking? He said, incredulously, like it was something that should be left to philosophers. 'Thinking? What about?'

I didn't have the answer then, but I do now. I've wandered all over the place, back to my childhood, forward to all sorts of things. I've been assembling memories all day. Some so long forgotten I'm not sure they're my memories at all. Maybe they're composite memories. Who knows, all I can say is that it's been incredibly relaxing. I recommend it. When I ran out of memories of my own I thought about the people on the train, what were they thinking, where were they going, what were they planning? Nosy bastard aren't I?

We start to track the Selenga River that feeds into the Lake behind us. Litter strewn village eyesores do their best to distract me from the Mayan Mountain range to my right but fail. Clouds sit on their majestic peaks like cotton wool hats. The journey along the valley is so beautiful it hurts. As does the gashes of logging that do their very best to blight it. Despite Russia's best efforts the scenery wins. Mile upon mile of green conifers cover the hillsides with occasional splurges of yellow beech for contrast. It's like God painted everywhere green, then walked back along this valley with a dripping yellow paintbrush.

The villages continue to do their best to spoil the beauty with their corrugated roofs sitting on washed out, grey wooden buildings. They look like boils: the buildings and the people. The approach to Ulan Ude is even more despairing. Its an experiment in concrete that has been repeated every ten years or so. Every time a new block of concrete goes up, an old one is abandoned, but only after its been stripped of anything of value. The result is empty concrete husks next to newer buildings of the same style. If these buildings were animals the only humane thing you could do is put them down. They're black teeth in the most attractive mouth on earth. I decide to get off at Ulan Ude for some fresh air, which to my surprise, they haven't managed to spoil yet. It's fresher than a poacher's rabbit. The station is ugly but not as bad as the twin sisters that walk past me. Bloody hell. They look like a couple of cabbage patch dolls. If there is a God he owns a wicked sense of humour. He probably looked at the first and thought, blimey, bet I can't do that again. Then promptly did. Or it might just be, like my mood, that everything is ugly here. Before I get back on the train the Nordics approach me. They are Finnish I discover, and the tall one is called Alice.

'Are you travelling alone,' she asks.

'Yes, I'm sharing with a Russian, he doesn't speak much.'

'Ah,' she says, nodding knowingly. 'We have found this also.' She translates for her friend who doesn't speak English, although she manages a perfectly good English nod.

'Where are you heading?' I ask in an effort to keep the conversation going. I want to make sure I can still speak English.

'We are going to Shanghai, and you?'

'Vietnam.'

'Perhaps we will find that people talk in China?' Alice says.

I spend a fruitless five minutes looking for a food stall but to no avail. It will be the restaurant car for me again tonight. At least it will be the last meal. The restaurant cars change at the border. I've organised fireworks and champagne. Bruce Forsyth is doing the after dinner entertainment.

Leaving Ulan Ude is no hardship, although this uniformly ugly concrete city is only replaced with sawmill after sawmill. Freight trains pass us with alarming regularity, some of them thirty or forty carriages long. We also pass the junction where the Trans-Mongolian line branches off from the Trans-Siberian. My train will branch off soon too. We skirt Mongolia rather than cross its border, which saves me the price of a new car in visa fees. The longer route means our train arrives in Beijing a day later than the Mongolian one.

It makes me think a little more about the effort involved in laying this railway. Siberia supports the three longest continuous rail routes in the world, and the majority of it was laid in the nineteenth century. Could you imagine undertaking such a project today? In a typical year over 63,000,000 cubic yards of earth was removed. Rather inconveniently the JCB hadn't been invented so it was all done by hand. Over 1,000,000 tons of rails were laid, and 60 miles of bridges and tunnels. At its height almost 90,000 people worked on it. And there was none of this hard-hat and high visibility vest malarkey. Just goes to show what you can achieve if you have the will and an endless supply of convicts.

I make a conscious effort to avoid looking outside, the towns are all vile and the litter they insist on dumping around them blights the countryside that surrounds them. It's like travelling through a landfill corridor that has managed to get planning permission through a nature reserve. Perversely, Janet sits up in bed and watches this wretchedness into the early evening. Perhaps Russians enjoy bleak vistas. He remains in the sitting position as we approach Petrosky Zavod and another time zone: we are now Moscow plus six. He settles back down for an afternoon nap, while I dress for a late dinner. That's to say I put my shoes on. I've hatched a cunning plan for this evening's gastronomic event.

I'm surprised to see some people in the restaurant car when I arrive. Three men and a woman: Australians. They are just finishing a bottle of wine. I can't work out the dynamics of the group, is it a husband and wife with two gay friends? Four gay friends? They look like teachers, so I plump for the latter.

Anyway, here's my cunning plan. To fool Bronson I'm going to ask for meatballs. Last time he suggested pork chop and bought me meatballs, so this is my attempt at reverse psychology. Surely If I ask for meatballs he'll bring me a pork chop. Clever eh? He brings me the menu. I notice today that he's dispensed with the blue slippers again and is wearing shoes: the sort accountants buy from C&A with a rim along the toe line. The laces are missing as usual. I ignore the menu in his outstretched hand.

'Meatballs please.'

'Niet, only pork chop.'

'No meatballs?'

'Da.'

'OK, pork chop please.'

'Da.'

Genius.

I eavesdrop on the two Aussies I can see from my seat while pretending to read the toothpick container. I notice for the first time that the brand name is "Fang," which lifts my spirits somewhat. From what I can gather they're going all the way to Beijing and debating what to see in the time they have available. I have a real urge to join in but am distracted by Bronson who looks a little agitated when he brings me a beer. He doesn't bother to ask if I want one anymore. Shortly after he returns with my dinner. Meatballs. Bugger, my double bluff has been double bluffed. At least the black bread is fresh, I saw the spindly-legged chef buy some at Slyudyanka. Looking down at my plate I discover that I have two meatballs. They've given me an extra one. They must really hate me. The Aussies leave soon after, each looking down at my meal like it should be on a Petri dish. I notice their plates have fish remains on them. Why have I never had fish?

Back in the cabin, Janet is sleeping. I undress for bed, that is to say I take my shoes off and climb in. Today has been a strange day. It's the last full one I will spend on Russian soil, a country that has both astounded me with its sheer beauty, and appalled me with it's hell bent desire to ruin it. Tomorrow I experience Russian border guards in the flesh. A sobering thought that forces me to start thinking about my delicate Western bottom.

Day 10

I wake to find the train dissecting a vast plain that stretches out to a range of hills on the horizon. Running parallel to the track is a road chock full of Ladas. I assure you there are no other makes of car on it and I get a good look because the train is going slower than the cars. In fact I could probably run faster. The sun is high in a clear blue sky, illuminating small black dots in the distance. They're cows, the first I have seen on this trip. I also catch glimpses of people, swathed in their puffa jackets, which look entirely out of place under such a beautiful sunny day.

During the night the train branched off the main Trans - Siberian line and we are now travelling south on the Trans-Manchurian section. I get up and move into the corridor. I want to get my bearings. Howard is standing by his door: he nods and smiles, then disappears back into his cabin. I look out of the window for the kilometre posts found on this side of the track. As the name suggests these mark kilometre intervals for the length of the journey across Siberia. On my side of the post is the kilometres travelled east. On the reverse, for trains travelling the other way, kilometres travelled west. Its not entirely accurate, but it helps. The other option is to try and memorise the Cyrillic construction of a station's name and attempt to find it in my guidebook. I calculate that the next station will be Borzya in the Zabaikalsk region of Siberia. This is, if you like, the last county in Russia before we enter China. Still worried about customs I dash to the bathroom for a wash.

If a digit is going to be inserted it will be into a clean orifice. I am British you know.

By the time I come back we are pulling into Borzya. It's a dreary town. The ethnicity of its inhabitants is markedly different. The people here are Buryrats, of Mongolian descent. It wasn't that many years ago they lived in Yurts out on the plains. These people come from hardy stock, so why are they all dressed for an arctic winter? I'll tell you why, because it is bloody freezing. I quickly buy some pistachio nuts for lunch from a stallholder who looks like he's been standing in this spot forever. I feel guilty buying my food from a third party but I can't face the restaurant car again. My stomach feels like a witches cauldron. It is groaning with this incessant delivery of food only digestible by ruminants. Forced through the human digestion process produces a foul by-product: the most putrid smelling wind. It's the main reason I got out at Borzya. The pressure build up has been worse than a steam train straining up a steep hill. The release has been like one coming down one. Careful to stand a good distance away from other people I sound like an idling speedway bike. When I'm finished my stomach contracts like a balloon with a puncture.

Back on the train I bump into Blondy and do my shower charade, the look of contempt I get back could have withered a cactus. In the cabin, Janet is busy. That's to say he's standing.

'Morning,' I say

'Morning Mike, soon Zabaikalsk, later China.'

'Yes, how long do you think we'll be at customs?

'I don't know,' he shrugs, walking off for a fag.

Not long after he returns Blondy comes in and hands both of us a form.

'Customs declaration,' Janet explains

'Its in Russian,' I say.

He shouts after Blondy, who returns, they jabber away for some while and she disappears again.

'No English forms,' he explains.

'None? Did they not think any foreigners would travel on this train? We're going into a different country.'

He shrugs, 'I will translate, no problem.'

And so it is that Janet takes me through the form, like I'm a simpleton, reading each question in Russian and then repeating it to me in English, VERY SLOWLY. At one point he asks me if I eat guns or explosives.

'Eat guns?'

'No, sorry, do you bring guns or explosives?'

We carry on like this until the form is complete. For all I know I've owned up to owning enough of an arsenal to take on the mentally deranged border guards.

We pull into Zabaikalsk station. It looks quite new and is essentially a very long, cream and brown building that occupies most of the platform. We pull alongside. At one end a footbridge leads up to a road that takes you into the town. There is another platform in the centre with rails on either side. It doesn't seem to have any access from any other part of the station, which is mildly intriguing. The sun shines brightly, but there is no warmth in it. Soon after we stop there is commotion in the carriage, I stand to investigate but Janet pulls me down.

'Better stay in cabin,' he says.

A man appears wearing green combat fatigues and boots that reach up to his middle shin. He looks like a 1970s Millwall fan. He is unsmiling and ignores us entirely as he looks around, presumably for my arsenal of weapons. He then steps aside and a man in a more formal uniform takes his place. He is wearing a peaked cap with gold braiding along the top of the peak, a shirt with pleats straighter than a German autobahn, matching trousers, and a brown leather attaché case under his arm. He looks at me and rattles off some Russian. Janet butts in and then turns to me with a translation.

'You must give him your passport.'

I hand it over. He puts it in the attaché without looking at it and snaps it shut. He rattles off some more Russian to Janet, takes his passport, which he does look at, then he's gone. I watch from the corridor as he disappears into one of the doors of the customs building and wonder if I'll ever see my passport again. Not long after, Blondy and the healthy one, who I haven't seen for some time, start moving through the carriage, jabbering away in Russian, despite at least fifty percent of their charges not speaking it.

'We must get off, they change wheels now,' Janet explains.

I forgot. The bogies need to be changed so the train can run on Chinese tracks.

'How, long do you think?

'I don't know,' he shrugs.

I hastily pull on my only sweater, grab my camera and jump off, nearly knocking over Alice from Finland.

'Sorry,' I say.

'No, problem,' she says, smiling.

'Do you know how long we'll be here?

'I asked the attendant, she said about three hours.'

'You can speak Russian?'

'Yes, I come here to practice.'

'But Russians don't speak.'

'No, it is difficult.'

'Have you been here before then?'

'Yes, I play Russia at Basketball in the 1970s. I played for Finland,' she adds needlessly.

'Really?'

'Yes, but this is my first time back.'

I want to ask her how it's all changed but I need to get back on the train. All my diabetic medication is on there and I will need it if I'm going to be here that long. I try to get back on but Blondy blocks my way.

'Niet.'

'But I need my medication. I'm a diabetic.' I point to the train, 'MEDICATION,' I enunciate.

The miserable cow still won't let me on despite Alice translating.

I step into line with Alice and her friend as we head for the bridge. She did tell me her name ages ago but I've forgotten it. The Belgians are already over the other side of the bridge and heading up the hill. The wind carries their voices, they sound in very high spirits. They've been regulars in the restaurant car, so I suspect they're celebrating the culinary liberation that the border might provide.

'They are from Holland,' Alice says, as if reading my mind.

'Ah, I thought they were Belgian.'

'They thought you was German,' she says.

'German, me?'

'I tell them only English wear wrong clothes in cold.'

And she is right, it's bloody freezing. As we cross the bridge and head up the hill the wind cuts through me like a Samurai sword.

There are a lot of men dressed in green passing us and heading towards the train. I suspect they're something to do with the border station. The men not in uniform all have leather jackets and Christmas jumpers on. They look like a 1970s Top of The Pops crowd. The women avoid eye contact and are all wearing narrow legged jeans. They all have straight, lank hair. The town itself is hard to describe, but here goes. Think of a long road with sink estates on either side. You know the places I mean, you see them on the telly when there's a news item on knife crime. Now consider what the after effects of a nuclear explosion would be. Add them together. Now, assume what remains has been carpet bombed with fag ends and litter. Get the picture? Still struggling? OK, think of Aldershot.

This place is like the overflow car park for hell. Shop windows display items you might see in a bric-a-brac shop. There is nothing in the stock that offers a clue to what the shop might specialise in. Mangy apples share the same shelf space as oily car parts. There are no lights to welcome you in, no signs, not even in Russian. This is a border town. They have a captive audience of, probably, 5000 passengers a week passing through, yet the only entertainment on offer is scraping fag ends of the soles of your shoes.

'Is this it? I ask Alice.

'I will ask if there is a restaurant,' she says, and walks over to a young lady outside a bank. I can tell it's a bank because it's the only building within two hundred yards with a light on. Alice asks a question, the girl becomes flustered and steps back into the bank.

'She says she doesn't know.'

'Doesn't know? Is this her first time in town?'

'I think she was a little shy,' Alice says, diplomatically.

Within ten minutes we are at the edge of town, that is to say we have walked the length of the one street. We turn around and start back on the other side of the road. We hear the Dutch laughing, but can't see them. The noise is coming from a dark cavernous doorway. It looks like the entrance to a crack den. Alice sticks her head in and reports back.

'It's a cafe, do you want to eat food here?'

I would rather eat athlete's foot. 'Ah, no thanks, I'm going to head back to the station.'

'OK, see you later,' she says, disappearing into the blackness. I have my doubts I'll ever see her again.

On the way back I bump into Janet, its nice to see him upright. He's wearing his heavy grey jacket over another grey jacket, and underneath are the grey clothes he's been sleeping in for the last five days. On his head is a grey baseball cap. When he smiles I discover his teeth are grey. Janet is the human equivalent of February.

'Hello Mike, you eat yet?'

'Ah, no, thought I would go back to the station.'

'No food there, you want come with me? I can translate.'

'No, really, that's very kind, but I think I'll head back.'

'OK,' he says, and lumbers off.

The platform is deserted, in contrast to the waiting room, which is full of people. I don't recognise any from our train. They have a local look to my eyes - knots of Mongolians and pockets of Russians. I find a seat and take it all in. The walls are the same dark green as the border guard uniforms. At either end of the seating area is a door, from which officials frequently appear. They stride across the main concourse where I'm sitting before disappearing through the door opposite. I avoid eye contact in case they're scanning for finger insertion victims and instead concentrate on a splendid chandelier hanging above me. I also spend some time trying to work out why the balcony surrounding it doesn't seem to have any means of access.

I am disturbed from my internal machinations by the large entrance doors bursting open. A young man enters through them dragging a huge bag across the floor. It's about three feet squared, as high as his thigh and obviously heavy. He wrestles it into position opposite me. Very shortly after another young man appears with a similar sized bag, quickly followed by another, and another. In no time at all a small procession of these street urchins have dragged in about twenty bags. They sit on them panting until a lady comes in and orders them to get off. She may look like a pantomime dame but she carries the authority of a staff sergeant. She sports a mono-brow hairier than a badger that moves independently of her facial muscles. A lengthy counting process takes place between her and the head street urchin, money changes hands, and they leave, presumably to return to the cast of Oliver! She now sets about rearranging the bags. Her very masculine hands lift them with some ease, although the stitching on the arse of her trousers reaches maximum torque. A second pantomime dame arrives and immediately starts to help her, followed by a young skinny girl with a spotty face and finally, a man dressed in the ubiquitous leather jacket and C&A jumper.

They all set about re-arranging the bags into some semblance of order. Eventually they are satisfied with their efforts and slump down in the chairs opposite me. I am now surrounded by bags and unable to move. The mono-browed pantomime dame takes charge again and orders the man back into the bag section for a couple of smaller ones. He lays them at her feet: a gnarly, crusted pair with hooked nails sticking out of her open-toed sandals like limpets. She is truly the ugliest human being I have ever seen and I went to discos in the 1970s.

They take it in turns to delve into the bags and pull out food. She produces a baguette the size of my arm and starts to munch her way down it. Because she is wearing so much lipstick each bite leaves a red ring. With every mouthful she fingers in a slice of luncheon meat from a plastic packet on her lap. Her podgy fingers have to push hard to get it all behind her teeth. The other pantomime dame is curiously eyebrow-less. Maybe they only have the one between them. In an effort to keep up with the other dame she has painted some on with a pencil. They arch like a couple of portcullis that make her look constantly surprised. She is eating a flan topped with green bogies. When she takes a bite they ping off in all directions. I'm so mesmerised I fail to notice Alice and her friend make their way through the forest of bags and sit next to me. Within seconds they are mesmerised too.

'They have a lot of bags,' Alice says.

'Yes, I think they're full of food.'

She's still chuckling when Hilda turns up and garbles off some Russian to Alice.

'She say follow her.'

'Why?'

'I don't know.' We get up and follow her out on to the platform.

Its bloody freezing, the sky is slate grey but we're not outside for long. Hilda grabs Alice by the hand and pulls her through a door further down the platform. I follow. It's another, much warmer, waiting room and entirely empty except for Howard and Hilda. Howard is standing at the front of a long row of chairs. We sit. He smiles at me, nods at the Finnish ladies, and then surprises me by speaking English.

'Much warmer in here.'

'You speak English?'

'A little, and German, some French, and Chinese.'

Alice interrupts. 'They travel to China to teach ballet. Before they were ballet dancers in the Kirov. At the mention of Kirov Hilda looks up and smiles. It knocks ten years off her. Ah, that explains the poise and the way they carry themselves to and from the samovar. I say this to Alice and she translates. Hilda smiles again and puts down the puzzle book she is working on. Howard smiles broadly at her, rolling back on the balls of his feet, like he's warming up.

'We dance everywhere with Kirov, he says, Germany, France, Japan, Finland, China.'

'Did you ever dance in England?'

'No, not England, Russia will not let us leave.'

I get the feeling he's enjoying his audience. 'Now, we teach in China. China girl big', he says, raising his hand parallel to his head. 'China boy small,' he places his hand palm down by his waist. 'Also no touch,' he shakes his finger at me for emphasis. 'It's true. Makes teach very difficult.'

I try to imagine non-touching ballet without success.

His wife speaks to me and Alice translates, 'do you do Suduko? Hilda points to her magazine.

'No, I prefer crosswords.'

'Tsk... much too difficult,' Alice translates for me.

'No yogurt!' Howard says, all of a sudden.

'Pardon?'

'No, yogurt, no milk.' He shakes his finger again. "Kill you in China.'

At first I think I've stumbled on the head of the anti-dairy league but then I realise he's talking about the dairy product health scare in China. Contaminated milk has been killing people all over the place: sadly the majority have been children. We continue to chat for a little while longer, with Alice translating, but I know I must find something to eat. I can feel my blood sugars getting low and passing out in a border station on the Russian, Chinese border without a lock on my zipper would be foolish. I make my excuses and leave. Heading back over the bridge I find the kiosk I'm looking for. I saw it earlier today but it was closed.

Like the ones in Moscow there is a small hatch at knee height. 'Hello.' I say through it to a lady who looks like she's about to be attacked by a mad axe-man. I don't expect her to speak any English, but who doesn't understand pointing? In the end, when it looks like I won't go away she puts something in a bag and takes my money. The hatch is shut quickly with considerable force, nearly taking my fingers with it. I'm not sure what's in the bag. It has the texture of a doughnut, but the filling is savoury, possible fish. Or meat. I finish it back on the platform just as Janet turns up. He's still vertical and looks happy. I think he might be pissed.

'I find restaurant. I point menu, they say "niet" I point again, they say, "niet." OK, I say, what you have?'

Welcome to my world.

'They tell me meat and potatoes.' He smiles his grey smile at me. I know what's coming.

'I get fish!' he laughs, which makes him look like a constipated Uncle Fester.

'You eat, Mike?'

'No, well, yes, a little.'

'We can go back to town, not far. I will translate.'

Luckily our train pulls back in.

'Ah, the train, we better not go back to town.'

We clamber aboard and shortly after I am re-united with my passport. The declaration though, is still sitting on the cabin table. I pick it up intending to follow the border guard down the corridor and hand it to him. Janet pulls me back.

'They haven't taken my declaration,' I say.

'You have passport back, better to stay quiet.'

I sit back down and shortly after one of the combat troops appears at the door. He looks me up and down and then peers at my holdall poking it with his baton.

'This is yours?'

Shit, here we go. 'Yes, it is.'

'Keep lock, China steal all time, keep safe,' he says, and leaves. Wow, I've cleared customs. I offer silent apologies to the receptionist at the Hotel Tourist.

'How long before we cross the border Janet?'

'Very soon,' he says, confidently.

I have been dumbfounded by the amount Janet has been talking, and he shows no sign of stopping.

'Mike, I am sorry I sleep so long.' He explains that this is his first holiday for over two years and in that period he has worked fourteen hours a day, six days a week. He's meeting his wife in Shenyang, she is already there having flown ahead a few days before.

'Why did you come by the train? I ask.

'I wanted to see something of my country.'

I check his face to see if he's joking. He's not. The only way he's seen what his country looks like is if he's painted Siberian panoramas on the inside of his eyelids.

'I am not very well, I have problem with my stomach, and I am depressed.'

I'd assumed all Russians were depressed, but I try to sound sympathetic.

'Oh, dear, are you seeing a doctor?'

'Doctor no good in Russia, buy certificate. I check on Internet to see what wrong and buy drugs there.'

'What about your depression?'

'I have friend, training for psychiatrist, he get me drugs.'

'Oh, dear, I'm sorry to hear that you have troubles.' I'm worried he might get morose and throw himself off the train, mind you if he did it now he'd simply fall on to the platform. He continues.

'Mike, Russia shit. My mother, she say better for me now. I say how better mother? Look at court system. Same. Look at regional authority. Same.' Pockets of thick saliva begin to accumulate in the corners of his mouth as he speaks. Maybe he was bitten by one of the stray dogs in town, or perhaps his stomach has just realised what he had for lunch.

'They have all power, Mike. Ordinary people, they have nothing. Why they not make rich like in West. In West, work hard, rise up.' I try to get off the subject of inequality in Russian society by asking him where he lives in Moscow.

'I move from centre, pollution killing me.' We lapse into silence. He, because he needs to regroup his thoughts and me because I'm frightened anything I say might send him over the edge.

Four hours later we are still sitting on the platform. Janet is back to his usual laying position with his coats on. It's dark now and from the corridor I can see into the customs hall that is lit up like a lantern. Three guards are busy. They have the contents of a suitcase laid out across the floor. One guard checks each piece and another photographs it. The third is writing an inventory.

'Do you think the delay is anything to do with that,' I ask. Janet gets up and looks.

'Mongol traders,' he says, raising his eyebrows.

'Really?'

'Yes, they come Russia for maybe six months, can only take three thousand Roubles (about £100) out of the country. They hide money but guards look everywhere.'

I bet they do.

Eventually the train pulls away and without us knowing it we pass into China and another time zone. It's now Moscow plus seven. So, despite it being pitch black outside the window, on Janet's side of the cabin its only four in the afternoon. It's only a very short journey to the Chinese border station of Manzhouli. As we approach a mist envelops the platform creating a yellow tinge to the light thrown down from the ornate lampposts, which are set out as uniformly as the Chinese border guards along the platform. Behind them is a grandiose building that shines newness. Light illuminates off the glass and aluminium, the mist smoothing its sharp edges a little.

I sit back on my bed and wait with Janet, who has managed a semi-sitting position for some time now. It's not long before a very smart uniformed female border official appears. The Chinese uniforms are a slightly lighter green than the Russians, but the creases are infinitely sharper. She is immaculately turned out as are the two officers standing behind her. We hand her our passports. She glances at them and then addresses me in better English than the owner of my local Chinese take-away.

'Welcome to China. You must complete this declaration.' She hands me a form, an English form, and then speaks to Janet in Russian, presumably repeating what she said to me. Then in English she says to Janet, 'we only use English or Chinese declaration forms. Would you like me to translate the form for you?'

'No, no, thank you,' Janet says, 'I understand English, no problem.'

She goes on to explain the customs procedure and roughly how long it will all take, then leaves. One of her assistants waits to collect our declaration forms. He takes the forms and says, 'you are welcome to use the facilities of the station but you cannot leave the premises until you have cleared customs. Understand? We both nod.

'That was easy,' I say to Janet.

'So, I hear you have many Indians in England,' he replies, which throws me a bit. Before I can work out what on earth he's talking about he adds, 'from when you own Kenya, they all come to England, yes?'

'Ah... yes,' I mumble, then, in an effort to get on to a subject I know more about I ask, 'shall we go and eat?'

'Good idea Mike, but you must take my coat, very cold.'

'No, really, I'll be fine, it's only a short walk.'

'No, you must, you will feel too cold.'

'Really, I'll be fine.'

We step on to the platform and the wind hits me so hard the muscles in my face contract and start to sting like I've been slapped.

'You have windy like this in England?' Janet asks, as we both lean into a force ten.

'Yes,' I say, 'we call it East Anglia.'

He is still trying to pronounce this as we reach the main doors. The nearest he gets is East Angrier. The heavy oak doors are exceedingly tall and take a shoulder to move them, but once on the other side the cutting wind disappears and is replaced with the cuddly warmth of the building. I find myself looking at a marbled waiting area about the size of a school gym. Corinthian columns rise up to a high ceiling. I try to recall a waiting room like this on the UK rail system without success. In truth it is more like a cathedral.

'The food hall is upstairs,' Janet says. 'I will meet you there, I need to use toilet first.'

I walk up a set of stairs, that wouldn't have looked out of place on the set of Wuthering Heights, and into another room similar to the size of the one downstairs. To my right is a long rectangular partitioned area with an opening at either end. I head to see what's behind it. Immediately a man approaches me. He looks Mongolian but is Chinese and very stocky. His leather jacket and red jeans look brand new.

'Ching Morney?'

'Pardon?'

'Ching Morney?' He pulls a wad of cash from the inside of his jacket: he's a currency dealer. My Chinese Yuan have spent most of their life next to a slowly decaying crutch but they should still be OK.

'No thanks,' I say, and wander behind the partition.

It is a market. The first thing that strikes me, apart from the abundance of things for sale on the ten or so stalls, is that all the stallholders are women with Hilda Ogden hairstyles. The tight perm isn't a style I usually associate with Asian women. The pace is frenetic. A small lady grabs my hand and pulls me to her stall. It's pretty much the same as all the others.

'Beer, noodle, fish?' The produce is mainly tins and packets, but there are vacuum-packed sausages and meats, and plenty of fresh fruit. The apples are the size of melons and the melons are the size of, well, really big melons.

'Ching Morney,' she offers, 'good price, no cheat.'

After the undertaker pace of Zabaikalsk I rejoice in the commercial energy sparking from every stallholder and quickly negotiate a deal on some grapes, apples and peaches, the size of, well, really big peaches. Language is no barrier as the translation is bashed out on calculators. My lady keeps holding my hand so that I won't leave, even after my purchase she tries to sell me something else.

'Noodle, very good,' she says banging out the price on her calculator. I am enjoying the raw commercialism so much I buy some vacuum packed sausage in return for very little Yuan and my hand back. As soon as she releases it, another Hilda

Ogden grabs it in what I suspect is the equivalent of a market trader relay race. I am the baton. She already has Janet in her other hand. This only leaves her knees to work the calculator.

'Noodle good, only add water, very good,' she says.

The noodles come in a pot the size of a large popcorn container. I buy one and we both fly back to the train as the wind is now at our back. Noodles prepared we sit in our cabin, eating a meal together for the first time since Janet ignored me, five days ago. He fires questions at me incessantly.

'So, Mike, you can explain to me free market economics?' I nearly choke on my noodles.

'Free market economic? Right... eh...yes...umm, right free market economics. The best way to explain it is with an example,' I say, playing for time.' Janet puts down his chopsticks and inclines his head slightly.

'OK... right, free market economics, well, Janet... earlier we spent about ten hours in Zabaikalsk. No one tried to sell me a thing. In fact when I did try to buy something I nearly lost the fingers of my right hand. As soon as we enter China everyone tries to sell us something. Umm... that's it in a nutshell.'

Janet mulls this over for a little while. 'But China not operate free market.'

'Well, no, strictly speaking...' Thankfully he moves on to another subject so I don't have to get into a philosophical debate on the economic systems of China.

'You know, Mike, Russia send logs to China to make planks. What difficult to make planks? I can understand maybe

Russia cannot make cars. But wood? Why so difficult?' He shuffles a little in his seat. 'Mike, Russia shit, everything the same as Soviet time. If alien come to Russia and say, do this, do that, we believe, not question what we are told.'

Carrying on in this vein for some time I get the impression he knows what's wrong with his country, he just doesn't know how to change it. And let's face it, ancestrally his people have been subjugated by the best of them, Ivan the Terrible, the Tsars, Stalin to name but a few. The list is an impressive one. I feel like the past is imprinted on Janet like a branding iron and he can't seem to escape from the corral. Sensing I am becoming as morose as he is, he attempts to lift the mood by asking me about my journey.

'So you go to North Vietnam, and South Vietnam?'

'It's the same country nowadays Janet,'

'Really?'

This is not the only gap in his geopolitical knowledge. He is shocked to find that Singapore isn't part of China or that Cambodia is no longer run by Pol Pot. He even baulks at my assurance that Margaret Thatcher no longer rules the UK. Then, sensing he's on sticky ground he asks me a bit about English.

'What mean, rain cat and dog? Crazy.'

I'm thankful for the diversion and spend an enjoyable hour teaching him other peculiarly English idioms, "sillier than a sack of elbows," "daft as a brush." Then, sensing he's enjoying this, I give him some cockney rhyming slang.

'Bag of sand - grand?' he says incredulously, what grand mean?

'£1000 pounds.'

'Crazy, you English very mad, my mother think same.'

Janet suddenly remembers he hasn't slept for nearly a whole day. 'Better sleep now Mike, tomorrow I leave train at Shenyang.'

I fall asleep thinking how friendly Russians are.

Day 11

I awake to my first day in China by being greeted by regimental rows of sunflowers bowing to a rising sun. They look like they've being told off. A carpet of cultivated land stretches out to rolling hills in the far distance and the bright blue sky magnifies the yellowness of the flowers tenfold. Breaking up this sea of yellow are fields of hay, bundled into small packages that look like headless Dulux dogs waiting for a stick to be thrown.

I celebrate arriving in China by crapping on to it from the mortar launcher. On the way back to my cabin I bump into Blondy and offer my shower charade. I can't speak Russian but you just know when someone swears at you. I also discover they've taped up the bin holes at each end of our carriage so any detritus in my carriage will have to stay there now. I don't know why we bother with provodnitsas. I'd replace them with a microwave and English instructions on how to maintain the samovar.

Before long, we're pulling into Angangxi and despite the long delay at the border we are back on schedule. The station is quite small with a building at its centre painted a fetching yellow with white piping along its edges. In front of the building, not too far from the track, is a two feet squared piece of platform painted black. Above it, suspended from a pole arching at about six feet, is an oversized policeman's helmet. This provides shade to the official who is standing smartly to attention below it. He is dressed in a light brown uniform that wouldn't look out of place on a five star general and is standing to attention and saluting. His white-gloved hand is stock still under an extravagantly peaked cap. This is the stationmaster. Only when the train comes to a complete halt does he bring his saluting hand down, snapping it next to his side.

The train stops here for ten minutes so I step out into a warm sunny day. After the chill of the border station the heat soothes and feels tingly on my skin. Slightly disconcertedly, a family rush towards me. There are two ladies, one much younger than the other, and an old man who is struggling to keep up. They are all grinning from ear to ear. The younger girl is carrying a bouquet of lilies. It's an extravagant welcome for a stranger but I slap on my best smile and wait to be hugged to death. They zoom past me and I turn to find them hugging a young man. The joy on their faces lifts my mood another load of notches and adds a huge dollop of optimism to an already over brimming cup. I think I'm going to enjoy China.

Mind you Angangxi wasn't much of a fun place to be in the past. In ancient times it was famous for the nearby Field of Death where public executions were performed. Most of the criminals were bandits and the favoured method of execution was decapitation. However, losing a head in China comes with more complications than an immediate lack of direction. You see, the Chinese at that time believed that Heaven was denied to mortals missing body parts so they sewed the heads back on after the execution, so as to afford them a proper burial. Re-attachment wasn't straight forward though, as it raised something of a moral dilemma: these bandits were bad people and sticking their heads back on gave them a sort of absolution and heavenly access that was totally unavailable to someone who, for example, did good all their life but had the misfortune to be born without an arm. The solution was simple: they sewed the heads on backwards so that everyone would know they were evil when they were alive. Clever buggers, Johnnie Chinese.

We pull out of the station and get saluted by a couple of three star generals at a level crossing who are holding back a million people on bicycles. The landscape beyond them immediately gives way to agriculture. Janet stirs and I bid him good morning. He nods, heads of for his first fag of the day, comes back, grunts, slips back under the covers and goes back to sleep. Normal service has been resumed.

Every field the train passes has a cluster of bicycles in the corner. Their owners are harvesting corn as yellow as marigolds. The labour is clearly divided. Some pluck cobs from stalks, others cut shorn stalks down and lay them on the floor, while others transport the produce to the edge of the field using carts pulled by water buffalo. Blackened rows of stubble contrasts with yellow rows of corn, from the air the fields must look like giant bees' abdomens. Hard as I try I cannot see a single mechanised vehicle. It's alarmingly therapeutic to watch such hard labour from a comfortable train. Especially when you consider that this line wouldn't even be here if it wasn't for the Japanese and some opportunistic Russian diplomats. After the

1894 Sino-Japanese war the victorious Japanese concocted a peace treaty that included the payment of a heavy indemnity by the Chinese. Around the same time the Russians were panicking over an expensive detour to their own train line that would have to skirt around Chinese territory. Knowing China couldn't pay Japan, Russia offered to loan them the money in return for a lease to use a thousand mile strip of land in Manchuria. So in a roundabout way I should be offering thanks to Japan for my approaching Beijing in such a fascinating way. Thank you Japan.

The train is passing through knots of homesteads with corn drying in their dusty yards. Vegetable cultivation, in contrast to Russian villages has been replaced with the rearing of livestock, mainly chickens, cows, and ducks. The latter might be better advised to move further away from Beijing, or as they know it Peking. Who'd be a duck in China?

I hear Howard in the corridor, he's talking to some Chinese we took on at the border, they laugh a lot and I get the feeling that it's where Howard likes to be: in front of an audience. I look back out of the window and am forced into a double take. Right next to the track is a bright yellow oil derrick. Ridiculous: oil derricks in the middle of the countryside? Then I spot another, and another, black this time. There's loads of them, some dipping like Japanese friends stuck on a perpetual hello, others still, like stick insects basking in the sun. I shouldn't really be surprised, I know the train will soon be approaching Daqing, a town in the centre of one of the largest oil fields in China. It's just they appear to be stationed so haphazardly. I see one right next to a flyover, another near a factory: a couple at either end of a housing estate. I spot one smack bang in the middle of a field of corn with a man working around it, loading his produce onto a cart pulled by a donkey. It's an exquisite metaphor for China. I'd love to have been a fly on the wall at the local council planning permission committee.

Bobbing oil derricks are not the only sign of new wealth. Everywhere I look major construction projects are underway. And it's all infrastructure, roads, drainage and large housing projects. It is such a contrast to Russia where there is plenty of wealth from natural resources. There, I didn't see one piece of what you might call infrastructure investment across the whole of Siberia, some 4400 miles. I'm less than 500 miles into China and that's all I've seen. This is one of the great advantages of travelling by train. You get a feel for a country's pulse at this level, which would simply pass you by in a plane. And my feel for China's pulse is that it has a very strong beat indeed.

The outskirts of Daqing announce themselves with rows of skyscrapers at different stages of completion. I suspect the oil is taking Daqing through a Dallas-ification process. Janet rouses, says good morning, for the second time and wanders out for a fag. Shortly after his nicotine induced departure a peculiar old lady comes in. She is European, stick thin and wearing a brown tabard. I have never seen her before and assume she's a cleaner. She stands at the door and smiles, exposing a not entirely full set of teeth. I smile back, not sure what I should be doing. Does she want me to move so she can clean? She starts jabbering away at me in Russian and produces two baseball caps from behind her back, holding them out in front of her and bowing slightly, like she's offering a sacrifice.

'I don't understand - An - Glee - Skee.'

She places the cap in my hand and it dawns on me. She's selling it. I'm taken aback. I've spent six days on this train, over a week in Russia and no one, and I mean absolutely no one, has tried to sell me anything. Not even in shops where they're supposed to sell things. And now I'm being hawked at by a three stone gonk. She pulls a calculator from her tabard and knocks out a price. I don't even bother to haggle and quickly become the proud owner of a black felt baseball cap, with Moscow - Beijing in Cyrillic, emblazoned above the peak. She looks pleased with her enterprise, clutches the money to her bosoms, or where her bosoms would reside if they weren't hanging just above her knees, and shuttles off. Janet returns shortly after.

'Look, I bought a hat,' I say, holding it up proudly.

'How much you pay?'

'Two hundred roubles (about a fiver).'

'They cheat you. Pay too much he says,' before slipping back into his bed for a nap (glasses on).

Not long after we cross the expansive Sungari River on our way into Harbin, a medium sized Chinese town with a population larger than London by only a few million. I spot some interesting signs that mingle English and Chinese. For example, smack bang in the middle of some Chinese script on a yellow restaurant awning is "Haughty, Happy, Frosty Free." Haughty? Do people sit and eat with disdain? I see another with "Holiday Eating."

I get out to stretch my legs at Harbin station and to watch millions of people trying to get to the same place at once. I'm especially intrigued by the Chinese queuing system. In essence it looks like a couple of hundred people simply milling about, passing the time of day by a carriage door. Don't be fooled. They're jockeying for position. As soon as the door opens a fraction they dive for the gap, like metal filings thrown in front of a magnet. One almighty scrum follows in which it is not unusual for a person to enter the carriage with someone else's shopping bag under one of their arms, and the owner's head under the other. The Chinese simply have no understanding of personal space. I suspect it's a consequence of living in the same country as 1.4 billion others. In England there would be bloodshed, or at least some aggressive harrumphing.

I spot two young Chinese girls trying to take a sneaky picture of Blondy standing in her uniform by the carriage door. She is aware of them also and rather than co-operate she turns away. Undaunted they take a few sneaky photos of some Western ladies and then turn their attention to me. I suspect this is because I am the only Western male in a sea of bobbing heads. Just at the point of snapping I turn and offer a cheesy grin that sends them into fits of giggles. Now their parents will think all Western men look like they've just shit out a foot of barbed wire. As we pull out of the station I swear the saluting female guard winked at me. An advertising hoarding also gives me the answer as to why Harbin has 10 million inhabitants. A forty feet high poster by the side of the track informs me in English: "Cure Male Problem - Call Harbin Clinic." I make a note of the number.

Rather than go back to my cabin I head straight to the restaurant car – the Chinese restaurant car. What a difference a border makes. The car is light and airy, yellow drapes, communal eating areas, red tablecloths. At the far end is the galley kitchen and seating is down either side of the aisle. The whole place is designed for eating, not for sitting and brooding over stinky fags and pork chops impersonating meatballs. The tempo is set by the upbeat clickety-click of spatula on wok and the singsong delivery of the head waitress. She is in total control of her environment. Calling out orders, taking food to tables, collecting more orders from the customers. The pace is frenetic. As soon as I sit down she is next to me with a menu. It has pictures and is in English, Russian and a couple of other European languages. She is rather dumpy with her hair tied into a tight bun. She has a mole on her chin, a gap between her front teeth, and is a little jowly. While doing the work of ten people she keeps up a constant banter with a man sitting near the kitchen and her two other waitresses. They regularly burst into laughter. The man near the kitchen is thick set with a flat face, wears a black suit in the Chinese style, crisp white shirt and owns a gruff voice. He's drinking from a jam jar. I notice the other waitresses are also drinking from receptacles more likely to be seen storing things, like coffee, or marmalade. The content offers no clues, but there is a thick bed of green leaves in each of them. Mint tea maybe? The Finnish ladies are already seated at a table. Next to them is group of four young Russian girls.

The head waitress takes my order quickly and the enzymes in my gut burst into song in anticipation of a meal that won't digest like a brick. They have been working flat out on the destruction of the Russian chef's meatballs and are looking forward to some light relief. I have to pay the waitress up front and she gives me my change from a huge wad of cash she struggles to pull from her pocket. Tipping is not on the menu. I make short work of spicy chicken and rice. In fact I have another plate. As I leave I look down at the leftovers on the Finnish ladies plates. They ordered loads but left most of the deep fried food. In contrast the Russians studiously avoided their vegetables.

Coming back from the restaurant car to my cabin via the loo I catch Blondy and Fatty in a clinch. She can see me, but he has his back to me. I fight back an overwhelming gagging reaction and do a shower charade. If eyes could swear... I spend the rest of the afternoon and early evening reading up on Beijing.

Around 9 pm Janet gets up. I soon realise this is a different getting up to his usual getting up. For a start he doesn't go for a fag but instead reaches for his wash bag. This is a significant development. Ten minutes later he returns and starts to re-assemble his belongings. I spend an enjoyable thirty minutes watching him. He fills one bag, then moves it into the corridor. Then he hauls down the gigantic carry case he had so much trouble with when he got on at Moscow and fills that. He then realises he hasn't packed any of the things on the table, so he gets the smaller bag from the corridor and unpacks it. He then partially unpacks the larger case and transfers some of the things from the smaller bag to a plastic carrier bag. He then goes for a fag. When he comes back, he empties the carrier bag and puts the contents into the large packing case they came from.

'Shenyang in ten minutes,' I tell him.

This spurs him into a packing frenzy and he simply stuffs things into empty areas. Satisfied, he hauls the big case out into the corridor, immediately blocking Howard and Hilda who are trying to pass. He hauls it back in to the cabin. Howard wishes me good luck, and Hilda smiles. Janet hauls his bag back out, realises the Finnish ladies want to pass and hauls it back in. They pass, and he hauls it back out, and then puts his smaller bag on top of it. Its the baggage equivalent of the hokey cokey. Finally he puts on his two grey coats and his grey cap, wishes me good luck, proffers a soft handshake, and leaves. I position myself by the window so I can watch him. His wife is meeting him at the station and I want to see what she's like. The Finnish ladies take it in turns to hug Howard and Hilda before they sashay down the platform and out of sight. Janet stands looking forlorn in the same clothes he was in six days ago. There is still no sign of his wife as we pull away. I suspect she's waiting for the air to circulate around him a little before she gets close. Meanwhile in the new luxurious solitude of my cabin I let the air circulate too. My body takes the opportunity to expel the remains of my Russian food without an audience. Some of the farts are so violent they make the windows shake.

Day 12

It is still dark when I wake. I check my watch: 3.30am. The train isn't due to arrive at Beijing Central for another ninety minutes so I set about packing. Packing takes me five minutes. I eat an apple, which disposes of another two minutes. I look at my watch again. Then out of the window. Its pitch black but I can make out shapes and occasionally I see a dimly lit road, but no one musters: not even in the carriage. My mind wanders a little though. I'm excited about arriving in Beijing, but at the same time, I feel a little nervous and I don't know why. I think I'm going to miss the train. It's been my companion for the last seven nights and I fear I may have fallen in love with it. It's done wonders with my need to reconnect to a machine I've for so long associated with evil.

I run down the clock a little more by going to the bathroom to re-grout myself with my nappy wipes. By the time I return to my cabin we are sliding through the outer suburbs of Beijing. Total darkness has been replaced with a misty dawn. Everything looks new and clean. The roads we pass are uniformly straight and the landscaping trim and tidy. I'm arriving only a few weeks after the Olympics and am expecting something of an end of party hangover, although everything looks pretty sober at this early hour.

The train pulls into a shiny white station that looks clean enough to eat my Peking duck off. I struggle off with my bags, test my land legs for defects, and look for my travel agent representative. She is by the door, holding up a sheet of paper with the name Milurd on it. Close enough. I point to the sheet and then to myself. The young lady holding up my name starts to jump up and down.

'He, he, he, lucky me! I guess correct carriage!' She says, clapping her hands in front of her and then pulling some MP3 earplugs from her ears. She is about five feet tall, but if she didn't have a gigantic mop of unruly hair she'd be four feet tall. When she smiles, which she does after every sentence, her eyes disappear into her cheeks. Her colouring is dark and her oval face owns a slightly oversized mouth. She's wearing black shiny trousers and a black jacket with a red top underneath. The red and black colour scheme is accessorised with red trainers and thick rimmed red and black glasses that rest on her dainty nose. She instinctively laughs before she speaks making the many scrunchies in her hair bounce about like flotsam and jetsam on an angry sea.

'He, he, he, I'm so lucky! You have good journey, Mr Miurd?'

'Yes, thank you, please call me Mike.'

'He, he, he, OK, Mr Miurd, Mike. He, he, he, I'm Jessica, welcome to Beijing.' I suspect this may not be the name her mother gave her. Her English is good, albeit with a slight American twang.

'We have driver wait outside, we can go now.' She moves to pick up my bag, but I stop her. It's only slightly smaller than she is and certainly more heavy.

'He, he, he, OK follow me Mike.'

I just have time to quickly say goodbye to my Finnish friends and I'm off. She sets a pretty brisk pace as we disappear into about a billion other people already in the underpass that she assures me will take us out onto the street. A rattling noise comes from Jessica as she walks. Some of the scrunchies in her unruly mop are ball shaped and have little peas in them, like the toy balls you find in budgie cages. It's like walking next to an out of tune barrel organ.

'He, he, he, so you have been to Beijing before?'

'No, this is my first time.'

'He, he, he, you will be sharing it with a lot of Chinese people. This week National Holiday, everyone come to Beijing.'

'Yes, they all seem to be in this underpass,' I say.

'He, he, he, no,' she says, with a little more seriousness than is necessary, 'more people upstairs, many people in Beijing, he, he, he.'

And she's right. As we emerge into a misty cool morning there are people everywhere, under my arms, between my legs, in my turn-ups, inside the crack of my knees. I've never seen so many black-haired people in the same place at the same time. One of them waves at us.

'He, he, he, taxi driver find good spot, lucky again! Come quick,' she grabs my arm and drags me across the road to a car. The driver smiles, pushes himself off the wing he has been leaning against, gobs a great big green grolly on the floor, takes my bags and puts them in the boot. Safely sitting in the back of the car I look all around me willing the rising sun to push the last remnants of darkness away so that I can soak everything up in Technicolor. In my experience trains usually deposit you in the parts of cities that have dull lighting and criminal shadows. By contrast this is clean and airy, the roads are expansive avenues, and despite the volumes of people everything is orderly and calm. As we pull away, Jessica turns in her seat and starts to give me, what I suspect, is a pre-prepared speech on certain aspects of Beijing.

'He, he, he, Mike, there are sixteen million people in Beijing. Yes it's true. And thirteen million bicycles.'

She continues in this vein, offering snippets on the Forbidden City and other tourist attractions, but I'm afraid to say she quickly becomes background noise. I am still pondering the bike situation. By my reckoning there are three million people without bicycles in this City. That is the equivalent of the combined populations of Birmingham, Glasgow, Edinburgh, Leeds, Bristol and Farnborough without a bike between them. It's a travesty.

Quickly realising she is talking to a half-wit she turns her attention away from me and to the driver. The Chinese language is wonderful: I could listen to it for hours. Every sentence sounds like an emergency, with high stresses at the end. Exchanges are swift and just when you think the two conversationalists are about to have a full scale punch up, they burst out laughing. I could have listened to Jessica and the driver all day, but it isn't long before we pull into the drive of the Capital Hotel. The fact it has a drive is something of a shock to me. My budget normally buys me a "functioning hotel" like Hotel Tourist in Moscow. This is most certainly not the Hotel Tourist. The lobby is grand and dressed in brown dappled marble. Corinthian columns stretch up to an ornate ceiling and spectacular chandeliers bathe the central lounge area in warm light. To the right of the lounge are a couple of restaurant areas, one that looks busy with breakfasters. I make a mental note of it. To my left is the reception area. It's only just after 6 am but is fully manned with pretty looking ladies in blue and white uniforms. Jessica takes my passport to the desk and motions me to sit in a seating area next to the reception. The tan leather seat is so soft it envelops me like a spongy marshmallow. I realise for the first time how tired I am.

'He, he, he, room will be ready at 7 o'clock,' she says sitting in a chair next to me. She is so light she hardly makes a dent in the upholstery.

'Do you have my ticket for Hanoi, my English travel agent said you would have it ready when I arrive.'

She looks a little sheepish, 'he, he, he, not worry about ticket now Mike, you look tired.'

I persevere, 'Only, I'm only here two days, Jessica, and it's the weekend...'

'Not worry, we can talk later.'

I immediately worry.

Jessica spends some time orientating me on a map I produce from my bag. I am only two blocks from Tiananmen Square. This is remarkable on the budget I set my travel agent.

Maybe she felt guilty after booking me into the Gulag Tourist in Moscow.

Forty minutes later a tall willowy young girl approaches us. She has slightly blotchy skin that she tries to hide, not too successfully, with make up. Her face is flattish with wide oval eyes and her long shoulder length hair is barrel straight. Jessica jumps up and down, clapping her hands, which sets off the budgie toys.

'He, he, he, this is Olive,' she says, 'she help you now, and to get ticket for Hanoi.' I suspect that Olive is not the name her parents gave her. Jessica smiles, waves at me, and bounces out of the lobby with the taxi driver, like an oversized baby rattle. Olive sits with me. I am slightly thrown by her deep voice. She sounds a bit like the film trailer voiceover man.

'Do you have passport?'

'Its with reception.'

'They not check you in yet?'

'Not till seven apparently.'

She looks bemused, heads over to them and within seconds I am clutching my room key.

'I will keep your passport Mike, for ticket to Hanoi.' She writes down her name and mobile number in the back of my notebook. 'You can phone me any time.'

The use of the name Olive intrigues me. I am aware that most Asians that come into contact with foreigners adopt a name that Westerners can get their tongues around, but why Olive? The only famous Olive I can bring to mind is the one from On The Buses – a right monger. Surely she could have gone for something more exotic.

'Olive,' I say, 'why did you choose the name Olive?' What is your Chinese name?

'Olive, ' she says. I'm glad I cleared that up then. She smiles and leaves with what looks like the Triad member responsible for passport cloning.

I am dismayed to find my room is being cleaned, which is a blow. I desperately need a shower. My pants are leaving vapour trails when I walk now. As a shower is out of the question I dump my bags and head for the breakfast restaurant.

This is situated just behind the central lounge area in the lobby and has two young girls standing sentinel at the entrance. They are wearing a green tartan: I think it might be the Emperor Ming clan. It matches the seating upholstery so well that waiters partially disappear when they walk past a chair. Beyond these Highland clad ladies is a nicely spaced out restaurant that circles a large podium groaning with food. Behind that, and to the side of it, are two smaller podiums equally heavy with produce. Although it's clearly self-service, the waiters and waitresses flit between tables with stainless steel coffee pots, constantly filling cups.

'Good morning Sir,' the taller guard says smiling, 'do you have a coupon?'

'I'm sorry I only checked in this morning, so I don't qualify for a free breakfast until tomorrow, but I'm happy to add it to my bill.'

'Oh, that's no problem Sir, please have a complimentary breakfast today.'

I resist the urge to kiss her and instead follow her friend to a table laid out for four. I'm the only one on it.

"It is a buffet breakfast sir, coffee, or tea?" With good old Scottish efficiency she comes back with a pot of coffee and leaves it on the table for me. I do what I always do when I find myself at an International hotel's buffet breakfast: guess the nationalities. The group of eight to my right is easy. They're all old, fat, loud, and dressed in matching sweatshirts: American. Further evidence if I needed it is the man in their centre. He has a huge head, and a mouth that looks like its been painted on by a cartoonist. He's shovelling in pancakes with a fork. Further along is a smaller group. They're nicely tanned. The men have grey, wispy, mullets and collectively look like they've only just discovered they're in China despite the fact they've been holidaying in it for the last fortnight. Their female companions are eating slices of ham and cake: Dutch. Directly opposite I spot a father, mother and small son. These are harder to place. For a start there is no food, they are all sipping tea. She looks hairier than her husband. Her eyebrows, in particular, indicate that she might once have been male. Greek maybe? The leather jacket hanging over his chair throws me. Possibly Russian. Then the boy speaks: its pure cockney innit.

The other great thing about International breakfast buffets is the dazzling array of cuisines on offer. It's the hotel's attempt to please everyone and I love them for it. I walk along the central podium first. No plate yet, I'm simply reconnoitring. One side is full of cereals, cake, sliced meats, yogurts, bread, jams, and other preserves. The other has a number of gleaming silver barrelled containers that gape open when you push the handle up. They have the items of a full English. A second podium holds all the drinks. These are mainly fruit juices in cylinders, with handles paddling inside to stop the pulp from turning into sediment at the bottom. The final podium has all the exotic stuff that would never be seen at your local Holiday Inn Express. Fish curry, noodles, eggs, fried rice, and congee, which is a sort of rice soup with chillies and pork meatballs. But what really makes International breakfast buffets truly entertaining is the innate desire to experiment. Its why I walk back to my table with a plate laden with noodles, fried egg, bacon, beans the size of walnuts, two potato waffles, and a large dollop of fish curry. It's also why I pass an Asian man trying to eat a fried egg with chopsticks. I make short work of my world buffet and contemplate a second visit but reconsider at the last minute and instead settle for a plate piled high with dragon fruit and melon. I finish off my pot of coffee, assiduously avoiding the milk, as instructed by Howard.

I have to manhandle my stomach into the shower cubicle but it's worth it. Standing under the first shower I've had in seven days almost makes me cry with sheer unadulterated joy. I select aloe vera and tee tree oil shampoo from my basket of goodies on the marbled top by the sink and work it into my scalp. Next, every nook and cranny of my body feels the zing of ginger and nutmeg body wash. As a scummy Russian residue congeals around the plughole I make noises more commonly associated with Turkish wrestling. When I finally step out the bathroom it's steamier than a South American mangrove. I inadvertently knock the toilet seat with my knee and reach to catch it before it clatters onto the bowl. But I needn't have bothered: it's a self-closing bog seat. I've never seen one, let alone used one, so I spend another ten minutes lifting it and dropping it. It's like watching an alligator yawning. Hard as it is to drag myself away from my new toilet toy, I dress quickly and head out towards Tiananmen Square.

The sky is electric blue and the sun is warming. My Russian death march has been replaced with a Chinese quick step and I feel light headed and excited. OK, I'm getting some funny looks from the locals but no matter. Quite a few appear to be spitting at me, or rather in my path, which is a little disconcerting, but I've got clean pants on and I'm ready to explore. I approach Tiananmen Square from the east, arriving just across the road from its southern gate, Qianmen. This was the original gate to the inner city and is suitably spectacular. I want to get a closer look, but how do I get to Tiananmen Square? I survey my options. The road is completely closed off with metal barriers: in fact the entire Square is, as far as I can see. Undaunted, I follow the half a billion people in front of me into an underpass. I may have touched the ground, it's hard to say, but within no time at all I exit into the largest urban Square in the world, although in reality it's a socking great rectangle. I make my way over to the gate, which isn't really a gate, more a fortification with an entrance through its centre. The first floor can best be described as battlements. It's oblong and brown and runs along the southern end of the Square. The texture of the walls is similar to a cobbled street. Above it are three more floors that become narrower, pagoda style. They are rich red, with blue inlay and gold leafing. Turning, so it's at my back, I look directly at Chairman Mao's Mausoleum. It's much bigger than Lenin's and a lot more ornate. Statues depicting armed struggle and sacrifice stand either side of the entrance gate. The bronze figures stand heroically behind a central soldier carrying a bayoneted rifle. Behind these and the gate are the steps leading up to the building itself, which is quite plain in comparison to the buildings that flank the Square. The columns that run along the top of the steps leading to the inner entrance offer a little grandeur. Soldiers circle the entire building at fifteen feet intervals: some appear to be guarding nothing more than the paving slab they are standing on.

The statues provide popular backdrops for photographs and I watch a family with some interest. There are seven of them, a child of about five, his parents and two sets of grandparents. The boy's father is in charge, directing them into a suitable family unit, waving his hand this way and that, and keeping up a continual stream of instructions. I've always enjoyed watching Asians take photographs. The sheer effort involved in preparing for the pictures is in direct contrast to the uniformly dull results. In my experience the subjects must stand, preferably by a tree, or some other innocuous item, and look solemn. Smiling is illegal. No sitting ever, always upright and erect. This family is no exception. Eventually he looks in the viewfinder one last time, re-arranges them again: he's ready. Arm aloft, he asks for the Chinese equivalent of cheese, simultaneously swinging his arm down in a chopping motion. This is his family's cue to look like extras in a zombie movie. Sadly all the effort is for nothing because at the critical moment a fellow countryman walks through the shot. This is to be expected in a Square that has twenty million people in it. Undeterred, they start the process again. Picture successfully taken they set off on a round robin, with each family member taking it in turns to be David Bailey. I would hate to sit through their family album. I'd be looking at seven versions of each snap.

I discover, with considerable disappointment that Chairman Mao is not in residence. He's in Moscow of all places, for his annual service. Be fair, he's been dead since 1976. I think the hot summer may have been melting his edges. Even mummies need pampering now and again. As well as being the surliest nation on earth Russia is the world leader in mummy servicing. They do Ho Chi Minh as well. I wonder if they're ever there together? I'd have an overwhelming urge to set them up like that picture you often see in golf clubs and snooker halls in which dogs play cards over a smoky gaming table. As I turn away from the entrance I'm approached by a young Chinese couple, aged, I would say, at about seventeen.

'Excuse me sir,' he says in pretty good English, 'could you take our photograph?' He offers his camera, but just before I take it he says, 'are you English?' Is it a condition of my taking the photograph I wonder?

'Yes, I am, and sure, I'll take it.'

His girlfriend is giggling behind him. I take a couple of suitably funereal snaps and his girlfriend collects the camera, 'thank you sir, do you live in England?' Her boyfriend is grinning now.

'Yes, I do, I live near London.' Her boyfriend joins her.

'Well, there you are,' I say handing back the camera, 'and where did you learn English,' I add, sensing they want to linger.

'High school,' they both say.

'Well, you speak excellent English, well done.'

They beam, then giggle, then leave. I may not be Sherlock Holmes but I reckon the only reason they asked me to take their picture was because they wanted to try out some English. Looking around I can see why they selected me: I'm the only Westerner in the entire Square.

I spend twenty minutes at the North Eastern end of the Square queuing up, to see why people are queuing up. When I get to the front of the line I find a security guard standing to attention in front of a beautiful flower display. He's dressed like a navy seal and marches the length of the display every five minutes or so. He salutes a bunch of marigolds after each bit of marching. This sets of a bank of camera flashes you'd more associate with the red carpet at the Oscars.

I spend a further twenty minutes ambling about taking pictures of the backs of Chinese heads and looking at real soldiers guarding trees, and policemen patrolling flowered lantern displays. This is no place for plant thieves. After I've had my fill of square bashing I head across the road to the entrance of the Grand Palace, or as it's more commonly known, the Forbidden City. It looks more like the entrance to an ant colony. Little black heads are bobbing about everywhere. Queuing here is not for me, even though I am desperate to get in. You can't argue with the statistics. It dates back over five hundred years and has been designated a World Heritage Site. There are nearly a thousand buildings, and nine thousand rooms to explore. It's the largest palace complex in the world, covering a whopping 7,800 square feet. The moat surrounding it is nearly two hundred feet wide and twenty feet deep. The wall surrounding the complex is nearly thirty feet high. All suitably impressive but the reason I'm desperate to get in is because Roger Moore provides the English speaking commentary for the audio tour. Roger Moore. OO7. How cool is that?

I decide to try the side entrance and take a route just east of the gate that takes me down Nanchang Jie, a road running parallel with the eastern edge of the complex. If I still can't get in that way I'll be close to the entrance to Jingshan Park, where I also plan to go. The early afternoon sun is getting warmer and the shade from this impressive tree lined road is most welcoming. There are a few restaurants down here that are aimed at attracting Westerners, although they are mainly rammed with Chinese. I get caught in a group of people blocking the pavement. There doesn't appear to be a way around them so I practice my Chinese queuing techniques and elbow myself to the front. It must be something interesting for this many people to be milling about. It's a bus queue and I only narrowly avoid being sucked onto the bus.

Feeling in need of a pee I dive into a public toilet and on my way to the urinal nearly knock over a man squatting on the floor. I'd fail to notice him because he's tucked just inside the door.

'Oh, I'm terribly sorry, I...' To my horror I find he's not simply squatting, as Asians are prone to do when loitering, he's squatting over a toilet. Its not partitioned off or secluded in any way - its just there by the urinals. He offers me the sort of look you would if you were knocked off your perch while having a dump. I don't know what to do. What is the protocol is this situation? Do I offer a hand, surely not? Should I drop to a similar height and then apologise, or wait until he's finished and apologise? I end up doing a curtsy bowing combination and apologise while he is still at knee height. I feel uncomfortable apologising to someone uncurling one into a hole in the ground but no one around me pays any attention. In the UK my errant shitter would have been wheeled off to an asylum and I would have been able to sue him for mental trauma using a no win-no fee solicitor.

My attempt to enter the Forbidden City from the side fails. There are ten million less people at this entrance but I would still have to queue behind the population of France to get in. By way of consolation I buy Chairman Mao's Little Red Book from a street hawker. He is a wiry fellow, holding on to a bike with a basket above the front wheel. It's full of Red Books and postcards.

'Mao, book, you buy?'

'How much?

'You buy first?'

'If I know how much....'

'OK, if you buy one hundred Yuan.'

'How much if I don't buy?'

'You buy first.'

'Fifty Yuan,' I say, totally bemused. Have I bought, or haven't I?

'OK, you give money, get book.'

Damn, no haggling, he would have gone lower. I hand him a one hundred yuan note.

'Fifty Yuan,' he says.

'No change,' I reply, shrugging my shoulders and taking back my note, as per the haggling handbook. I start to walk away. He tugs me back by the arm and hands me his bike.

'Wait,' he says. I lose him in the crowd in seconds. A couple of minutes go by and I feel a little conscious. I clearly don't own the bike and I'm worried people might think I've nicked it. I contemplate resting it by a wall and leaving, but eventually he re-emerges and hands me fifty Yuan and the book. He mounts his bike and prepares to pedal off. Now it's my turn to grab his arm.

'Don't forget this,' I say handing him my one hundred Yuan note. The smile on his face indicates to me that he would be well advised to spend some of his new wealth on dentistry.

The reason I planned to visit Jingshan Park is twofold. Firstly, city parks are the souls of a city and they offer so much about the character of the locals. Secondly, there is a hill in its centre called Long Live Hill. What a great name. This 100 yard incline is entirely man made using the earth removed form the moat surrounding the Forbidden Palace. The view from its peak is supposed to be spectacular, not least because it offers a vantage point from which to look down into the Palace complex. If I can't get in, at least I'll be able to look in.

I can see the five summits of the hill as soon as I enter the park. Each one is capped with a pagoda styled pavilion. The roofs of each peek out above the tree line, like ornate chevrons pointing to the sky. The park is immaculately manicured with small plaques announcing the names of the plants and trees in English and Latin as well as Chinese. Take note Russia. The lawns are cropped as tight as the centre court at Wimbledon. The whole place is a miniature Bonsai garden on a grand scale, if that makes sense. Birdsong takes over from the hum of the Beijing traffic. I feel eleven days of almost non-stop travel peel away and immediately relax by watching a group of old age pensioners practicing their Tai Chi under the shade thrown out by a huge sycamore tree.

The only hurly burly to be found is in the tour groups that march through the park's lattice of pathways. Sitting on a bench to soak up the tranquillity I watch one progressing. The lady leading them is corporately decked out in a yellow company cap and tee shirt. Her charges are also decked out in yellow caps and tee shirts. It looks like a gathering for a giant canary symposium. Holding aloft her yellow company umbrella she shouts continually through a megaphone. This instrument is totally unnecessary as the entire group is within touching distance. They display the sort of attentiveness that puppies offer at feeding time. When they move to the next stopping point, they do so in unison, like a big yellow battering ram.

The hundred yards of Long Live Hill doesn't take too long to climb. I stop at each pavilion to take photographs of the backs of the heads of the other ten million other people sharing it with me. The highest pavilion offers the best views and I take some time to wander about the pagoda looking across at this great city. In the south I can see directly into the Palace complex. Each of the red-topped buildings is visible and it's easy to imagine Emperors living in the luxury and safety of this walled city within a city. To the north are the skyscrapers of the new Beijing. The distance between these two vistas may only be one hundred and eighty degrees on a compass, and a couple of miles as the crow flies, but in reality the gulf between them is colossal. They might easily be two different worlds. I spend a little more time taking photographs of the backs of Chinese heads and wander down the hill. I've caught a familiar sound on the wind, and if I'm right it will provide me with some more free entertainment. Time to investigate.

Just as I suspected I find a gaggle of families in a shady spot under a large tree. They are between a picnic area in front of them and banks of red and yellow peonies behind them. A man in the centre of the group is producing the noise I heard on the hill. He's about seventy, smartly dressed in a black suit and crisp white shirt undone at the collar. He's singing into a microphone with the accompaniment of a backing tape. Its karaoke Asian style and he's the Chinese equivalent of Daniel O'Donnell. He is accompanied by a lady of a similar age, adorned in a black sequined dress, that shimmies as she moves through the crowd in a sort of Thai Chi, ballet, ballroom dancing, sashay that enthrals the crowd. I'm no Len Goodman but it doesn't take an expert to notice that her moves are totally independent of her crooning partner and the backing track. This lack of timing extends to the crooner who stops for breath whenever he runs out, which is rarely at the end of a musical interlude. The backing track they are all enjoying sounds like Joe Pasquale being battered to death with a cello. Nevertheless, at the very end of each song the crowd claps enthusiastically. They also clap enthusiastically when the crooner runs out of breath just in case he is actually finishing. I am tempted to tarry a while longer, the scene is somewhat mesmerising, but I have a date with a Hutong.

Hutongs are essentially pockets of old Beijing and they're becoming endangered by the developers never ending appetite to swallow them up in a seemingly unending quest to rip the heart out of the City. Gongjian Hutong is only a short walk from the northeast tip of the park and I soon find myself in its tangle of narrow alleys. The sun is hotter now and magnified by the closeness of the white buildings. There is very little distinction between commercial and private property. Living rooms double up as shop fronts. I pass a school sitting cheek by jowl with a police station. I carefully navigate myself past a game of Mah Jong that is being played in the middle of the road. It looks like it's going to erupt into violence but I relax when one of the players slams down his counter and they all break into fits of laughter. I decide to stand and watch for a bit to see if I can pick up the rules and station myself by a house selling fruit. The owner points to a melon and mimes cutting it with a knife. She is small and weather beaten like a sun drenched prune. The lines on her face are deep and her brown eyes, rheumy. I shake my head but she cuts me some anyway. She waves away my money dismissively and turns back into the darkness beyond the beaded curtain hanging from the entrance to her door.

Munching away on my succulent melon slice I walk deeper into the lanes. The further I travel the narrower they become until bicycles are the only suitable form of transport.

Washing hangs from electricity lines like homemade flags, fluttering on gusts of invisible thermals. I'm so close to homes it feels like I'm intruding. I can see old people in yards dozing in the sun, or peeling vegetables for the evening meal. Living rooms almost spill out into the road. It's an enjoyable way to spend an hour and I'm sorry to leave it, as I do, unexpectedly, by turning on to a road that is not where it's supposed to be according to my map. I dig it out for a quick consultation. Before it's fully unfolded a young Chinese lady approaches me.

'Are you lost? Can I help with direction?' She is about five feet tall, shoulder length hair, compact in stature and light skinned. Two friends stand a little further away smiling, but keep their distance, just in case I bite.

'Well, actually I want to head back to my hotel. It's near Tiananmen Square.'

'We go to Jingshan Park, on way, you can come with us.'

I'm slightly taken aback by their offer, but agree anyway. 'OK, that's kind, thank you,' I say refolding my map. My new friend walks alongside me but her friends continue to hold back.

'We are teachers,' she says waving a hand in her friends direction, 'we come to Beijing for National Holiday, stay with my uncle.'

'That's nice. What do you teach?

'I teach English in junior school. How old are you?

We continue to walk and chat, all the time slightly ahead of her friends then suddenly, she stops.

'Oh, I forget to look, now lost. Wait I ask in shop.'

I realise I'm close to where I entered the Hutong. 'Wait, I know the way.'

'You know? You come Beijing before?'

'No, but I was here earlier, follow me, I'll show you the way to Jingshan Park.'

In the space of two hundred yards I've converted myself from lost tourist to tour guide and within another two hundred yards we're at the entrance to the park.

'There you are, Jingshan Park.'

'Very kind, thank you for help,' she says bowing slightly.

'You're welcome, enjoy the park.'

'Yes, enjoy Beijing,' she says waving. Her friends join in. Perhaps waving is the only English they know.

On the way back to the hotel I mull over these small encounters. Teenagers practicing their English, old ladies offering free fruit, my new teacher friend willing to help me, despite having no sense of direction at all. It's all too bloody, oh I don't know, all too bloody good to be true. I make it back to my hotel without incident. My room key doesn't work. I take it back to reception, they give me another. It doesn't work.

'Sorry sir, we send someone look.'

I decide on a coffee in the central lounge while I'm waiting. Five quid. Granted I don't have to add pepper to make it quaffable but five quid? Three gulps and its gone. Now I'm hungry. I look at the menu. Its mainly sandwiches, the cheapest being seven quid. I decide on the restaurant where I had breakfast. In contrast to this morning its empty and my tartan clad lady friends have been replaced with an older man and a young girl. I order rice soup and another coffee. The coffee here is three quid. In less than one hundred yards I've saved two quid. The coffee came from the same pot. What is it about those hundred yards? Are they crocodile infested? Is that why coffee is cheaper here? I ponder this coffee problem sufficiently long enough to have another coffee. Well, at these prices...

Safely back in my room I open and shut the toilet seat a few times and have another shower. I'm not particularly dirty but the novelty of showering has not worn off yet. It's why I'm sopping wet and wearing only a towel when Olive arrives with my train tickets. It's probably an image she will take to her grave. She passes me reams of paperwork and my passport and explains everything quickly, resolutely refusing my offer to come in.

'If you need anything Mike, ring my number,' she says, looking down at the hall carpet. I decide it's time for a nap.

I wake some time later in a darkened room watching a Jackie Chan film dubbed into Chinese with English subtitles. Confused, I realise my planned doze has lasted a few hours. This is disappointing, as I wanted to watch the lowering of the flag ceremony in Tiananmen Square, a ritual more precise than a Swiss clock. The national flag is lowered every night at sunset. The soldiers are drilled to march at precisely 108 paces per minute. Each pace is exactly 75 centimetres long. It's so accurately timed that the flag disappears under Tiananmen Gate at exactly the same time as the sun disappearing.

Never mind, I quickly dress and head out. I have a cunning plan B for this evening and it revolves around eating. Wangfujing Dajie is described in my guidebook as "full of stalls bursting with food from all over China, including flat bread, oodles of noodles and pancakes." When I get there I discover another reason to ignore guidebooks. The only thing it's bursting with is neon. Banks of fluorescent lighting cast unnatural shadows behind an army of shoppers. Rip off shops are situated next to genuine designer ones. For example, next to a Rolex retailer is another, decked out in exactly the same livery, same font, same colours, essentially the same stock, only it's called Tudor. This kind of street is my kind of nightmare but I spot an English bookshop and go in to look for an accurate guidebook on China. I come out with an Agatha Christie whodunit. I continue to traipse up and down this Mecca to consumerism in the vain hope of finding food, to no avail. No matter, according to my map there is a street near here that hosts the Donghuamen night market. Beijing being based on a grid system I calculate I'm only two blocks away.

An hour later I arrive, via a narrow alley that doesn't exist on my guidebook map. Donghuamen market is actually a street of about seventy stalls. Each stall is covered in a red and white, striped awning. Nothing unusual in that I hear you say. Well no. The interesting stuff is the produce underneath them, because this food market specialises in ingredients that

Westerners would normally bludgeon with the heal of a stout shoe.

The first stall I look at is typical. In fact, its pretty much repeated all the way along the row. There are a few things that are obvious. Scorpions piled next to mountains of ants. Skewered grasshoppers and deep fried frogs, although some of these have lost their original shape due to their fat partially melting in the cooking process. Other items look like the content of an autopsy bucket and are, I suspect, the internal organs of larger species. I walk up for a closer inspection.

'You try this,' the stallholder says, in passable English, offering me a worm impaled on a toothpick. He's large and fat, not unlike the worm. I pull it off its spear with my teeth and bite. It's been deep fried, and to be honest, the overwhelming taste I get is garlic and ginger. I open my mouth to show him it's gone. He laughs the high-pitched laugh of a helium addict.

'Ha, ha, ok, where you from?'

'England.'

'You have this in England?' He produces a small handful of ants in his podgy palm.

'Ants?' I say. 'We love them in England.' I scoop them off his hand and munch them down. I notice, as does the stallholder that I'm starting to draw a small crowd. When I say small what I mean is it's like having five million people to dinner. On the upside I'm getting fed for free. My new best friend says something to the crowd in Chinese and they all burst out laughing. He then offers me a water cockroach. I'm struck by the silence as I push it in. The texture is disgusting and the wings give way almost immediately. I then bite down into the body. If you want to know what it tastes like ask a teenager if you can chew on his acne. Nevertheless, I am acutely aware that I am representing the UK now and manage to turn my gag into a gentle cough.

'Ha, Ha, England, you Chinese!' He translates for the crowd that is now at least ten million strong, and they clap. Honestly, they clap. I contemplate a bow, but I don't have time. He moves on to a jar of bile, from which he ladles a small spoonful into a plastic bowl. A hush falls over the crowd as he hands it over to me. It's so viscous I can't keep it balanced on the spoon, so in the end I just upend the bowl and let it slide down. It's like blowing your nose backwards and very hard to describe the taste, but here goes anyway. Run three hundred miles in the same pair of pants. Cut out the crutch section. Soak that in paraffin and bury it in a dung heap until flies have eaten the dung. Retrieve the cloth and boil it in the putrefied remains of a dozen skunks. Add pepper to taste. It made it as far as my tonsils before it came back with the velocity of a discharging shotgun cartridge. The cockroach and scorpions followed it, but curiously not the worm or the ants. The crowd burst into spontaneous laughter.

'Ha, ha, not Chinese!' my fat friend shouts and then repeats this obvious deduction to the crowd. He hands me over half a dozen dumplings, which I eye suspiciously.

'This you can eat England.'

Its pork, and delicious, and better still he refuses my offer to pay, waving me off with another high pitched whinny. The crowd I've pulled is sufficient reward and he sets about serving them, still laughing at my pathetically weak Western stomach. While I'm working my way through the dumplings a young lady approaches me. At first I think it's Jessica, she has that same bouncy way about her, but then I realise she is taller, and her hair doesn't have any budgie toys in it. She tells me without any prompting on my part that she works in Hong Kong.

'I have English boss like you.'

'Do you?' I reply, very much doubting it.

There is something about this girl that makes me uncomfortable. For starters, despite my teacher friend and the snap happy teenagers, young women rarely spontaneously approach me. I suspect it's to do with my face. Its not intentional but I always look like I've won the lottery but lost the ticket.

'Dumpling?' I say.

'Oh, thank you, very nice, you like Chinese food?' I think of the puddle of sick by the stall.

'Oh, yes, delicious.'

'I watch you eat food - I don't think you like...' she points to her head, 'I don't know name in English.'

'Head?'

'No, inside.'

'Brain?'

'Yes, I not like too.' So that's what it was.

Meanwhile my brain goes on to red alert. I'd read in my guidebook about tea scams. Basically a nice young girl will approach you, make friends and then suggest going for a traditional Chinese tea, served by the Triad. Tea with the Triad naturally comes at a significant price. They offer you two options, pay the highly inflated bill and leave quickly or refuse and die slowly. Sure enough she suggests tea.

'Not very far from here, I can practice my English.'

Yes and I can practice breathing without a nose.

'Oh, that's very kind but I'm meeting some Chinese friends in a minute. Can they come too?'

She couldn't leave fast enough. Ah, ah, perhaps Beijing's halo is slipping. I make a mental note not to be rude about guidebooks in the future.

Tiring quickly of eating stuff that you generally find listed on the back of a donor card I traipse off towards the northern end of Tiananmen Square. I'd spotted a restaurant earlier that I want to try for no other reason than the pathetically sad sign in its window. Made of cardboard and written in thick red marker pen it informed me: "we have menu in England, please come in and try traditional food." Under that it had another sign informing me: "we boil tripe." How could I resist? I walk in and am greeted warmly by a small lady, mind you, this is China, and people can be inscrutable. Behind the smile she could actually be weighing up how to dispose of my body.

'Table for one please.'

She looks at her husband with the look of someone who has been vindicated. She knew the sign would reel them in. He nods slowly at me and leads me into the eating area. The walls and floor are covered in small white tiles. It's like a urinal. The table is protected with a sheet of Formica and the menu he offers me is covered in Perspex. I point to a poster of a beer on the wall and he shuffles off to get it. To my left is a party of six or seven chain smokers. Empty beer bottles fight for space with plates of half eaten food. Grains of rice are scattered about over their Perspex like a heavy dusting of dandruff. The man at the head of the table smiles at me exposing a couple of gold teeth and half a pound of rice. He rattles off something in Chinese, raises his bottle and takes a swig. The table erupts into laughter setting his wife off on a coughing fit. She turns this into a gob, which she dispatches to the floor. It hits the tiles with a plop.

At the far end of the restaurant is a Chinese family of four, father, mother, son and daughter. The daughter is playing with her food and being constantly scolded by her mother. The father looks on disinterestedly, picking his nose. To my right are two young men. Both are as thin as breadsticks and own scraggy crops of hair. One has his tied back in a ponytail and the other constantly pushes the mop from his eyes and the plates of food the lank tresses errantly dip into. They are having the conversation all young men have at least once in their life when they are totally pissed. My translation is as follows. Firstly, they take it in turns to accuse each other of sleeping with their respective girlfriends. This involves much finger pointing and raised voices. Then, after a suitably melancholic pause, they each reassure the other they are better off without the evil bitches. Morose introspection, and some contemplative quietness ensue, underpinned with the odd gruff murmur. They then agree the world would be a better place without women, click glasses, offer a toast to men, and gob on the floor to cement their brotherhood. I watch with some interest, as each cycle of fraternity ends with an ejection of such velocity they are in danger of splashing my trousers.

My food arrives and it's delicious: spicy chicken noodle soup followed by chilli pork. The big man with the entourage watches me with the sort of anthropological interest a botanist might offer to a new species of insect. When I catch my breath on a particularly hot chilli he bursts into laughter and underlines his disdain by dispatching a rice-laden gob to the floor.

Gobbing, I have discovered, is the national pastime, although I have to admit, this is the first time I've witnessed it in a restaurant. I have yet to walk down a road without hearing the hoiking and dispatch of puddles of green, gooey, grolly. Here's what you need to do if you want to join in with the locals. Start with the collection. This is combination of coughing, inward nose snorting, and gagging. Store the result. The best way to do this is by pushing your tongue down to the base of your mouth and pouting like a blow up doll. You're now set up perfectly for the dispatch. Think blowpipe. With practice you'll quickly produce gobs the size of a small lake. I've stepped over some today that would have covered a Wellington boot. With a fervent wish to avoid drowning, I decline dessert. The bill is about eight quid and I hand the nice lady the equivalent of a tenner.

'Keep the change,' I say, getting up to leave.

Before I get to the door she grabs my arm and levers me over to the till. Lifting my hundred Yuan note and pointing to it like a magician about to do a trick, she carefully taps out one hundred on her calculator. She then minuses eighty and points to the twenty remaining. Slowly she unrolls two ten Yuan notes and hands them to me smiling, pointing once again at the calculator. I want to argue that it's a tip, but the grolly orchestra behind me is reaching a crescendo. I reluctantly take my change and leave with a wave.

On the way back to my hotel I encounter two tramps and a beggar, who I give the refused tip to. He offers a cough and a grolly in thanks. Maybe, just maybe, this city's halo has a rusty underside. I've had a great day, and tomorrow promises to be even better. I mean, I'm meeting Johnny Yellow Cab, and I can't wait. But before I drop off, I can't help wondering: this country has 1.4 billion people and twenty million are currently in Beijing. So why haven't I seen anyone who is pregnant yet?

Day 13

Johnny Yellow Cab is also known as the Beijing Taxi Driver, which is just as well because Johnny is not the name his parents gave him and he doesn't own a yellow cab. I found him on the Internet when I was planning my trip. What we are going to do today is the culmination of a joint planning initiative negotiated via extensive e-mail correspondence and Skype. It sounds complicated but it was far less painful than trying to get a cab to my local train station, and he spoke better English.

We agreed to meet today outside my hotel at 7 am. This meant I only had time for a small breakfast of noodles, steamed dumplings, bacon, boiled ham, and a strawberry jam baguette. Oh yes, and a bowl of fruit. And some cold meat. Flying through the lobby's revolving door I scan the car park for his black Hyundai and the number plate he asked me to look out for. The doorman notices me scanning.

'You look for taxi John?'

'Yes.'

He points to a dapper looking chap leaning against a car. It's parked in a prime position to the side of the main doors. John pushes himself off the bonnet and walks towards me smiling. I've seen a head shot from his website and recognise him immediately. He's about five feet six, wearing a cream jacket, slightly darker trousers and a white shirt. His feet are ensconced in a pair of white trainers with yellow flashing. He's wearing sunglasses, is tanned, and looks fit and healthy, aged about twenty five. There's something of Miami Vice about him, maybe it's the way his jacket sleeves are rolled up his forearms. His English is great and delivered at speed with intonations in unusual places. He also stretches out the end sounds of every sentence, each of which is preceded with a laugh.

'Ha, you Mike?' he says, offering me his outstretched hand, 'so yessss, you arrive on time, good, good, please sit in car, ha ha.' He opens the car and I slide into the front passenger seat. It's immaculately clean and I notice he has a jam jar half full of brackish liquid and leafy sediment resting at the bottom. It fits nicely into the bottle holder on the console. In a very short space of time we're on the dual carriageway that will take us into the climbing hills on the northeast outskirts of the city. John chats incessantly.

'Ha, so Mike, you arrive Beijing before.'

'Yes, I arrived yesterday.'

'No, before, yessss?'

'No, yesterday, I arrived yesterday.'

'No, come Beijing before, yessss?'

'Ah... no, this is my first time.'

'Ha, that is good, Okaaaay, this morning we go Great Wall. This you love. Mike, I take you Mutianyu, best for the Wall this time of day. Must come early better no crowds.'

He'd already explained this to me in various e-mails. Mutianyu is about forty five miles out of the city and reputedly one of the best sections of the Wall accessible to tourists. Most people go to the more commercial Badaling section. You don't get a yellow taxi with Johnny Yellow Cab but you do get local knowledge.

To be totally honest the Great Wall was not really on my agenda when I planned my journey. It is such a familiar image that I felt I already knew it but John's enthusiasm persuaded me that if I came to Beijing I should see the Wall. OK, for wall anoraks I can see the attraction. For a start it's nearly as long as the Siberian leg of my train trip. In ancient times over a million men guarded it, and as everyone knows, it's the only man made object visible from space. Or is it? When Chinese astronaut, Yang Lewei emerged from his landing capsule on the Mongolian border in 2003, the assembled press wanted to know the answer to this most important question. Who better to provide it than a Chinese patriot who'd just orbited the earth fourteen times? With a phalanx of microphones and intrepid reporters hanging on his every word the question was asked.

'Can the Great Wall be seen from outer space?' Hush fell over the crowd. An expectant nation of nearly one and a half billion people huddled around their television sets, nudging each other knowingly.

'Errm... no,' he said.

A convoy of black Mercedes flash past us. They are followed by an even faster Toyota pick up truck, which stations itself in front of them. There is a cameraman on the back filming the convoy.

'Are they making a film?' I ask John.

'Ha, oh, no, they make marriage.'

I wonder how many collective points the English courts would meter out if we tried this back home.

'What date today? John asks.

'Date? Mmm... 4th October.'

'Ah, okaaaay, day 4, month 10. Lucky numbers, I think marriage will be good.'

'Did you marry on a lucky day?'

'Me? Oh yes, yes, of course, ha, ha. Very lucky, day 8 month 8 - lucky for me. I have one daughter and wife, yessss, good luck.' He continues to tell me about his family as we start the climb into the hills. There is moisture in the air and many of the people going about their business are wearing light waterproof tops with umbrellas tucked under their arms. It is still warm enough for wispy strands of steam to rise from the trees. John tells me his daughter is eight, and loves school. His wife stays at home now, but before she was a teacher.

'Now, she look after my parents, they are old and live with us now.'

'Does she mind?'

'Why?' He seemed genuinely confused by my question. 'My parents look after me, when young, now we must look after them.'

We are bridging achingly beautiful streams as he speaks, water cascades over rocky outcrops. Thick, dark green, foliage hang into the water's edge like a trailing hand. The sky is grey and heavy.

'Ha, but my parents, they come live so I say goodbye Japanese.'

'Japanese?'

'Yessss, no camera, no machine for grill bread, no television. My car, Korean, yessss, no Japanese.'

'Why.'

'Nanking,' he says in hushed tones. 'My father, remember Nanking, cannot forget.'

It's easy to understand why this event might stick in the mind. The Japanese reputedly killed over a quarter of a million people, mainly civilians, many by the most barbaric means. But even so, it was over seventy years ago, I try to work out how old John's father might be.

'But me, I say okaaay, time to forget. If I have Japanese customer, I am polite, okaaay, must forget.'

'Would you buy a Japanese car?' I say, trying to lighten the mood a little.

'Ahh, not Japanese. When I make more money, I buy Mercedes, or maybe Audi. Ah, ah, maybe my business do well, I buy both, ha, ha, ha, me best entrepreneur in China, make money, ha, ha, ha.' I find his upbeat demeanour infectious, and we continue to chat about his business. Then he asks me about my family. I tell him I have three older sisters.

'And you, John, how many brothers and sisters do you have?'

'Ah, no, Mike, no brother, no sister, in China, only one child.'

It suddenly dawns on me. Nearly everyone I meet in China will be a single child. No siblings. It's a weird thought and slightly melancholic. But it has an upside. John has never suffered at the hands of a big sister practicing her make up techniques on him.

The climb is getting steeper, and the villages that we pass are coming to life. We stop in one to let a donkey pull a large slab of concrete across the road. There is no apparent reason for this but the donkey doesn't seem to mind. I am surprised to see many of the shops have English signage so am aware we pass "Good Fish Shop," and the intriguingly named "Donkey Meat & Fish Store." I'm tempted to ask John to make a detour when I spot an enticing sign for a bottle lid factory. Fruit stalls are dotted along the road. Melons, jackfruit, others I don't recognise, and piles of walnuts, sit under awnings, usually with a lady stallholder in attendance, dressed for a Siberian winter. We also pass some restaurants with spectacular vistas of the valley below, yellow and orange lanterns swinging gently from their wooden balconies.

When we arrive at the entrance, I get the impression John is a bit of a face around these parts. He opens his window, waves at the security guards, who smile and direct him towards the car parks. John ignores these instructions.

'Ah, Mike, car parks always busy, better we see my friend near Wall gate.'

At the highest car park he engages the security guards in a little light banter, and eventually parks on a slip road, all the while keeping up a conversation in Chinese with security and a travelogue in English with me. It's only a short walk to the entrance gate from the car, through a small market. The market is an eclectic mixture with stalls offering fruit and vegetables, others selling surplus Chinese and Russian army gear. Many sell Che Guevara tee shirts and military survival kits. How high are these mountains? John deposits me at the gate and addresses me as he might his daughter.

'Ah, ah, OK Mike. You pay seventy five Yuan to lady. This include cable car and toboggan back down.'

'Toboggan?'

'Ah, suuuure,yessss, its fun. I think two and half hours enough, by then you tired. Meet me in tea house.' He points to a red brick building near the entrance. 'Okaaay Mike, see you later.'

Still musing over the toboggan, I forget to ask him if there is a way up that doesn't involve a cable car, which in truth is not much better than a ski lift. I have a morbid fear of them. Sitting on a seat dangling from a few strands of cheese wire, half a mile above the ground seems to me to be, literally, the height of folly. But before I can think about it a large Chinese man is manhandling me on to a board.

'Stand on board,' he says, as I'm swept up at the knees by the lift. He clamps the safety bar over my lap just before my feet leave the ground. I hold the bar so tightly my knuckles threaten to break out of my skin. It wouldn't be so bad if I could see my final destination, but I can't. The crest of the hill in front of me is covered in deep green foliage and a range of trees that blocks out any view beyond it. I try to take comfort from the greenery directly below me. It looks so lush it might act like a plump cushion if I fall. Once I crest the first line of trees, I'm faced with another section of hill and another restricted horizon, and another, and another. People heading down who wave at me as they pass are met with the maniacal stare of a serial killer.

Eventually, cresting the last ridge, I'm rewarded with a panoramic view of the Wall stretching out to both my right and left like billowing ribbons of stone. There are watchtowers in either direction, some atop impossibly high ridges. Each is connected by the grey stone artery of the Wall, which drapes itself along the ridgeline of the mountains for as far as the horizon in either direction. The early morning mist shrouding the uppermost reaches of the mountain peaks lends the view an eerie feel, like I'm just about to land on the set of the Water Margin. I judder to a halt, skipping off the slowing ski lift and make my way up a short flight of stairs to a vista point. I am genuinely astounded. The surrounding mountainside is heart-skippingly beautiful. I simply don't have an experience I can draw on to describe it. This might explain why I text a friend and write: "I'm on the Great Wall - Fuck me." John told me to walk the Wall to the right of the cable car station first.

'This section not too crowded Mike, and better views, yessss, you like this.'

It's a little after 8 am and I'm pleased we've arrived so early. Hardly anyone followed me up on the ski lift and I feel like I almost have the Wall to myself. I set off for the first watchtower. It doesn't take long before the path's gradient climbs sharply. The few people up here with me employ both hands and feet to clamber up. I can't help thinking that the soldiers that manned it must have been knackered just travelling to a breach by insurgents, let alone fighting them off. After five minutes my calves are burning and my lungs are working like a pair of bellows with a broken handle. I stop frequently, each time rewarded with an ageless view. I am accompanied in my ascent by a gaggle of Chinese families who, amazingly, are less fit than I am. I know they're Chinese because the effort required at this altitude to climb steps pushes the Chinese gob-ometer off the scale. Some of the phlegm I side step looks as ancient as the Wall. The fact they're prepared to gob on one of the world's most beautiful monuments is irritating, but at least it's biodegradable. Which is more than can be said for the graffiti I find scratched into the stone on the inside turrets of the first watchtower. I hope 'Josh, 2007, Idaho,' and 'Jon, New York, 2008,' had fun scratching it. I also hope the cable car gave way on their descent, fucking philistines. Americans don't have history because they don't deserve it.

The battlement at the top of the tower offers another vocabulary sapping view. A man decked out in all weather walking gear, including a stout pair of boots stands next to me. I know he's English as soon as he opens his mouth.

'Fuck me,' he says.

'Fantastic isn't it,' I say, looking out at the view.

'Fucking knackering, he says, turning around and heading back down to the ramparts. Perhaps we don't deserve history either.

I follow him down and am collared by a man selling water. There are quite a few of these traders dotted along the Wall.

'Hello, where you from, friend?' he says, grinning. He's swathed in what looks like a yak's skin with its head removed. He has a pair of flip flops on his feet.

'England,' I reply.

'Ah! UK, good friend, China. God Bless UK Queen! You want water?'

'How much?'

'Twenty Yuan.'

'Twenty? Its only two Yuan in Beijing.'

'Beijing?' he stands up and points down the mountain, and then at the five or six crates of water bottles next to him. 'Beijing not carry water up mountain, so you can drink when thirsty! Fifteen Yuan - good price.'

Good point, well made I think. We haggle a little more and I say no higher than six Yuan, fair I think at three times the going rate. Grudgingly he hands me the water, and even when it's in my hand tries to force me up to eight Yuan.

'Ok, you have water, now you give me two more Yuan.' Doesn't he know possession is nine tenths of the law?

'I'm Mongolian,' he shouts after me, as if this is going to make me walk back up a one in ten incline to give him another two Yuan.

Heading back towards the ski lift station I fall into step behind two American ladies, one is black with an unfeasibility large rear end that she advertises by encasing it in a pair of bright red corduroy trousers. It looks like her buttocks have been removed and replaced with two space-hoppers. Her companion is white and petite with a bushy crop of blond hair. The black one is doing all the talking. It's a bellowing voice that resonates around the valley like a fugal horn.

'... So there I am with my two hundred Dollar sonic hair, brushing my teeth, and I'm thinking, like, there are people here who don't have enough to eat.' Her blond companion nods.

'And I'm like letting the water run, and like, people don't have enough to drink. But you know, these people, are like, so lucky. They have so much culture...' Whilst she is informing the world of how lucky these starving people are she passes up the opportunity to help their economy by brushing away every hawker who approaches her.

'They have such beauty around them all the time,' then in hushed tones, 'but I do wish these people wouldn't hassle me so. I mean can't they see I have water? The hotel give them free with the room.'

Hypocritical moron. What's a fucking sonic haircut anyway? Perhaps if she spent some of that two hundred Dollars in the real local economy, instead of the International Hotel chain where she lives, eating hamburgers that are "just like home," she might actually help these poor people have full bellies so they can enjoy their culture. And, she wouldn't have a haircut that looks like its been fashioned by a crow on LSD.

Back at the ski lift station I encounter two Chinese ladies selling postcards. They laugh when I get near. One points to my legs poking out from my shorts. The weather is closing in a little. I can see heavy rain clouds across the valley, slowly making their way towards me. Even I have to admit I'm probably inappropriately dressed.

'Hello mister! You mad!' She translates for her mate and they both fall about laughing.

'Wan't buy water?'

'No thanks,' I say waving my half full bottle.

'Beer? You want beer?'

'No, thanks,' I say walking past.

'OK, maybe you come back later if you still alive!' She translates again for her friend and they have another laughing frenzy at the expense of my goose pimpled knees.

By now the clouds are above us and there is a light drizzle falling. I decide to head for the toboggan, as I know it will close if it gets too wet. The only way down then is the ski lift, or walking. Neither fills me with excitement. There is a small queue so I while away the time reading the safety notice. I'm pleased to discover that no one with mental diseases is allowed on or anyone with firearms. It may seem a little odd that one of the world's most iconic historical sites effectively turns the descent into a joy ride, but sliding down on my arse is more preferable than my other options.

The toboggan is actually a plastic seat on wheels. The lever now protruding between my legs is the brake. Pull it towards my gonads and the plastic seat slows down, push it towards my knees and it speeds up. So, one moving part, what can go wrong? Well, nothing to begin with. I am held back initially to ensure plenty of space between me and the toboggan in front, and upon release start out at the sort of pace associated with maiden aunts in Morris Minors. Marshals are stationed at each bend and call out instructions in English and Chinese as I pass, although there doesn't seem to be any communication between Marshals in any language. After only two bends of being told to speed up I am forced to pull the lever towards me so hard I nearly crush my tackle. I avoid the pile up in front of me by a whisker. The carnage has been caused by a girl stopping to get off. I don't have time to be smug about avoiding the ensuing pile up though because the joy riders behind me are soon piling in to my rear end. The carnage is dealt with swiftly by the Marshals and we soon set off again despite the rain getting harder and turning the aluminium shute into the Cresta Run. A few sharp bends follow and then some longer straights. I estimate I'm doing about thirty miles per hour at the next pile up. This one sandwiches me in the middle of a train of at least ten toboggans. Marshals appear from nowhere waving hands and shouting in a sort of Chinese, English mix. Despite my protestations they declare that bad weather stops play. The cause of this latest pile up is another girl who didn't like the speed and stopped to get off. I walk past her laid out on the side of the run. She is clutching what I suspect is a broken ankle. Either that or her left foot always points towards her bottom. She makes surprisingly little noise. The rest of us are forced to take the only other route to the bottom - a winding set of steps. Thankfully it's not too far, because the rain has upgraded itself from a misty mizzle to a full-blown storm. Raindrops bounce off the steps like gunshots. I dip into the tearoom in search of John. He's chatting to the ladies behind a large tea urn and munching on a piece of cake.

On the way back down to Beijing John stops at a restaurant so he can drop something off for a friend. It's quite a large place with sweeping verandas and a mountain stream meandering through it. In the car park I'm surprised to see a pond surrounded by people. I get out of the car to investigate and discover customers catching goldfish for their lunch. They stand with concentration etched across their brows holding rods similar to the ones garden gnomes carry and they are catching their dinner at an alarming rate. Once landed one of the waiters rushes over, unhooks the unlucky fish and clumps it over the head with an auctioneer's gavel. We should do this in our fast food chains. Think about it, if we got the fat lardy arses to chase down each cow they eat, we'd solve the obesity crisis in a week. We're soon on our way and John suggests some music.

'Ah, International radio Mike, okaaay, you like I think.' It occurs to me that John might make a good DJ. Immediately we get a jingle, "Beijing International, with Dave G," and then a load of Chinese, then back to English, "This week's top twenty," more Chinese, then, "The Charts!"

And so I find myself listening to the top twenty with Dave G, whom I suspect was given a different name by his parents. John passes comments on all of the tracks. Apparently Avril Lavigne has too much guitar, Justin Timberlake is pretty good, and Madonna is fantastic. All the while he fires questions at me about them, which is a totally pointless exercise, as I know less about them than him. Soon we are listening to "Everything I do".

'Ah, ah, Mike, this good song, yessss, you like I think, very goodddd. I think singer Michael Bolton.'

'Really?' I'm sure he's wrong. 'You sure its not someone else?'

'Ah, maybe, he have blond hair.' Then I experience a rare flash of inspiration, mainly because the song irritated me for months when it was number one.

'Bryan Adams,' I say, 'that's it: Bryan Adams.'

'Ah, yes, yes, you right Mike, yes, I like this very much. But I not like that noisy music.'

'What noisy music?'

'Ha, I think you know, that Hip music, not like, too much shouting.'

'Hip Hop?'

'Yessss, no, I don't like it.' Thankfully Dave G finishes and we turn off the radio so he can give me instructions on my next destination: the Temple of Heaven.

The Temple of Heaven is my second World Heritage site today and another place I hadn't made plans to see. John suggested it. The grounds in which the Temple majestically sits are, in fact, a park with the Hall of Prayer at their heart. This is where the Emperors went to pray for good harvests.

'Ha, ha, okaaay Mike, I drop you north entrance, you walk to south entrance, I meet there, under bridge, you see me, no problem. You have my telephone number, you can call you lost, okaaay.'

Thirty minutes later I'm in the queue with ten million others at the entrance. I employ my now finely honed Chinese queuing techniques and elbow my way to the front in no time. The entrance to the park is suitably grand with gigantic brass studded doors standing at least sixty feet high. I walk through them under a slightly murky sky. The temperature is dropping and once again I feel underdressed in my shorts, but at least no one is laughing at my knees here. I can just make out the Temple's uppermost roof over the tree-lined pathway. The pathway is the central avenue through the park and has lantern styled lampposts on each side at about twenty step intervals. They don't emit light. What they actually do is provide a running commentary of some sort, in Chinese. Then again, it might simply be a message warning dog owners not to let their canine chums piss up them. Additional speakers are strategically placed and play 'The Sound of Silence,' on a continuous loop, which at first I find mildly ironic. After ten minutes I find it a little irritating and after another ten minutes excruciating. I make for the Hall of Prayer as quickly as possible.

The Hall is a magnificent triple gabled circular building, over 90 yards in diameter, and a little over 100 yards high. It sits within a round battlement and is built on a marble base. The building itself is wooden and constructed entirely without nails. No B&Q in those days. I decide to give it a wide berth just in case it collapses. It's impossible to get near anyway because sixty million people are queuing to see the interior. I settle for some photos of the queue and head off towards the southern gate. I'm painfully aware I haven't done this monument justice but it's starting to get colder and the drizzle is turning to rain. It doesn't take me long to find John leaning against his car under the motorway bridge and we are soon on our way. Back at the hotel we exchange gifts. He gives me some ornamental lanterns to bring me good luck and I give him some foreign coins for his daughter. He'd told me in our e-mail correspondence that she collected them.

'Oh, ha, yessss, thank you Mike, my daughter not have English coin or Russia, but maybe too much. I can pay you for coin?' It takes me a full ten minutes to persuade him that I have no need for the £1.50 the combined coinage is worth. He grasps my elbow as we shake hands.

'Okaaay, Mike, have safe time in your journey, yessss, I hope you have great time in China.' As I walk back through the revolving door into the lobby I think I may have just met the nicest taxi driver in the world.

By the time I walk out in search of an evening meal the rain has relented but there is still dampness in the air. Within minutes I find myself in the food market. My new best friend shouts across at me to join him, presumably to try and get me to puke up in front of a new crowd. I wave back but slip behind a stall and up the stairs to a restaurant that I'd noticed the night before. It specialises in Szechwan cuisine, my favourite. The waitress leads me to a table near the window so I can look out on the market and watch other people hooting up cockroaches.

A man and woman are enjoying a meal on the table immediately next to mine. I soon discover she is American and working in one of the Chinese Universities. She is about fifty and has a shrewish nervousness that I find hard to warm to. Perhaps it's the aura of perpetual victim that shrouds her. He's of Indian extraction, strong features, large aquiline nose and lusty black hair. His eyes are as black as a raven. He tells me, rather mysteriously, that he works on "special projects." It's the only thing he's not very explicit about as he ploughs into how British housing development is blighting UK cities. He's also strikingly certain that London couldn't possibly hope to compete with other countries on cuisine. Proving his international credentials he further informs me what's wrong with the Middle East, America, Russia, and how these countries are neglecting a growing underclass that will rise up one day and cause chaos. I assume it's an oversight on his part that he neglects to mention that half a billion people live below the poverty line in India.

'You must try some of these vegetables. They are called Pak Choi. Most delicious and not available in England.'

'Ah, Pak Choi' I say, 'yes I grow it in my garden, but no thanks, my order will be here in a minute.' He totally ignores my vegetable sleight. 'Of course, you English are used to eating food from your own plate. Here in Asia it is customary to share.' Well, I fucking never, really?

In no time at all I know he has three bedrooms and three bathrooms in his apartment on the outskirts of Beijing and what the square footage is. His wife says nothing at all but occasionally twitches her nose. Surely she must be as bored as me because I suspect she's heard all this verbal claptrap before. By the time he offers me some spring rolls I'm getting a little tetchy.

'Really you English should learn to share your food, you will enjoy it far more.'

Not for the first time in my life, my mouth decided to take action without prior collaboration with my brain.

'I'd enjoy it far more if you shut the fuck up for a few seconds...'

They paid the bill in silence and left. I finished my spicy prawn noodles without offering to share them with anyone. Amazingly I still enjoyed it.

Halfway back I need a pee. By the time I'm at the end of the road to my hotel I need more than a pee. When I turn into the hotel drive something more solid is forming and I have to develop the gait of a man with a Cornish pasty wedged up his backside. On the other side of the revolving door I fear the worst – I might not make it to my room. Then I remember some toilets by the elevators. I combine a shuffle and a cha cha cha on my way towards them. By the time I reach the door I've given up the dancing and pretty much hit it at a full sprint. The door hits the wall with such force the handle gouges a hole in the wall behind it. Then it gets surreal. Standing by the door of the disabled cubicle is a very tall, very toothy, Chinese man. He's dressed in a grey morning suit that his arms are patently too long for. The trousers only reach down to the middle of his shin. He flicks the tails back, theatrically, before he speaks.

'Good evening Sirrrrr,' he says sweeping a hand along the cubicles like a game show model fanning a hand across a stage full of prizes. Then he bows.

'Pereeeesssse,' he says, opening the door to trap one with another flourishing hand movement. I cautiously walk past him and shut the door. I've never been comfortable with the notion of communal crapping. I know the Romans were big fans but I feel decidedly awkward doing my business when I know someone is so close. Especially when the event itself is preceded by a combination of pig noises, exploding fireworks and an army squelching through a swamp in Wellington boots. In an attempt to retain my dignity I finish as quietly as I can, tidy myself up and unbolt the door. Before I can open it fully he's pushing it back for me.

'Pereeeesse,' he says, offering another hand flourish towards the sink. Watching attentively at my shoulder as I wash my hands, he offers another extravagant bow.

'Pereeeesse,' he says holding out a paper towel in his outstretched palms. When I finish drying my hands he takes it from me and throws it in the bin, then turns towards me again, this time offering only a small bow, and once again stretching out his hands palms up. I give him some change form my pocket, he offers a big grin, opens the door for me and bows again.

'Pereeeesse,' he says, and watches me through his eyebrows as I walk past. It is a most bizarre encounter so when I collect my room key I ask the receptionist if all the toilet attendants are so attentive.

'Attendants? Sorry sir, the hotel doesn't employ toilet attendants.'

Day 14

It's just as well that I have nothing planned for today other than catching my train to Hanoi. There is a constant drum of rain on my window and the slate sky offers little hope of improvement. I have to be out of the room by midday so plan a lazy morning, starting with an around the world breakfast. I eat my fill by ten and return to my room. Bored, I start exploring. That is to say I check out what I can nick. Most of the toiletries make it to my bag. I add the shoeshine and the sewing kits, and then I play with the self-closing toilet seat for a while. I work my way through the complimentary drinks by having a coffee, a Lipton's tea, another coffee, and a green tea. This makes me want to pee, which gives me the opportunity to play with the toilet seat a little more. At 11 am I pack. I then unpack and pack again, and then check and re-check my documents. Then the phone rings.

'Hello Mike, its me Olive.'

'Hello Olive,' I am just about to ask her if freelance toilet attendants are common in Beijing, but she gets in first.

'I will collect you at 2 o'clock to take you train station. I speak with hotel, you can have room until 2 o'clock - no charge, OK?'

I say it's fine but to be honest I'm ready to leave now. I feel the pull of the train and the need for motion. Beijing has been great but, if I'm honest, a little too sterile for me. As cities go, it's missing something. I'm not sure what: an undercurrent maybe. The surface is all calm and inviting but a city this big has to have an undercurrent. Even the cleanest rivers have the odd eddy. This place is like a gleaming new computer that hasn't had any viruses downloaded on to it yet.

After an eternity Olive arrives and we set off for Beijing West train station where I encounter, for the first time in my life, two hundred thousand people trying to walk on my bit of pavement. If you viewed this station through a microscope it would look like an outbreak of the E-Coli bacteria. Everyone is walking in the opposite direction to me. Olive seems only mildly surprised by the amount of people.

'Normally not too busy but many people go back to village after celebrate National holiday,' she says, taking my hand to avoid my getting swallowed up in this human swamp. I thank God she is six feet tall, it will make her easier to spot if she loses her grip. Employing my elbows in a sort of threshing movement helps me to reach the waiting room on platform 4a. Olive tells me she must see me off, so wanders off to get a platform ticket.

The waiting room would be better described as a hall. It looks like a refugee camp. People are everywhere, on rows of chairs, under them, cross-legged on the floor, leaning on walls, perched on windowsills, under each of my armpits, between my legs. Some are eating, others chatting, reading, and many are staring directly at me. I am the only Westerner in the hall and therefore a subject worthy of bemused scrutiny. I'm getting used to this sort of close inspection, as the population has subjected me to continued examination ever since I arrived in

Beijing. The Chinese simply have no concept of privacy. If I behaved like them in England I would be constantly fighting. Soon after my arrival a couple of other Westerners turn up so the gawping is spread a little more fairly. Without much delay we are called forward for boarding.

I'm travelling first class again, but if you're thinking a nice bed, en-suite bathrooms, and perhaps a butler, think again. Mine is a four-berth cabin about the size of a small family bathroom. Thankfully I'm in a bottom bunk. A young Chinese man enters soon after me with a suitcase that comes up to his lower chest. With my assistance we heft it onto the bunk above me, leaving him about an inch of sleeping space. He offers me a crooked smile that elongates a scar on his upper lip into a tick. He quickly disappears back into the corridor. Shortly afterwards two more youngsters arrive, early twenties I would say, they're carrying about twelve bags between them. Its clear they've done a lot of shopping in C&A and McDonalds. He has a very healthy thatch of black hair and South East Asian colouring, like very milky chocolate. He's wearing cream jeans and a beige top. The girl has long hair, slightly under five feet, and a little podgy. She's wearing blue jeans and a black top. Immediately after they stow all their bags they start arguing, or at least it sounds like a row. They then start frantically searching through their pockets and bags.

'You have telephone?' he asks me.

'Yes, ' I reply.

'I need quickly.'

If it wasn't for the panic on his face I would have told him I need a please even quicker but instead I hand it over to him. While he tries to make a connection she pulls out two sets of train tickets and passports from a compartment in her bag. They both start laughing and he hands me back the phone.

'Sorry, thank you,' he says handing back my phone with a beaming smile that exposes a perfectly straight set of gleaming white teeth. I think he might be Donny and Marie Osmond's secret love child. Panic over, the train gently pulls away. True to her word Olive stands on the platform, waving. I'm sure I see a tear in her eye. Once she is out of sight I settle back onto my bunk. The rhythm of the train is comforting and I while away an enjoyable ten minutes watching my new sharers get comfortable. She takes the lower bunk and he clambers up onto the top and pulls out a Harry Potter book. She makes do with Roald Dahl. The script on the covers confirms my suspicion that they are Vietnamese. I dig out my guidebook to Vietnam, which I notice, for the first time, was published in 1997. No wonder it was so cheap. I start to bone up on all the stuff that will, by now, be totally out of date. I notice both of them sneak glances at me when they think I'm not looking. Eventually, curiosity gets the better of the boy, and he asks me, in passable English, what I'm reading.

'Its a guidebook to Vietnam,' I say. 'Are you from there?'

He sits up and flicks his legs over the edge of his bed so he can look at me directly. 'Oh yes, me and my sister have holiday, four day Beijing, four day Shanghai. Brother study in

Beijing, we stay him.' His sister sits up also and they pool their vocabulary. I soon find myself in a sort of triangular conversation. His sister is an accountant and he is studying in Hanoi. He's eighteen and I'm surprised to discover that his sister is thirty.

'Thirty? Never!' I say. He translates and she blushes.

'Yes, she very old,' he says, pityingly.

They go on to explain how their eight days in China has been really enjoyable.

'We go to the Haggis building in Shanghai,' she says.

'Haggis building?'

'Yes, Haggis,' he repeats. He can see I'm confused. 'Wait.' He digs out his mobile phone, jumps down from his bunk and comes and sits next to me. His sister joins him on the other side of me. They both cross their legs under their bodies in a fashion that would break both my knees if I tried it. He finds the picture he's looking for. Its shows him, his sister and a taller man, who I assume is his older brother, standing in front of a skyscraper. They all carry the expressions of the newly bereaved. 'Very hag, building, haggis in Shanghai.'

'Highest, ah, you mean highest.' My translation is rewarded with a picture history of their Chinese vacation. It's basically combinations of the three of them posing, erectly and soberly, beside something significant, like a park bench. I persuade him not to look for the memory card with the other pictures on by suggesting we look at them tomorrow.

'You like football?' he asks.

'Yes, I do. Let me guess, I bet I know what team you support?'

'Really, OK, who you think?'

'Manchester United,' I say confidently.

'How you know?' he says, shocked at my ability to read minds.

'OK, you know my father team?'

'Manchester United? I say, with a swagger of confidence.

'No, Arsenal.'

'And you team? He asks.'

'West Ham,' I say, expecting at least a muffled guffaw, but if he finds it funny he hides it well.

He proceeds to offer me a run down on the state of the Premiership, and rather delightfully, why he thinks Spurs will never challenge for anything. He then offers me a full appraisal of each Manchester United player, including some of the youth team prospects, finishing off with a eulogy on both Scholes and Giggs. This boy knows his stuff.

'Oh, I am Tie,' he says pointing to himself, and my sister called Twee.'

'I'm Mike.'

'Nice to meet you Mike.'

'Nice to meet you Tie, and nice to meet you Twee,' I say smiling directly at her, and seeing for the first time in my life Vietnamese coquettishness.

There's still no sign of the Chinaman residing above me when we put out the cabin lights. I stay awake watching neon station signs and village streetlamps pierce the thin curtain and illuminate the wall opposite. I am in reflective mood and muse on the progress of my revenge. There's no question I have regained some of my lost commuting days, however I measure it. If I use days as my benchmark I've recouped fourteen and in mileage terms it's even more impressive. I think about putting on my table light and doing the mathematics to see just how much progress I have made and reach for the light. As I do so I hear the gentle breathing of my two new friends sleeping and decide against it. It can wait until tomorrow: after all, its not like I have to be anywhere.

Day 15

I wake to the sound of a Chinese accented Dolly Parton wishing me a lovely journey. She's the automated announcer at Changsha train station and she is saying goodbye to my departing train and suggesting how nice it would be to see me again. Its 6 am, an hour I normally associate with getting up for my commuter train, so despite the early hour, I rise to see what the world is like outside. Careful not to disturb my slumbering sharers I grab my wash bag and step out into the corridor. It's my first real look at the train interior and I discover it's rather shabby. The clean contours of the train that took me to Beijing have been replaced with British Rail rolling stock circa Slade. The red carpet running along the centre of the corridor bears testament to an army of shuffling passengers searching for the bathroom. Some of the stains indicate they didn't all make it. The carpet curls up like stale bread in the corners. Any self respecting Health and Safety Officer would declare the whole corridor a trip hazard. The cream walls are grubby and more than a few imprints of outstretched palms can be seen on the windows. Outside, rice has replaced the corn of the north, taking up every available inch of land. Paddies buttress the track, steam rising and trapping as condensation that trickles down fronds of heavily leafed trees and bushes. It's hard to tell whether the rice paddies have followed the contours of the land or shaped them. Even at this early hour I see farmers hunched over, up to their knees in paddy water, or leading reluctant water buffalo by tugging aggressively at ropes attached to the beast's nostrils. Snorts of breath are expelled from both man and beast forming clouds that float upwards until they evaporate into the bright blue sky.

The bathroom door is locked so I stand a while and take some more of the scenery in. The vista is a much less wealthier one than the north. The villages and towns we pass are well established, the buildings much older, and there is a total absence of suburbs. English signage is practically non-existent. Gigantic spring onions and leaks compete for space with washing that flaps like skittish spectres on every balcony. Most have a birdcage hanging from a hook with small finches inside hopping from perch to perch. When we leave the towns the water buffalo count is significantly higher than cars. What is the delay in the bathroom? Don't they know there's a queue of one out here? While I wait, I consider this part of my journey. Beijing to Hanoi is about 1700 miles as the crow flies, but I know little about the regions I'll be passing through. And, I'm on my own from here: no travel agent assisted itinerary and no being met at the station. When I booked my Hanoi accommodation from the UK I asked them about meeting me at the station. They would be pleased to, they said, for more than the cost of the room. I decided I'd get my own taxi. How hard can it be? Thinking about it, all I really know about this part of my train journey is that I am scheduled to arrive in Hanoi tomorrow morning.

I notice a five star general or a slightly worn carriage attendant depending on whether your eyes are Eastern or

Western, walking towards me so I take the opportunity to ask about the bathroom. He looks at me confused: maybe he's struggling with my English. I up the volume.

'BATHROOM...' he holds up his hand to stop me and opens the door next to the bathroom. It's the bathroom. I've been standing outside the toilet. This bathroom is palatial in comparison to the Russian offering. Three gleaming aluminium sinks in a row and plenty of running water. I have a choice of cold or instant frostbite. Selecting cold, I make short work of stripping down to my under-crackers and set to work. Two minutes later the door flies open and a woman so old she may have been the original Eve shuffles in. She is stooped like an upturned hockey stick, but not quite as broad. As soon as she clocks me her eyes widen in the same way they might if she'd walked off a cliff unexpectedly. She retreats, in what I suspect, is the fastest backwards shuffle ever recorded. I hope I haven't offended her because you just don't know what you're dealing with in this part of the world. Don't forget, people like her fought off the mighty American armed forces with only a hairpin, three boiled sweets and inscrutable guile.

On the way back to my cabin I'm nearly trampled by a platoon of five star generals. In perfect formation, eyes ahead, backs straight, they march past at the double, in metronymic unison. I only just manage to stop myself saluting as I dip back into the cabin. Still no sign of the Chinaman, dirty little stop out, but my new friends seem to be stirring, albeit, slowly.

I soon hear the sales call of the trolley girl. It sounds like she's grieving for a recently murdered relative but I know better. I discovered this little gem last night. Basically the buffet car doesn't function like the one travelling down to Beijing. On this train they package up whatever they're cooking and bring it around on trolleys. I have no idea what's in her sales spiel, or indeed what's in her trolley but I stop her anyway. Her hot plated perambulator is essentially an oven on wheels, with a storage area on top for housing the condiments, soy sauce, chilli powder, sugar and so on. The front of the trolley displays the content and price. So I know it's going to cost me five Yuan (about 40p), I just don't know what it is. The trolley lady is about fifteen with hair rolled into a bun, which is partially covered with a small white hat. She's wearing a green tabard and tries, without success, to avoid eye contact with me throughout the transaction. I point to the sort of plastic box you get burgers in. She opens it to avoid any translation issues and shows me a pile of noodles nestled in like a pit of blanched vipers. I stick up a thumb and she then points to the chilli sauce. I offer my thumb again and her eyebrows knit together. Obviously she was expecting thumbs down. Nevertheless she ladles on a healthy dollop. I grin, trying to look like I always have half a pint of chilli on my breakfast. Finally she spoons on a steamy beef broth with tofu and spring onion. Et voila - breakfast.

My sharers linger in their beds as I work my way through it, the boy especially, eyeing me carefully. I feel a warm sensation between my legs, which is a little disconcerting and when I look down I discover I've spilled some of my breakfast on my bed. He follows my gaze, jumps off his bunk and offers me some tissues to mop it up. I do my best but it leaves a brown stain on the sheets. Whichever way you look at it, and I try most angles, it looks suspiciously like I've shit the bed. I put my flannel over it so as not to upset the perfect impression his sister undoubtedly has of me.

'What food is this?' he asks, pointing to my flannel.

'Fang,' I reply, offering the only word the waitress had said when I asked the same question of her. For all I know she could have been calling me a shit and I've told Tie I'm eating shit.

'Chinese food?'

I give this due consideration. Let me think, I'm on a Chinese train, in China, being served by a Chinese waitress.

'I think it might be,' I say.

'Oh, Chinese food no good, ' he says, waking his sister and pointing at my flannel. After they finish laughing they tuck into a couple of cold McDonald's apples pies from their stash.

After eating I pull the curtains back and look out of the window. We're passing through a village where I spot a mother washing down her naked offspring in a pond by their weather beaten red brick house. The paddy fields are more substantial now, graduating up into the hilly terrain like steps on a massive green escalator. Inside, the train is bustling. When the corridor isn't being used for platoon drill by the generals it's filled with

Chinese and Vietnamese going about their business. Many congregate by the samovar, which on this train looks more like a contraption for dispensing golf balls on driving ranges. Old people wander past frequently and many stop to scrutinise our cabin. Some show the same level of interest as customs officials, standing in the doorway for quite a few minutes, shamelessly staring at each occupant. In an effort to mingle I've had a pretty good nose myself, and have discovered there are far more Westerners in my carriage than any of the others trains I've taken. The next cabin down has three. One is an Irishman with an exceedingly loud voice. I caught a glimpse of him earlier on his way to the golf ball machine. He's in his mid twenties, very thin and has dark hair. He has kept up a constant dialogue with anyone that will listen and many that won't, so I felt like I knew him long before I saw him. It's why I know he's been trekking around China and will be getting out at Guilin for another trek.

'I don't have all the right kit, but so what,' I heard him say to no one in particular while I was in the corridor.

I have spoken to the other man in his cabin though. We met on one of my gazing out of the corridor window expeditions after my breakfast. In his early fifties, he owns the remnants of a 1970s grey mullet with a weak centre parting. He has slightly protruding teeth and his ensemble of khaki combats and checked shirt screamed Marks and Spencer at me. I discovered he's doing his gap year in reverse, at the end of his working life, courtesy of redundancy and early retirement from the Civil Service. So basically I'm funding his bloody holiday.

From Moscow onwards his route has pretty much mirrored mine.

'We rented a flat in Moscow, private rental, you know to save some money.'

'We?'

'Yes, me and my girlfriend.'

'Is she the lady you and the Irishman is sharing with?'

'No, she flew home from Moscow, she had to get back to work.'

I'd place his accent's origins in South London or Home Counties.

'This is something I've wanted to do all my life and never had the chance, what with getting married, and bringing up a family.'

'You're married?'

'Was,' he said, gazing down at his feet. 'The flat was a little grim. My girlfriend wasn't too happy.'

'How did you find Moscow?' I ask.

He gave the question some serious thought, 'mmmm... miserable, I think.'

I discover his plans are sketchier than mine. He will spend some time in Hanoi, then make his way down the coast to Saigon, then maybe Thailand, possibly Malaysia, or Singapore.

'Have you had breakfast?' he asks me.

I tell him I have and how to go about organising it. Fortuitously the trolley makes an appearance while I'm offering instruction. It's serving completely different food now, but after some wasted requests for information from the trolley girl about the food he makes a purchase and disappears into his cabin.

As he steps into the cabin the girl comes out into the corridor. She is, I think, Australian, rangy, light haired with a sallow complexion that is a little blotchy. My guess is she's in her early twenties. She watches the trolley exit the corridor whilst preparing her own breakfast. I watch with interest. She pulls out a large pot of noodles from her grubby looking backpack: it's crumpled around the edges due to it being squeezed into her pack. Padding bare-footed down to the golf ball machine she fills it with hot water and carefully carries it back, leaving it to stand on her bunk. Then she pulls out a carrot that looks old enough to have been pulled by Confucius. Pulling a penknife from her trouser pocket she peels it half way down. She then cuts the peeled half away from the unpeeled half and slices it into her pot of noodles. The unpeeled half is returned to the bowels of her dusty backpack where I calculate it will putrefy in about twenty minutes. Breakfast fully prepared she tucks in.

I've said already you get a lot of time to think on trains, which is why I have time to consider the economics of what I've just witnessed. The pot noodle retails at about three Yuan, twenty five pence, say. The carrot is about another Yuan so her meal cost her about thirty pence. My breakfast, of fresh, highly nutritious ingredients, cost me about forty pence. OK, there is no denying she's saved ten pence. Lets be even fairer and assume she's travelling for a whole year. Three meals a day, at a saving of ten pence each soon adds up. She is likely, using my example, to save a whopping £110 in the whole year. Or put another way, just over two pounds a week. Get a fucking life. If you can't afford an extra two quid a week to ensure you have enough nutritious food to stop you looking like you've got yellow fever, why bother? It's not just the money. She's missing out on a genuine experience. The food on this train is not cooked for the benefits of tourists. This is a working train stuffed with local people. It cooks local food, with local ingredients, for local palettes. It's the real deal. Not that backpackers look for genuine travel experiences. They simply follow a well-trodden backpacker trail on which they only experience backpacking and other backpackers. Its a pastime primarily undertaken by people who penny pinch their way across continents and return home to wallow in the considerable affluence from which they came and boast about how they saved two pounds a week by eating shit. Like cockroaches they serve no purpose whatsoever. And, that in a nutshell is what's wrong with backpackers.

We pull into a station that I can find no reference to in any of my guidebooks. It's called Yong Zhou Zhuan. The station is a little beaten around the edges but scrupulously clean. Stepping out onto the platform I find the sun warming, which is a pleasant contrast to the air conditioning of the train. I buy some grapes with the intention of sharing them with my new cabin compatriots. When I get back I'm pleased to see we have recovered our missing Chinaman. He is sitting on his bunk, legs dangling, receiving a lesson on Vietnamese vocabulary from Tie. The gulf between the Chinaman's Cantonese and Tie's Vietnamese is bridged with English. Tie offers a word in Vietnamese which he will not leave until the Chinaman's pronunciation is exactly right. When it's spoken perfectly he translates the word in English, or a close facsimile of it. I find it most entertaining and listen for about an hour until Tie says in English, 'maybe we stop now, you can rest.' Or as I translate it, Tie is knackered. The Chinaman takes the hint and curls up for a rest on the inch of bed available to him between his case and the window.

Guilan is the next big stop and I spend the afternoon watching the landscape change as we head towards it. Large, jagged, limestone escarpments break up the landscape, at first sporadically, then more regularly. These impressive edifices reach skywards like giant podgy thumbs. After we leave Guilan the vista turns into expansive valley floors and the podgy thumbs become even more numerous. They look like the result of hundreds of small eruptions that have solidified at the apex of their journey upwards. Rice paddies fill the gaps between the mammoth molehills and I encounter scenes familiar to me from antique Ming vases. Conical hatted farmers wash down water buffalo, some with suckling young, in babbling streams. The fresh blue sky and the strong sun bring everything into sharp focus. Greenery is greener, streams are clearer. It's truly stunning. Only darkness drags me away. As the day slips into the dim light of dusk I dip into my thirteen year old Vietnamese guidebook and discover that the train to Hanoi from Beijing is actually two trains. Really? I'm sure I only have a ticket for one train. I check my itinerary notes. No mention of a train change. Strange.

'Tie,' I say, disturbing him from his Harry Potter adventure, 'does this train go directly to Hanoi.'

'Directly? What this?'

'You know, no stop, leave Beijing, get out Hanoi, no change.'

His sister gabbles something to him and a light goes on in his head.

'Oh, no, must change at Dong Dang. Dong Dang in Vietnam, very good, quick.'

I dig out my tickets. Sure enough, there are two coupons. How did I miss that? More to the point, why didn't Olive mention it?

'When do we get to Dong Dang, Tie.'

'Later,' he offers helpfully, laying back down and working his way through a Quiddich match.

The Irishman left us a Guilan along with quite a few Chinese. They were replaced with a rather loud Australian couple and a young English couple.

I bump into the Aussie, literally, in the corridor, and he immediately starts chatting, mainly about himself. I find the accent difficult to place.

'Where are you from?' I manage to squeeze in when he draws a breath.

'Me?' he says needlessly: I'm not talking to anyone else. 'I'm Canadian by birth, but have lived in Aussie for the last forty years. Been trekking, fucking fantastic, met up with the young couple from England, nice people, very friendly, heading down to Hanoi.'

We pull into Nanning and are ordered off the train, so he heads of to collect his stuff before he can run through everything he's done in the last fifty years. I'm not sure why we are being asked to get off so I ask Tie.

'Not, sure but carriage locked, can leave everything in cabin. Not here long'

I gather up all my documents, valuables, and medication. I've been down this road before. I snatch the rest of the grapes before I'm ejected. On the platform we are herded into a group. One of the five star generals claps her hands and we follow her to a waiting room. She switches on the lights to reveal rows of comfy chairs, covered in gold velour. We settle in. The Canadian talking machine sits near me, as does the Civil Servant who is poncing a holiday on the back of us hard working taxpayers.

'So,' the Canadian says, at the top of his voice, turning to the Civil Servant. 'What are you doing here?'

'I'm having my gap year late... holiday of a lifetime,' he replies, meekly. This is the opening the Canadian is looking for and he launches into what he's doing here, which was, of course, the purpose of his question.

'Me and the wife do a few trips every year, Europe, Asia mainly though. We have a lovely farm property in tropical Queensland. It's beautiful, stunning place Queensland. Went there on holiday from Canada when I was a young man, never left. Don't get me wrong, proud to be Canadian, just wouldn't want to live there, ' he nudges the Civil Servant for emphasis, who visibly shrinks into the chair.

'Anyway we like to get away. 'How much you think, Aussie to Beijing?' This is purely a rhetorical question: he has no intention of letting anyone answer it. 'A hundred and ninety nine, bloody Aussie Dollars, that's what. How cheap is that? Still, financially we're very fortunate. We can do it.'

He turns to me, 'why'd you think we've stopped mate?'

I hate being called mate by people I don't know.

'I think the carriage attendants like to rummage through guest's dirty pants before they get to the border.'

I listen to my sense of humour rattle around his head like a rolled up ball of paper in a draughty cathedral. The Civil Servant sniggers quietly. So he should. I've been paying his wages for the last thirty years.

An hour later the five star general returns and we follow her back to our train, or rather the remnants of our twenty carriage train. There are now only four. It's late so in pretty quick time I'm hunkered down and asleep.

Day 16

I'm woken at 1 am by a knock on the door. Tie reaches down and opens it from his top bunk, using his other hand to rub his eyes. We are met with a blast of cold air and three Chinese customs officials, two women and a man. Their olive green uniforms look almost black in the half-light of the corridor. The man addresses me, 'this your bag?'

'Yes,' I reply.

'Open please.'

I open the bag and one of his assistance offers a cursory prod with his middle digit.

'What is your job?'

What's shifty chancer in Cantonese?

'Businessman,' I say.

This seems to satisfy him and he hands me a declaration. Tie and Twee are handed the same.

'Who lives here?' he asks pointing to the Chinaman's bunk. He's gone missing again, which I find rather sinister. Maybe his cover story of going to study in Vietnam was a load of baloney, but then again why would a Chinaman try and hoodwink his own customs officials?

'I'm not sure, I think he's with a friend in another cabin.'

Thankfully he turns up as I'm finishing my sentence, jabbers off an explanation and sits up on his bunk. I look at my declaration form, which is hard to read through my stinging eyes. Twee is equally groggy.

'I'm falling in love,' she says, after completing the form.

I knew this would happen. A woman can't be in such close proximity to me for this long and not fall for me. Then her brother speaks to her.

'Oh,' she says blushing, 'sorry I mean I'm falling asleep.'

That's the other effect I have on women.

Two hours later we get our passports back, dutifully stamped. I'm pleased to find my paperwork is in order. More pleased than the Russian lady and her lanky son three cabins down from mine facing a jury of customs officials. I've seen little of these two. I noticed them getting on in Beijing, but they've kept to their cabin ever since. I've certainly never seen it open and I do a lot of corridor loitering. I poke my head out of our cabin door so I can get a better view. She is undeniably ugly. Standing at a little below five feet, she is shaped like a novelty potato. Her oval face is framed with wispy blond hair. She has no eyebrows above her squinty brown eyes and has the dubious distinction of owning a chin and nose that bump into each other when she talks. She can't speak English so she's roped in the assistance of a young man who, up to this point, I hadn't realised was Russian. The reason I assumed he was anything but Russian is that every time I've encountered him he's been smiling. Perhaps he doesn't live there any more. He's acting as the conduit between her and the customs official translating her words into English. The essence of it is that she doesn't have the right paperwork.

'She is asking if she can ring her travel agent in Russia,' he says to the head customs officer.

I do a quick calculation. Russia is eight hours behind China, so its 10pm there. Timing is irrelevant because the customs man, who remains polite throughout the debate, isn't going to be moved. The paperwork is wrong. She has more chance of making the front cover of Vogue than winning this argument. Eventually they gather up their belongings and I watch them disappear, flanked with customs officials, into the darkness of the customs building. I kiss my passport and visa before I go back to sleep.

I've only been asleep about twenty minutes when we are woken again. This time it's Vietnamese customs officials – do these people only work at night? The blackness of the night adds to my growing disorientation. My throat is dry from the air-conditioning and the constant disturbances to my sleep are making me grouchy. Looking over the officials' shoulders, I see the lights of a building winking at me through the gloom. Illuminated on a large green board above the door is the words Dong Dang. We're in Vietnam. We are told to leave the train and take all of our belongings with us. I help the Chinaman get his case down from his bunk and we all struggle onto the platform. Like a line of war refugees we haul everything we own off the platform, drag it across a railway line, up onto another platform, and finally into a waiting area. The love affair with green continues into the interior. To my left there is a large table standing next to a glass-partitioned counter. In fact there is a glass-partitioned counter in each corner of the room with differently uniformed Vietnamese officials stationed behind each of them. The clamminess of the outside permeates the inside giving all the surfaces a sheen of moisture, like the room is sweating in sympathy with the occupants. Insects dance around the single lighting strip that hangs loosely from the crumbling ceiling. On one wall there are a row of clocks, each with a plaque underneath displaying a destination, London, Paris, Rome, Hanoi, Beijing. None have been troubled with the guiding principles of Greenwich Mean Time. Even the Hanoi clock is wrong. I drop my bags down sending a cloud of dust up to mix with the heavy air. What now?

The Civil Servant, who lets face it, has probably spent his life swimming in bureaucracy must know what's happening. I walk over and ask.

'No idea, but I think you need to have your temperature checked,' he says, pointing to a glass partition behind him. It appears to be manned by dental assistants with white smocks and little square hats.

'Temperature?'

'Yes, to make sure you're not bringing in any diseases.'

I think about this. What if you have a temperature, are you declined entry? That means you might not get in if you have a cold. Ridiculous. I look for Tie, he must know. Tie and Twee are sitting on the million or so bags they hauled from the train.

'Go to counter one, get form, take with passport to next counter.

'What about that counter,' I say pointing to the one with a queue of people in front of it, paying two Dollars (cash only) to get a thermometer shoved in their ears.

'I don't know, ' he shrugs, then continues, 'when passport back take to counter by door, get train ticket stamped.'

I am now ahead of the game so I go to counter one and complete my declaration, get it stamped, and fly over to counter two and hand in my declaration and passport to a bewildered looking border guard. I image all this night work must take its toll. Despite handing in my declaration and passport first I am, as is usual for me, the last to be processed. By the time it's passed to me under the glass partition everyone has left the waiting area. I'm alone with twenty customs officers and a couple of pseudo nurses who are frankly unnerving. I don't bother with the ear scam, or get my ticket stamped and run out the door dragging my bags. I'm stopped just outside. It could be a railway official or possibly an Admiral. He looks at my ticket, looks at me, looks at my ticket again and then waves me towards the train that's replaced the old one. It is the poor relation of my last train, which was, lets face it, a peasant of a train. Each new train I get on is scruffier than the last. At this rate my last train to Saigon will be an open carriage with broken wheels.

At the carriage entrance my ticket is scrutinised again before I'm allowed on, and again in the corridor by a Vietnamese lady who looks as pissed off as I do at being woken in the middle of the night. She manhandles me into a cabin with the Aussie/Canadian talking machine. Great. Thankfully before he can get into his stride about how he came to be born and what he's done ever since, she comes back, grabs my arm and drags me out. I scamper along the dirty corridor that in these parts is known as Vietnamese first class and I'm deposited in another cabin. I nod towards the Russian translator and his girlfriend who are already in residence and haul my bag onto the top bunk, quickly following it. Laying flat on the bed my nose is about three inches away from the air conditioning vent. Good, it might cool me down. Within twenty minutes I'm asleep. Forty minutes later I'm awake and so cold my face is numb, like I've been to the dentist for a full root canal job. I am in danger of sticking to the air-conditioning vent. I spend a fruitless couple of hours trying positions that keep me out of the direct flow from the vent but eventually I give up and step out into the corridor. I'm the only one there. The corridor in daylight is grubbier than my nocturnal impression. A film of rust coloured dust covers every surface, but by way of compensation the view out of the window is spectacular. It's a steamy rainforest. Thick green foliage carpets the far distance and copses release steam from exotic trees with huge leaves. It's like all the trees in the rainforest are having a crafty smoke before anyone wakes up. In the middle distance every available space is a rice paddy. The train track is following a small stream. The red clay banks on either side are water logged, and small tributaries have developed, like the land is bleeding into the stream. Lots of the paddy fields we pass have cemeteries, or solitary gravestones within them. I suspect some of the inhabitants were born in the paddy fields, toiled there all their lives and died there. And people say there's no such thing as a job for life these days. I discover I can slide the window down by undoing a clipping mechanism. I unclip it and push down as far as it can go. Despite the early hour the hot air hits me like the back draft of a jet engine. This wanton act of window opening would easily be twenty years hard labour on the Russian train so I keep an eye out for carriage generals.

The train may not live up to its first class billing but it is the perfect vantage point from which to watch the small stream we've been following grow into a river. We ford it regularly by way of small, heavily riveted bridges that are the same rusty colour as the soil. I'm starting to see more farmers working the land, many using bullocks and water buffalo for the heavy work. Activity is increasing in the carriage too. The Canadian and his wife appear, thankfully offering only a nod, rather than a minute-by-minute account of how they slept. They seem, like me, content enough to watch Vietnam unfold outside the window. I catch a glimpse of a snaking line of school children on bikes weaving their way along a rusty red dirt track that melts away into the jungle. Immaculately turned out in white blouses and blue pleated skirts they turn towards the train offering wide grinning faces and wave like they've never seen one before. I wave back which sends them into fits of giggles.

The scene outside the window continues to get busier and in the corridor. There is a constant line of older Vietnamese, bent like willows in a stiff wind, shuffling backwards and forwards to the bathroom. Their toileting involves the sort of hoiking the Chinese would be proud of and often includes a preliminary bout of lung sapping coughs. I try to search out Tie and Twee but can't find them. They must be in another carriage. I'll try and grab them before I get off but I'm not hopeful. I have some experience of South East Asian train stations: when a train arrives the station turns into an ignited ants nest.

The vista from my window is becoming steadily more urban and the towns we pass buttress the tracks: literally. We travel so close to some homes I can see and hear what they are watching on the television. If I had a longish stick I could probably turn the telly off and really piss them off. Most of the properties are no more than shacks, which is a complete contrast to the homes on the outskirts of towns. These houses are just plain odd. They have all the main attributes required of a house, windows, a front door and so on. Indeed many are quite grand, standing three or four stories high with brightly coloured facades. Some of the cornices are ornate enough to embarrass an Arabian Sheikh and the sweeping balconies house marbled columns and French windows that wouldn't look out of place in the Palace of Versailles. But, and here is the weird thing, the majority are only about ten paces wide. You wouldn't be able to cartwheel from one side to the other without bashing your feet on a wall. No wonder you never see any Vietnamese in the gymnastics at the Olympics.

In contrast to the fantastically ornate fronts the sidewalls are only half rendered, exposing poorly finished brickwork. It's like looking at rotten teeth that have been given gleaming white acrylic fronts. The smile looks great but try to eat anything harder than a noodle and they fall apart. Each house has a build date etched into the front and I notice that many have been constructed in the last few years. The newer ones are grander than the older, which may be indicative of the new affluence in Vietnam. Or it might just be they were tight bastards years ago.

The bathroom finally becomes free of lung expelling octogenarians and I briefly consider washing but once I catch sight of the high rise office and apartment blocks of Hanoi I decide to wait until I'm in my new hotel room where I can luxuriate in cascades of water that doesn't necessitate my ladling it over myself with cupped hands.

Hanoi is often referred to as the disapproving uncle of its wayward nephew Saigon, but nevertheless, I'm looking forward to it immensely. If my internet booking worked my hotel will be in the Old Quarter. If it didn't I will have to revert to plan B. Plan B will only be formulated if Plan A fails. As the name suggests, the Old Quarter is in the heart of the city. So, what does a quarter get you these days? I'll tell you what. Spread over thirty six small streets you get a warren of commerce where you can buy anything from a gravestone to silk pyjamas. According to my book it's like a human beehive, which means it will be only half as crowded as China was.

The train pulls us across the mighty Red River, which is technically a murky brown, and into the suburbs of Hanoi. Stickiness increases by a factor of ten and once again we pass within an arms length of family homes. Women stand outside washing down everything, small yards, children, grandparents, anyone passing by, the train. The constant watering does nothing more than temporarily solidify the dust into clingy dirt, which in the steamy heat, quickly turns back to dust. We pass so close to one restaurant, I can see the contents of the soup in the diners' bowls and a cat playing with a rat in the kitchen beyond. When I say playing, what I actually mean is killing, but I don't want to offend rat or cat lovers.

Meanwhile, I gird my loins in preparation of meeting my first Hanoi taxi driver. Taxi drivers are genetically linked. If you review their DNA you will see they are all descendants of a thieving shyster who operated a camel taxi across the caravan routes of the Eastern Sahara. His trick was to agree a mutually acceptable charge for conveying customers across the great expanse and then increase the rate half way across. Over the years their scams have become more sophisticated but essentially they are the same dromedary owning, thieving bastards. No sooner have I lugged my bags from the train than I discover a representative of the Hanoi branch of shysters standing beside me.

'Official taxi, Sir?'

Official? Sir? He has oily olive skin, is about five feet five inches high and owns a skin condition that runs along his upper lip. It makes him look like he's been playing the trumpet non-stop for a month.

'Official taxi, meter.'

'Meter?' I say.

'Meter,' repeats.

'How much to Hanoi Capital Hotel, Old Quarter?'

'Meter, Sir.'

'OK, official taxi meter?'

'Yes,' he says, pointing to an official looking train crest on the breast pocket of his light blue shirt. I'm knackered, I've had hardly any sleep, it's hot and I need a shower. All of these things run through my head, each of which will do as an excuse for being ripped off if anyone asks.

'OK, where's the taxi?'

He picks up my bag and I follow him out into a wall of screaming motorcycle noise. This is what it would be like if you entered a hornet's nest licking an ice cream, wearing pants made of syrup, swinging a flaming stick and blowing on a vuvuzela. These particular hornets are dressed as extras in Good Morning Vietnam. We walk past the official taxi rank. Usually I'm all for queue jumping but when a taxi driver is involved this is a bad sign.

'The official taxi rank is here,' I shout after my bag and the shyster striding purposefully away from the official taxi rank with it. He stops by a small minivan with a dent in the front driver's side wing. The dent looks suspiciously like the outline of a motorcycle.

'Air-con inside, quickly please.' He throws my bags into the cab. He knows I'll follow them.

'Official taxi, right?' I say, standing by the side door he's opened for me. He points to the meter. I swear I see it move before the taxi does. We nearly wipe out a dozen motorcyclists as we swerve sharply into the traffic tsunami. He points to the meter once again.

'Taxi meter,' he repeats with extra emphasis, in case I don't understand taxi driver double talk. I slump back in my chair and watch it spin around so fast the numbers become a red neon blur. If this taxi is on the meter its attached to the pistons. I notice the meter slows when he steps off the accelerator, which is infrequent. On these rare non-accelerating occasions I encounter the additional complication of converting the ever-increasing bill into a currency I can understand. The Vietnamese Dong is not for the mathematically challenged. I know I get 28,000 of them for a pound but how quick can you divide 28,000 into 350,000?

It's late morning as we skirt around Hoan Kiem Lake, which I know is near the Old Quarter. Even my ancient guidebook can't get that wrong. Lakes in my experience very rarely move. The sun is sparkling like a golden button floating in a tin of blue paint. We've only travelled a mile or so but have, nevertheless, nearly managed to kill two hundred motorcyclists, but then, they do all seem to be students of Kamikaze. The roads are entirely bereft of any form of traffic control measures, save the occasional set of traffic lights. These are treated as starting grids. The racers are a giant swarm of crash helmeted bees. The motorcyclists communicate through blasts on the horn that vary in length depending on the rider's proximity to death. Prolonged use normally precedes a collision. The fact these communications are universally ignored by other road users is not an issue. The important thing is to press down as hard as you can and as much as you can.

We soon swerve off the main drag and start scouring the Old Quarter for my hotel, the one my driver promised he knew like the back of his officially stamped taxi licence. Every road it's not in is costing me thousands of Dong and there are an awful lot of roads in which you won't find my hotel. One road was so chocked with motorcycles he had to reverse back. This manoeuvre alone cost me twenty thousand Dong. I finally spot the hotel sign and with some effort, mainly the avoidance of two or three million parked motorcycles, we pull up outside. The meter is showing 467,000 Dong. Half a million Dong? Who does he think I am Simon Cowell?

'How much for Dollar, ' I ask.

'Ten Dollar.'

I furrow my brow in concentration, which must have been a little disconcerting for him. It's the same look I have when suffering from constipation. Right: 28,000 Dong to the pound, 1.67 Dollars to the pound. Do I simply times the Pound - Dong rate by .67? No, that's no right. What about divide by 1.67? Could be. What the fuck does that make it then? The meter is still running at 5,000 Dong per second. This flight into the unknown world of long division is bankrupting me.

'OK,' I say digging into my bag, turn off your meter.'

I am dismayed to discover the smallest denomination I have is twenty Dollars, because I'm now faced with the other unifying fact about taxi drivers. I soldier on anyway.

'I've only got a Twenty, do you have change?'

The shock by which taxi drivers across the world react to this simply question never ceases to amaze me. He starts to pat his pockets like he's on fire. The expression on his face turns from a man about to become the richest taxi driver in Hanoi to one who's been told he only has an hour to live.

'No change.'

'No change: what happens when you collect a fare? Do you immediately drive home and deposit it under your grandmother's arse?'

He can't understand a word I'm saying but he gets the sentiment and he knows I will not part with this note without seeing something in return. I manage to extricate enough change for the taxi fare to cost me about nine pounds. Three times the going rate, but respectable. Come on, I'm knackered, I've hardly slept, I'm hot...

I soon discover that the only thing my Chinese hotel and my Hanoi one have in common is the name. I'd say the total square footage of my new hotel would fit into the reception desk of my Chinese one. A smiling young lady greets me at reception. She's wearing a traditional red silk dress, which matches the colour of my eyes perfectly. I'm checked in within seconds, and then she gets down to the serious business of trying to sell me some tours.

I cut her short, 'maybe we can talk later, I need a shower,' I say. She wrinkles up her nose in tacit acknowledgement, smiles, and hands my room key to a young man who appears at her side as if by magic. She then hands me a card with the hotel's name and address on it in both English and Vietnamese.

'You can show this to anyone when you get lost.' When?

My new best friend manhandles my bags along the short corridor and past a small eating area, which in reality is part of the corridor. He is dressed in a plain white shirt and black trousers, which I notice have a split under the pocket. He smiles continuously. I try to return an everlasting grin but find, after a few moments, the corners of my mouth drop and my face returns to its usual slapped arse demeanour.

'Are you happy today?' he asks, with almost unrestrained joy.

'Oh, yes, my face is just having a few minutes off.'

'Good, good,' he repeats, grin fixed like The Joker.

The lift creaks open, we step in with my bags and it groans all the way up to the fifth floor, offers a sigh on opening and spits me out. I follow him up a short flight of stairs and along a corridor to my room. It's the furthest a guest can be from the hotel entrance without being in a different postcode. The room is adequate for my needs although I discover with a crash that toilet seat isn't self-closing. I quickly shower and hit the streets with my guidebook and a calculator. I need to find a bank.

The thing about the Old Quarter is, the names of the streets are supposed to denote what you can buy there. For example, my hotel is in Hang But. Hang means street and But means brushes. Obviously the street should be teeming with brush shops. I should be witnessing brushes hanging from every available space. Shopkeepers should be leaning on brushes. In reality if I was in desperate need of a brush I wouldn't find one here. It's full of travel agents and small hotels like mine. I try, with the help of a map that refuses to fold properly, to make my way back towards the Lake. I saw a bank there on the way here that will do very nicely. I walk down Basket street, discovering its mainly hardware these days, and take a right onto Stringed Instrument street, now specialising in cheap tee shirts, and straight on to Raft street that has a thing these days for handbags. So far I have only had to cross the narrow roads of the Old Quarter, no more than ten strides. But, even these roads are not for the faint hearted. If the Olympic Committee ever introduce pedestrian killing as a sport, Vietnam will take a clean sweep of the medals. The motorcyclists especially are mental.

Successfully disgorged from the narrowness of the Old Quarter I rather smugly spot the bank I saw earlier. I'm not smug for long. The road splitting the pavement I'm standing on and the one the bank lives on is wider than your average French Boulevard. How to cross without dying? I quickly hatch a plan and decide to out psyche the swarms of motorcyclists in a high stakes strategy of bluff and counter bluff. My limited experience in the Old Quarter has already indicated that any signs of timidity from pedestrians will be seized upon. The only option, as I see it, is to stand tall and stride out purposefully, look straight ahead, and do not, under any circumstances, hesitate. These motorcycles come at you like bullets.

Before I fell upon my cunning plan, I considered the pedestrian crossing. There is one. That is to say there is a series of alternately painted black and white rectangles on the road stretching from one side to the other. That is where the similarity with a pedestrian crossing stops. I was dissuaded from using it after watching a gaggle of unsuspecting backpackers only make it to the middle of the crossing, and only then by taking evasive action from a motorcyclist in a blue cape. They had to abandon their kit and sprint back to their starting positions. It took a full fifteen minutes and as many near misses to retrieve their bags from the road. No, the pedestrian crossing is not for me.

I wait for a lull in the traffic, which I calculate is when the motorcycle count drops to below one million per square meter per minute, and I step off the pavement. Keep the line. Keep the line. Eyes right. Fuck that was close. Keep moving. Oh shit. Steady, steady. Fuck, fuck, fuck, bollocks shit, that was close. Nearly there, keep your nerve, nearly, fuck, bugger, arse. Over. Easy. I walk into the bank, thirty shades lighter than I was on the other side of the road. My pants are thirty shades darker.

Twenty minutes, four forms, in triplicate, and a copy of my passport and library card later, I walk out a millionaire. To celebrate my new wealth I have a coffee next door. Right down to the names of the coffees on offer it's Costa Coffee but this place is called Gloria Jane's. They stiff me for a seventy five thousand Dong coffee and muffin. Daylight robbery.

After my coffee I make a mad dash across the road to the lake. It looks like a pretty good spot for lunch. From my side of the road I can see plenty of eateries tucked away in the shade of trees. A billowing ribbon of walkways hugs the lake like the trailing tail of a kite. From where I'm standing it looks like an oasis of calm in a desert of motorbikes. I get across safely but my shoe doesn't. I retrieve it quite elegantly, although to the casual observer it looks like someone from the Ministry of Funny Walks competing in a shin-kicking contest with an epileptic break-dancer. I look so absurd the motorcyclists have to slow down to wipe away tears of laughter.

'Postcard?' A small lady falls into step with me. She's shabbily dressed in loose fitting trousers and a stained white top. She carries a small brightly coloured shoulder bag under her arm.

'No thanks.'

'Guidebook?'

'No thanks.

'Phrase-book?'

'No thanks.'

'Fan?'

'No thanks.'

'Book marker?'

'No thanks.'

'Why you so difficult?'

The look of astonishment on my face makes her laugh. This makes me laugh. I buy a fan.

Stopping for a drink at a lakeside cafe I idly thumb through the menu. It informs me, "Another high end dishes begs distinguished guests bespoken when eaten two hours," then a little further down, "from Italy with love." I can't resist this sort of sales pitch and order an orange juice. While I'm drinking it I notice a painfully thin old lady walking by. She is stooped at the perfect angle for spotting dropped coins. Her hair is almost transparent making her look bald. When she looks up I discover she is entirely toothless and has either been chewing red tobacco or has recently coughed up a lung. The loose bags under her eyes droop like saggy tears onto sunken cheeks that billow like sails when she breathes. A rivulet of foamy dribble runs from the corner of her mouth, a consequence I think, of the argument she appears to be having with an invisible friend. Quite suddenly she pulls up, stands erect, and looks in my direction. Then, with agility I would never have credited her with, she skips over the cafe's small picket fence, side steps me, grabs an empty tin of Coke from a table behind me, and scampers back out. With a ghostly smile of satisfaction she plops into a black plastic bag under her arm and continues on her way. Recycling Vietnamese style.

Across the road I catch sight of the Civil Servant, he's by a cash-point machine looking bewildered. Bewildered on my tax money I might add. With no regard whatsoever for my personal safety I sprint across the road, adopting a commando style zig zag pattern to make me harder to hit, and join him.

'Hello, everything all right?'

'Ah, hello, mmm... yes, slight problem with the cash-point.'

'Really? Card not working?'

'Oh, no, well yes, no, not really... I tried to get 10,000 Dong but it wouldn't let me.'

I explain that he's only trying to get a little over fifty pence out. He blushes slightly.

'Anyway I was just about to get a beer, fancy one?' I say, 'I'll pay if you're skint.'

'Oh, no, no, I'm not..., getting used to the money and what have you... beer? Good idea.'

Within no time at all we manage to find a bar without crossing a road and I discover the Civil Servant I have been bankrolling all his life is called Peter. The bar has a Mexican theme going on but sells Vietnamese booze. I order a bottle of Saigon Beer.

'Shall we buy our own beer?'

'Eh? Oh, no, I'm happy to buy you a beer Peter.'

'Perhaps we can split the bill?'

'If you like. The truth is Peter, I haven't had a good drink in weeks, and I intend to have a few.' Best to get these things out in the open I think. He can beat a hasty retreat then, if he's not on my wavelength.

'Yes, ok, well... I'll have one of those,' he says, pointing to a draft beer of unknown origin. I get the feeling Peter would describe a good drink as a small schooner of sherry, whereas my definition involves waking up trouser-less with your head in a spittoon. Five or six rounds later, I'm starting to feel the beat of Hanoi. Peter though, seems to be getting shorter, either that or he's lowered his chair.

'Are you all right Peter?'

'Me? Yes... fine, fine... you see, Mike, the thing is, its my birthday in a couple of weeks. Do I follow my dream and travel, or go back home?'

'Well, Peter, that's a bit of a no brainer, I mean....'

'Only, I don't know. She says she doesn't mind if we don't celebrate my birthday together, but, oh, I don't know...'

I order more beers and pretend I'm sympathetic but I'm not a natural sympathiser so quickly revert to type.

'Listen mate, if she says she doesn't mind, you can bet your arse what she really means is...'

He quickly interrupts, 'because you see, I really want to travel, and now I've got the opportunity, but I don't want to... Oh I don't know...'

'Have another beer.'

'Good idea,' he says.

After another hour of enduring my individual style of relationship counselling, and in an effort to avoid drinking his weight in female conundrums, he decides to leave. We agree to meet up later and go to the Don Xuan night market together.

'Meet me in Ho Chi Minh's Jazz Bar at seven, OK?' I give him directions.

'It's on the road that specialises in bamboo screens. Or leather, one of the two'

Leaving the bar soon after, a little less steadier than when I went in, I continue to explore the Old Quarter and stumble upon the best way to cross the roads - do it drunk. I spend the rest of the afternoon testing this theory. It doesn't take me long to get to grips with it. Find a bar: drink a beer: cross a road. Then repeat. I get cheerfully lost but run out of bars. Then I happen upon a small gaggle of Vietnamese squatting on the floor in front of a shop. They are surrounding a table full of beer bottles. Am I in Off-license Street? No, when I check my guidebook I discover I'm in Coffin Makers Street. Needless to say there are no coffins to be seen but in the middle of this small group squatting at knee level, is a prime candidate for one. His face is so wrinkled I can't see his eyes and the hand he's using to hold his beer is entirely made up of liver spots. His younger companions keep topping up his glass from the bottles of Saigon beer on the table. They are all sitting on miniature plastic stools that have legs up to about ankle high. Next to the table, on a rattan mat, are all the utensils needed for a barbecue. Next to the mat is a small pestle shaped cooking pot resting on a grill above a pot of unlit coals. Vegetables of various shapes and colours bob about in a plastic bowl of water by the shop door. I point to the old man's bottle of beer and then to the shop.

'Can I buy beer here?' I ask the men.

The old man's face breaks into a toothless smile and he garbles out something towards the cavernous darkness of the shop. It's not immediately obvious what they specialise in. There's a small glass fronted cabinet across the entrance housing medicines, tee shirts hang from the walls, and toys adorn the shelves. A lady comes out squinting slightly at the late afternoon sun. She is about sixty and has immaculately permed hair and polished nails. She is dressed simply in a pair of three quarter trousers and shirt. She points to one of the chairs.

'Saigon beer? She asks.

'Yes, please,' I say. She points again to the chair.

I fully understand the sentiment here: she wants me to sit. It's the execution that I'm struggling with. These small chairs are everywhere. Outside all the shops, they form impromptu al fresco sitting rooms for families and friends. In Hanoi life is lived on the street. But the Vietnamese have an advantage because they can squat for hours. I've seen countless examples of them lowering themselves down so that their arse is only inches off the floor, and staying there balanced on their haunches like a weightlifter that never learned to clean and jerk.

I can only get down onto the seat by inserting a half of kneel into the process. Even then I only maintain my balance by putting a hand out in front of me. The old man watches my journey to the chair with unrestrained joy. This is heightened even more when we both discover that the actual seating area of the seat is not designed for a fat Western bottom. There is only room for one and half of my buttocks, so the surplus half is forced to dangle over the edge and rest on the pavement. This unfamiliar sitting position pushes my knees so high my pockets empty onto the pavement. One of the younger men helps me collect all the detritus. The woman speaks to the other young man, handing him some money. He scampers off. The old man continues to watch me intently. I need to make some re-adjustments so as not to join my money on the floor. I try placing my feet further apart but this causes my arms to hang hopelessly by my side. Thus positioned I look like an enormous fat crab sitting on a miniature throne. Passers by can see down my shorts without impediment and the strain of trying to retain my dignity is making me sweat.

The young man returns and disappears into the shop with four bottles of Saigon beer. A few moments later the lady comes out with one opened bottle and a frosted glass. Realising that I cannot remain balanced if I am forced to pour, she does it for me and hands it over.

'Cheers,' I say to the old man and raise my glass, almost losing my balance in the process. He chuckles some more. I finish my beer in total silence and attempt to get up. This is complicated by the need to hold both the bottle and glass at the same time as shifting to the vertical. The muscles in my legs simply cannot carry my weight so I try to push up from the waist. Each attempt looks like a Michael Jackson crutch thrust. Eventually the old man, rising like a feather in an updraft, takes pity and divests me of the bottle and glass. The lady returns and with the help of the young man they haul me up. Now, the uncharitable might say that my level of inebriation had something to do with my inability to negotiate a stool, but I assure you its impossible for a Westerner to look elegant on a piece of furniture proportioned for a Wendy House.

By now, it's nearly time to meet with Peter so I dispense with my planned return to my hotel and get directions to Ho's Jazz bar from the old man. I pass him again five minutes later. He grabs me by the hand and walks me to the road junction and points at Ho's neon sign, flashing like a beacon in the gathering gloom of early evening. It's no more than two hundred yards away. I thank him, he smiles the smile of a man that's seen it all before, and within minutes I'm sitting at the bar with another Saigon beer. Ho's Jazz bar is empty so when Peter arrives he increases the customer base by one hundred percent.

The rest of the evening is a blur. I vaguely remember walking up to the market with Peter only to discover it was closed. I half recollect selecting a restaurant with a balcony over a busy intersection so we could watch motorcycle crashes all night, and worse of all I am certain I blabbered on like only the truly pissed can. I may have mentioned how timidity and Asia do not mix, or I may have thought it. I really hope I thought it, because I can be quite direct when I've had a few. I certainly recall him worrying about the traffic, food, catching malaria, and being trapped by fire in his hotel. Basically all the things I hadn't given one ounce of thought to up to that point. I'm also sure that when we parted we didn't make arrangements to meet the next day. But we might have. I have no idea how I found my hotel, only that the receptionist, who had turned into a man, was relieved to see me.

'Ahhh, Mr. Mike, you not get lost.'

'No, young man I didn't, but I took the long route,' I remember saying while he escorted me all the way to my room.

'Have you ever had a fire here?' I ask, as he took my key from me to open the door.

'Fire? No, no fire here.'

'Good,' I said, handing him thousands of Dong in gratitude.

The last thing I remember was watching Midsomer Murders dubbed in Vietnamese. John Nettles mouth continued moving long after the words had been spoken. Or it might have been in perfect sync. I just don't know.

Day 17

A cyclo driver accosts me in Brush Street. I've stopped to look at my map so I can plot a course to the Woman's museum that will involve the least number of road crossings. These purveyors of people are endemic in the Old Quarter and this one has been shadowing me for the last ten minutes. Essentially they ride a three-wheeled bicycle that is the wrong way around. The single wheel is below the saddle, upon which a crusty old man sits, and over the front two wheels is a small carriage with a hood for shade. It's big enough for two people, or one American.

'Cyclo Sir?'

'No thanks.'

He follows me for about two blocks, peddling slowly and offering a new question about every twenty yards.

'What your name?'

'Mike.'

'Where you from?'

'England.'

'Manchester United! Very good!'

'West Ham better.'

'Where you go?'

'Nowhere in particular, just walking about.'

'Cyclo easy than walking, you take my cyclo, one hour free.'

I'm not tempted because I've heard this spiel before. The second hour is free. Who wants to sit in a bicycle basket for two hours?

'No thanks.'

I stop at a junction to get my bearings and a motorcycle screeches to a halt in front of me just missing my foot. A young lady is piloting but the chap behind her riding pillion springs off. The cyclo driver stops nearby, smiling.

'Hi, where you go my friend?' he's trendily dressed, sports jacket and jet black hair protruding from his small crash helmet.

'Nowhere in particular, just walking about.'

'What's your name?'

'Mike.'

'Where you from?'

'England.'

'Ah, England, very good.'

'Yes, very good.' I don't know why Scotland hates us so much because Asia loves us.

'Hi Mike, you need guidebook?'

'No.'

'You need map.'

I wave the one in my hand in front of him.

Then, lowering his voice, 'you want boom boom, good massage, very cheap, not far?'

'No, I say, 'I just want to get across the road without dying, so if you can move your motorbike...'

'OK, you want postcards.'

'No, just you to get out of my way please.'

'OK, have a good time,' he says, jumping back on the bike and speeding off.

The cyclo driver then blocks my path.

'One hour free,' he says, hopefully.

'No, I just want to cross the fucking road.'

'OK, next time,' he says, cycling off, smiling. The thing is, I should have employed him. He's probably the safest mode of transport in the whole of Hanoi. But I know I'll end up miles from where I want to be because he'll follow a tour of Hanoi designed to last two hours.

I decided on the Woman's museum over breakfast for two reasons. Firstly I've never been to a museum about women before, and secondly, Ho Chi Minh's mausoleum is closed.

'He go Russia for repairing.' My young receptionist said when I asked her about it. 'He have holiday in Russia, ha, ha, ha.' I can't think of a more appropriate holiday destination for dead people.

I've plotted a course to the museum that takes me down Travel Agent street. It doesn't take me long to work out that it should be re-named Cartel street. I'm after a train ticket to Saigon and the prices are within a Dong of each other. So much for free market reforms.

My mood, like the weather, is overcast and oppressive. I've only walked three blocks and have already been involved in five near misses. Crossing the road when pissed may have been a solution yesterday but trying it with a hangover today just adds another layer of danger. By way of respite I drop into the bank and change up some more money. Becoming a multi-millionaire lightens my mood a little. As does thinking about the train. Just picturing it pulling out of the station is cheering. But then I remember it will be my last train journey of this trip and my mood returns to the colour of the sky, black and foreboding.

I find the museum, which is not far from the Old Quarter, with little difficulty, albeit somewhat shaken. The roads are much wider in this part of town so to help people travelling on foot there is a pedestrian crossing at each junction. However, the strident green man symbol is misleading. One on a crutch holding up an outstretched hand would be more accurate. These junctions are lethal because traffic can make a right turn at any time. At best the green man only gives pedestrians a clear run at half the road. The other half is still as manic as ever. The luxury of sauntering across half the road is quickly replaced with a swarm of hornets on amphetamines. It's mental. By the time I'm standing outside the Woman's museum I've endured about ten of these junctions and my nerves are completely shot. Not only am I a nervous wreck, I'm sweating profusely from a mixture of pure fear and the steamy output of the tropical storm that is brewing. The sweat is dripping from me in a continuous cascade of body odour and creating perfect growing conditions for mustard cress in my pants.

Wiping the continuous flow of sweat from my eyes, it doesn't take me long to discover that the Woman's museum has been replaced with the Ministry of Commerce, and they're not open to the public. This is what happens when your guide is thirteen years out of date. Stopping too long to review my options isn't advisable in Hanoi because it is considered an invitation to hawkers of every sort to approach. I walk on purposefully towards the Melia hotel, which is only about four death defying junctions away. I decide it's time for tea and, more importantly, a blast of air conditioning.

The Melia is one of the best hotels in Vietnam and is suitably palatial. It has more marble than the pyramids and all the employees are immaculately turned out. Which is more than can be said for me. The juices being disgorged as a result of my enforced road sprinting means my tee shirt is clinging to me like drowning man. The moisture that has been sucked out of me has made my khaki shorts two sizes too big and caused them to pucker all along the belt line. I'm not helping myself by unforgivably wearing dark woollen socks with my trainers. Realising that I look like a man who has had a recent encounter with a shark I decide to bluff it by affecting the look, and walk, of an eccentric billionaire. I transverse the lobby to the plush seating area by reception like Max Wall missing a hip. Meanwhile the cold air conditioning envelops my clammy body and produces a vapour trail behind me. When I go to the reception desk the receptionist smiles, looks me over, then glances across to her colleagues and stifles a laugh behind her hand before asking if she can help.

'Do you do afternoon tea?' I ask in my 1930s BBC announcer voice. She points to a lounge area and suggests I pick jasmine tea from the menu, as it is very "cooling."

While drinking my jasmine tea that costs me more than the taxi fare from the train station, I notice a sign for a travel agent. I finish my tea and head straight for it. I'm going to book my train ticket to Saigon here. I'm not bothered if they're more expensive than Travel Agent street because they have the distinct advantage of being air-conditioned. A most exquisite young lady dressed in a tailored business suit greets me. Her hair is tied in a bun that has been stabbed with a pair of chopsticks. Her English is deliberate, but very good. I explain I want a first class train ticket to Saigon and a hotel for a couple of nights.

'You want a hotel similar to the Melia, we have sister hotels in Sai...

'No, no, um... it's not necessary to look at a five star option,' I say. She thinks I'm resident here. 'Three star will suffice.' Running a professional eye over me she professionally ignores the flies circling my crutch and taps out a tune on her keyboard.

'Ahhh, problem with computer. Shall I send the information to your room?' Her pen is poised over a writing pad: she looks at me expectantly.

'No, no, I'll come back later, if that's OK.'

'No problem Sir.'

We make a date for 1 pm. I've got two hours to kill.

Before leaving my air-conditioned sanctuary I take a trip to the toilet to see what type of slasher you get for five hundred Dollars a night. It has more attendants than urinals. What do they do? On the way out I notice a cleaning schedule on the back of the door. What is the point of this? Do they honestly get complaints if the 11.10 am clean was missed? Why can't the manager keep his cleaning roster to himself? I decide to fill my time with a visit to the December 19th market, which rather misleadingly is open every day. Its a market for locals and has the added advantage of being near the Melia. Most importantly of all though, getting there doesn't involve a road crossing.

I make my way to the market entrance and am immediately distracted by three ladies sporting conical hats. They're Vietnam's equivalent of mobile fruit and vegetable vans but their conveyance is two baskets hanging from each end of a thick pole. Slung across one shoulder they deftly balance the heavy produce, stopping from time to time at seemingly random spots. Despite selecting the market's busy entrance as their next pit stop, these ladies are inundated with orders. A constant stream of motorcyclists buzzes around their baskets shouting out muffled requests from under crash helmets. The ladies set to work on the orders by pulling out chopping boards and hefty cleavers that they employ with great skill and dexterity. Each transaction is over in seconds.

Their cleaver skills are truly astounding. I approach one and point to a pineapple. Less than a minute later, after a blur of steel and hands, I walk away with a piece of fruit sculpture that wouldn't look out of place as a table centrepiece in a Buckingham Palace banquet. Mind you these cleavers are not always employed for such beauty. On the way here I watched a woman sitting outside her shop using her cleaver to cut her toenails.

The market is two parallel walkways, the whole being roofed with heavy, dark brown tarpaulin. It does its job of shielding the sun but it also acts as a thermal blanket. Within seconds my clothing clings to me like smouldering polyester. Because the market is situated between two main thoroughfares a constant stream of nut-case motorbike riders use the walkways as rat runs. I frequently have to dive in between stalls to avoid a collision. Despite my vigilance, and flattening myself against the wall of a shop, I watch in static horror as a moped comes so close his handlebar brushes my arm. He has a young child of about two squeezed between himself and his mother who is perched at the back of the passenger seat carrying a box. A boxed TV set rests in the foot well, which he grips with his knees to stop it falling out. Thanks to my evasive action I avoided wiping out three generations and a perfectly good telly.

Motorbike avoidance aside I enjoy the stroll. The fruit stalls sag with produce. I see furry red rambutins, durians like knobbly green beach balls, pineapples, blushed pink apples, and massive hands of bananas. The butchery stalls offer intrigue. They are raised plinths and entirely tiled in white. All the butchers are rotund ladies who squat cross legged in the centre of their plinth totally surrounded by body parts, like Buddhas who have just performed a frenzied autopsy. Some of the bits are recognisable, pig heads, trotters, kidneys and ribs. Others are totally alien to me. All, including the butchers themselves, have their own cloud of flies.

I turn round at the end of the first walkway and start walking down the second. Here I discover a butcher of a different variety and the undeniable truth that a dog is not just for Christmas: sometimes it's for dinner. One particular specialist butcher is doing a roaring trade. A steady stream of dog lovers pitch up and point to various dogs hanging from meat hooks. The odd thing is they all look like they're been shot jumping a fence and retained that shape into death. They've all been pre-cooked and are coloured the deep bronze of a glazed Peking duck. You can buy half a dog or if you're really hungry, a whole one. I resist the urge to whistle as I pass by just in case they have raw ones under the counter. I exit back out into a hot and fetid blanket of cloudy daylight. The weather is now close enough to touch.

Back at the Melia I'm dismayed to find my efficient young lady has been replaced with an equally pretty, but less friendly colleague.

'Better you come back in an hour,' she offers as a solution, rather than take on my aroma single-handed. I make a beeline for the lake. That's to say I take a route three miles out of my way to avoid crossing too many roads. Safely by the water's edge I wander along the paths, batting away hawkers like I've lived here for years, while simultaneously looking for a suitable watering hole. The near death experiences I'm enduring every time I cross a road are playing havoc with my nerves. Alcohol is the only solution I can think of at short notice.

'Hello,' someone shouts. I ignore it, it might be Peter and I don't have a suitable excuse ready.

'Hello, you, hello.'

The voice belongs to a lady sitting on a bench. She has a lovely view of the lake. Beside her rests an unusual pair of wooden crutches. Intrigued I walk over.

'Hello, how are you? She asks. She's about forty five, slightly unruly hair, a round face, kind eyes, and a small mole on her left cheek. She smiles quickly and often.

'I'm fine thanks, how are you?'

'Oh, very happy thank you, come sit here,' she pats the space next to her. I sit and we both stare out towards the lake for a few moments and watch the kites swoop across the sky in figures of eight and dive-bomb the water before looping upwards in frenzied spirals. She's wearing a nice white shirt with a small motif on each sleeve and a pair of trousers. The trousers have been rolled up and are resting on the seat. There is only space below her knees where her shins and feet should be. I absorb this information with surreptitious glances when I think she isn't looking my way.

I say, 'you have a great view here.'

'Yes, this is my favourite place, are you American?'

'Americ... ah, no, not American, English.'

'Oh, English, very nice country.'

We spend a little time swapping information. In return for my going through the 'my name is Mike' routine, she tells me she's from Hue, the ancient capital of Vietnam and how her parents fought the Americans in the war. She is single, never been married, and has no children. Being English I avoid at all costs asking why because it might be connected to space where her legs are supposed to be. She touches my arm.

'You know America never declare war on Vietnam?' she says, quietly.

'No, I didn't know that.'

'I know a lot of history. Before I teach in school to children.'

'Really, why did you stop?'

'Lose second leg, she says pointing down at her lap.' Now she's mentioned the leg situation I feel more comfortable about talking about them. Or lack of them.

'Ah, yes, I can see... how'd you lose it?'

'Stand on American bomb.'

'Oh dear, and the first one, how did you lose that one?

'Stand on American bomb again.'

'I'm really sorry to hear that,' I say totally inadequately.

'Not sorry please, I like American, very nice people.' This comment is genuinely delivered and immediately alerts the compassionate section in my brain to get ready for a major outpouring. Here's a woman who has lost two limbs, her livelihood, any chance of marriage and children as a direct result of faulty military hardware, delivered by a nation that forgot to declare war on the people it was bombing. I start to elevate my new friend into the Mother Theresa bracket. Not only has she shown such great forgiveness, she hasn't once tried to sell me anything or beg from me. In most parts of South East Asia someone as disabled as her would make a good living simply begging. And I'm not being heartless here. The width to which a rich Westerner's wallet opens has a direct correlation to the severity of the disability. The fact of the matter is a one-legged person would make less money begging than someone with no legs. Sadly, this says more about us than it does about the disabled. This train of thought brings another thought to my mind. Despite the continued problems of unexploded ordnance in this country, I haven't seen one disabled beggar. Yes, I've been hassled on every corner by hawkers, but they've all been entirely able bodied. Irritating they may be, but lacking legs they're not.

'I can teach you about Hanoi.'

'Really? You take classes?'

'No, I can be your guide.'

Ah...

'We can go Old Quarter, I know history, very good. One hour not long.'

I have to admit that a walking tour of the Old Quarter with this lady is so very tempting, but she is lacking the most basic physical equipment for a walking tour. I think about how to approach this.

'Ah, well...yes... but what about... you know.' I point to where her legs should be.

'Oh, I have these,' she says pointing to her crutches. I take a closer look. They are similar to normal crutches but have very wide plunger shaped bases. However, I still can't see how she uses them to travel any distance.'

'Well, the thing is I have to be back at the Hotel Melia soon, so I don't have time.'

'I can take you through Old Quarter to Melia, no problem.'

'Mmmm... look, I tell you what. Will you be here tomorrow?'

'I'm here, everyday, but you not come back.'

I feel wretched, but I don't want to go on a walking tour with anyone, let alone someone lacking the basic ingredients to take me on one. She'd never get across the road alive and I don't want to be responsible for her damaging her torso.

'OK, I'll be honest. I don't have time now, and I may not have time tomorrow, but can I reserve your time just in case I can make it?'

'Not understand, sorry.'

'OK, I'll pay you for one hour. We meet tomorrow this time. But if I cannot come, you keep money. Deal?'

'But you pay today?'

'Yes, I pay now.'

I haggle, because I feel I should, but my heart's not in it. We agree a price and I hand over the cash.

'Make sure you come back tomorrow,' she says as I walk off.

'Sure I will,' I reply, lying through my teeth.

I do a circuit of the lake to try and shake off a melancholic cloak hanging over me like the oppressive storm laden skies above me. It doesn't work so in a desperate effort to raise my spirits I once again take my life in my hands, dodge the traffic and skip into the Thang Long Water Puppet Theatre.

Quite clearly the theatre was once very grandiose but now it looks like a frayed old Odeon. I buy a ticket to the 8.30 pm showing and tuck it into my shirt pocket. Back out into the heat I decide to while away some time at a café with seats under dappled shade that makes the tables look like they have been draped in camouflage. It's only ten yards from the main road so I have a great view. The traffic roars past in a barrage of noise and exhaust fumes. Within no time I'm sipping strong Vietnamese coffee and watching Hanoi parade past on motorbikes.

From my camouflaged vantage point I quickly learn that not everything on the street is in perpetual motion. For example, squatting down in the Vietnamese style, across the road from me under the shade of a maple tree, is a scruffily dressed man. He is resting his right hand on a bright orange foot pump. He's exceedingly old and I fancy he could easily have been in the war of independence against the French. Beside his pump is a small carrier bag and a brown medicine sized bottle that he regularly takes a draught from. Cyclists pull up regularly, dismount in a single motion, and point to one or other of their tyres. He responds by attaching his pump, rises from his haunches and pumps away on the foot pedal, like a Yankee at a hoedown, periodically feeling the pressure in the tyre. Occasionally he dips into his carrier and pulls out a dust cap and screws it onto a wheel. Cash is handed down, nods of thanks are exchanged and he resumes his squat position until the next customer arrives.

Not too far away are two men sitting on a wall. Initially I think they're a couple of drunks, as they appear to be continuously laughing at the pavement in front of them. Between them are two large brown bottles and a pile of squashed cigarette cartons by a carrier bag. Every now and then someone pulls up on the side of the road and shouts over. A noisy exchange ensues and then, after dipping into the carrier bag, one or other of them dismounts from the wall and runs over with cigarettes. Sometimes it's a whole packet, sometimes only one or two. After the money is paid they resume their wall sitting. Each time a packet is emptied it's squashed flat and added to the pile between them. Much closer to me I watch a man walking up and down rows of motorbikes with padlocks hanging over both shoulders like he is about to climb a mountain. He is renting them to the bike owners and is very busy dispensing them to a constant flow of customers. If you take the time to look there is more to Hanoi than lunatic traffic.

Back at the Melia my little friend has struck gold. Her train fare is cheaper than the chiselling weasels in Travel Agent street and the accommodation looks good for the price.

'This hotel, very good, same group as Melia, very close to our sister hotel, Riverside Hotel, same name. Good position.'

The train leaves early afternoon tomorrow and arrives in Saigon the day after in the evening.

'This train, before called "Reunification Express." I think you like travel in day, see everything.'

The Reunification Express: perfect. I'll finish my train journey on the Reunification Express. How appropriate for a man who's spent the last month exacting his revenge on trains, to finally be reunified with them. I'm pleased at the symmetry of it all and pay the money.

My high spirits last about one road junction. Two schoolgirls come at me full pelt on a motorcycle that looks like it's been constructed out of spare washing machine parts. In an effort to avoid a head on collision with them I jump on to the pavement and am immediately hit by a motorcyclist who is not satisfied with the level of pedestrian killing he achieves on the road. Despite a spectacular skid he rams into my leg with some force.

'Fuck,' I say instinctively

The motorcyclist looks at me with utter contempt, looks down at his bike to check for damage, says something that is most definitely not an apology and roars off, nearly taking my arm with him. I empty every swear word I know into the space he's left behind. Then it starts to rain. Not gentle, old fashioned watery rain but the sort of rain that leaves dents in steel. It starts pinging off motorbike helmets like ricocheting bullets. Good, I think, that should get rid of some of these bloody lunatic bikers. But within seconds rain capes are donned and they continue in their quest to murder and maim. I head back to my hotel to dry out and swear a little more. The receptionist congratulates me on finding it, 'well done, you find us again,' she says, laughing.

Despite it being within walking distance of my hotel I decide to take a taxi to the Water Puppet Theatre. I'm not prepared to risk my life walking to a fucking puppet show. Needless to say the taxi driver didn't have any change so I end up paying three times the going rate, but at least I am still alive. A little after eight I'm sitting in the foyer. The performance bell rings and I follow a mixture of fat Germans dressed in shorts and old Vietnamese dressed in silk ball gowns and dinner suits into the auditorium. The women are wearing the gowns in case you were thinking otherwise.

The auditorium seats about two hundred people in ascending rows that are so close together only the Vietnamese can comfortably fit in to the seats of luxuriant red velour. Mine is at the very back and, as luck would have it, on the end of an extended row. The exit stairs are the only thing in front of me so I luxuriate in the leg space and watch with unrestrained joy as fat Westerners try to slide knees under armpits in a pitiful attempt to get seated. Dominating the stage is the façade of a pagoda styled building, painted the deepest red. The ends of the eaves sweep up into crested waves of gold leaf with spitting dragons adorning the tops. The lower part of the pagoda is completely covered by ornate curtains behind which the puppeteers work. In front of this building is a large rectangular pool of water. The shimmering reflection of stage lights ripple over the surface. To the left, barely visible from my seat, is the orchestra who sound as though they are breaking their instruments on each other's heads rather than warming up with them. Piped music from the auditorium speakers competes with them and the combined result is something you'd expect to hear from an orchestra of tone-deaf chimps.

Being acutely aware that I come from a nation that considers Morris dancing to be an art form, I realise that I am not exactly qualified to make comment on what another country might consider to be high culture. But here goes anyway. The puppets are attached to the ends of long poles that are about the length of a pole vaulter's pole. The puppeteers are at the other end hidden behind the ornate curtains. They stay there, up to their arse in water, for the whole seventeen acts. Their nads must be like shrivelled prunes by the time the show finishes. The story starts with the raising of "The Festival Flag' and ends with the 'Dance of Four Holy Animals.' In between, to offer only a flavour, you get little side stories with nattily descriptive names. So I watch, with varying degrees of interest,

'Catching Frogs', 'On a Buffalo with a Flute', and 'Unicorns Playing with a Ball.' At one point, a young puppet dressed in nothing but a thong had sex with a fox but that scene may have been lost in the cultural translation. I found it impossible to work out how these events were connected and if the expressions on the Vietnamese in the audience were anything to go by neither did they. The ball gowned ladies looked as confused as a Vietnamese motorcyclist would if you gave him a Highway Code.

A couple of Americans sitting next to me left in the fifth act: Agriculture. I don't think they had anything against agriculture per se, I think it was more to do with the lack of commercial breaks: a show with no advertising must have taken its toll. In total the performance lasted fifty minutes, which I would say is about forty nine minutes too long. When it ended the cast stepped out from behind the curtains and, knee deep in water, clapped the audience. The fact they clapped us is telling.

I leave in search of a restaurant and nearly stumble over a puppy dog outside the theatre doors. Before I can warn him about jumping over fences his owner picks him up and walks off. I select a restaurant overlooking the lake, not because of its wonderful views, or indeed for its cuisine. No, I pick it because it involves only one road crossing. Its only three hundred yards away, which is enough time to be accosted by four postcard sellers and a motorcycle - you want boom, boom - hit squad. The drip, drip effect of this constant effort by the local population to part me from my money is becoming wearing. Today it has been relentless. Normally, I can cope with this sort of attention: in fact I generally enjoy the banter. But today, combined with every motorcyclist in Hanoi trying to kill me, it has placed my patience on a hair trigger.

The restaurant is long and thin, just like the waiters, and I suspect, this is the sort of Vietnamese restaurant you'd find in London, under an "authentic" tag. Staff are dressed in national dress, or pyjamas, it's hard to tell the difference. There is a musical trio on a small stage knocking out Minny the Moocher on bamboo xylophones. One of the trip mistakenly assumes that combining some tracing paper with a comb produces a musical instrument. Unfortunately he is ill equipped to play anything that requires a lung as I suspect he would have trouble breathing when standing still. The resulting accompaniment sounds like a wasp with asthma. Both musicians are fat in Vietnamese terms, or anorexic in Western ones. The asthmatic wasp has a shiny pate sporting about four strands of hair. The female singer, by contrast, is strikingly beautiful and adorned in a pale blue satin gown. She has a purple and white lotus blossom in her long raven coloured hair.

The music changes to something elevator-ish and she walks over to my table and sings whatever it is you sing in elevators, directly to me. After a cringe curdling verse, in which I apply the sort of stoical face you'd more associate with the Duke of Edinburgh, she hands me a flower and smiles. I smile back despite pricking my thumb on one of the thorns. The waiter offers me a napkin to stem the blood flow and while he's there, takes my order. I select a lotus and chicken soup, simply because its called 'dung' in Vietnamese and I can tell my friends that I bought some dung with my dong.

While I wait for my dung to be delivered I eavesdrop on a couple sitting by the window. They're both Westerners. He is a portly sixty year old with grey thinning hair. She is younger, I'd say, early fifties, very tidily put together, pearls, a white blouse, rust coloured waistcoat and matching knee length skirt. Her face looks like the ones you see at department store perfume counters and she is the proud owner of a cut glass English accent. His has more of an edge, like he's lived away from his native land for years. They're talking business, high finance, and swapping stories about deals won and lost, mutual acquaintances and so on. Eventually she calls for the bill, and I expect him to get it. I think she does too because it sits there until all the small talk dries up. Tired of waiting she picks it up.

'1,800,000 Dong (about £65). Shall we go halves?'

'OK, I'll have to pay by credit card,' he says.

'Me too.'

She calls over the headwaiter and explains how they want to pay, handing over the bill and their two credit cards. She scuttles off to put this major financial transaction together. When she returns the bills have been split as requested but converted to Dollars.

'Why's it in Dollars?' he asks.

'Can only accept credit card payment in Dollar Sir.'

This is perfectly reasonable when you have a currency as unstable as the Dong and a method of payment that will delay settlement to the retailer. The currency conversion could be staggeringly different between these two events.

'Uh, you didn't tell us that before we sat down.'

'Its on the menu Sir.'

'Uh... well, what exchange rate are we getting?'

'1650 to the Dollar, Sir.'

The lady furrows a brow, 'but the rate today was 1657,' she says.

'The headwaiter smiles a smile that says, if you want to split a bill and both pay by credit card, for which we get charged but don't pass on to you, I'll offer any exchange rate I fucking well like.

'We are happy to accept cash in Dong if you prefer, she offers politely.'

They ignore this and the man looks up directly at her, 'bet you want the tip in Dong, don't you?'

'No need for tip Sir, service charge included in bill.'

They sign the credit card slips with the same depth of thought as went into the Declaration of Independence. Rising up to his full six feet, he flings down some Dong.

'There's six thousand Dong there, that should be plenty.'

Yes, I'm sure the waiting staff will enjoy splitting thirty pence between themselves. Tight fisted bastards.

Finishing my lotus and chicken soup I realise why the Vietnamese call it dung. Bill paid, in cash, with sufficient tip I leave just as baldy starts murdering the Yellow Rose of Texas on bamboo poles that I'd mistakenly thought were part of the stage construction, not musical instruments. I head for home. It's still early but frankly the sooner I get to sleep the sooner I get on the train. My mood is still several shades darker than purple.

About two blocks from my hotel a woman falls into step with me. She's wearing jeans and a bright red tee shirt, has short hair, and is overly made up, in particular her lipstick, which is red as her shirt. She looks like a post box in legs. I go through the now weary routine of who I am, where I'm from and where I'm going.

'You want boom, boom? Good massage.'

'No thanks.'

'Boom, boom, good price, nice massage.'

'Really, no thanks.'

'I give nice massage, good boom, boom, good price.'

I wonder whether she's going to go through every combination of the words boom, boom, good price, and nice massage.

'No, really, I'm going home to bed.'

'Go bed, good massage, boom, boom.' She makes a lunge for my nether regions, 'good boom, boom.' Then another lunge, 'you like, good price.' Another lunge. I stop and grab both her hands, holding them down by her side.

'Look, I'm trying to be polite here. I don't want fucking boom, boom, or a massage. Please stop trying to touch me.' She immediately takes my actions as a definite declaration of interest, 'Ahhh, you like boom, boom, massage.' She breaks free of my grip and makes another lunge.

'Fuck off!' I say louder than I intend. 'Do you fucking understand. I don't want you touching me. I'd rather fuck a barbecued dog in the market. You go near my gonads again I'll stick a motorbike up your arse. So please, leave me the fuck alone.' I am, by now, shaking with anger, and she is getting a whole day worth of frustration dumped on her over lip-sticked head. I'm confident she doesn't know what my exact words mean, but she finally understands me.

The night watchman at my hotel claps as I enter.

'Ha, ha, you not get lost!'

I watch another episode of Midsomer Murders to calm myself down. John Nettle's lips really do carry on way after his dubbed voice.

Day 18

It's amazing what waking up with a purpose does to your mood. I'm travelling again today. I will miss Hanoi, in spite of its constant desire to try and kill me and the never ending desire of its citizens to get me into bed or divest my of my money. It's a place I definitely want to come back to and if I do I will commission a tee shirt that I will wear daily. On the front it will have:

Thank you for asking but no, I don't want:

Postcards

Books

Maps

Massage

Boom, boom

Cyclo tour

Motorbike taxi

On the back I will have printed:

My name is Mike

I'm from England

Yes I'm on my own

No I'm not going anywhere in particular

Over a breakfast of fresh crusty baguette and jam I read up on the Reunification Express in my ancient guidebook. In the context of my journey it's only a short hop of about 1100 miles, but how it got its name gets to the nub of my quest. My commuting years turned trains into objects of loathing. I hated them so much I worked out a way to quantify it. Every commuting year represented days of unwanted train travel. I've blamed trains for stealing this time from me for most of my working life. I plotted this trip as my revenge. Hanoi to Saigon represents the final chapter in that revenge. So how does it feel? Well, appropriate. My reunification with the train will be complete on the Reunification Express. It's almost poetic.

The Reunification Express has also acted as a unifying instrument for Vietnam. The very first piece of track was laid in 1899 by the then ruling French, although with typical Gallic laissez-faire the last one only got laid in time for the Japanese to commandeer the line for WW2 duties. Not for the first time in history this irritated the Viet Minh. They set about dismantling it at every opportunity, often by using copious amounts of American, yes I said American, donated dynamite. No sooner had they seen off the Japanese than the French ambled back in under plumes of Gauloises smoke. Finding their American dynamite supplier less than co-operative to provide ordnance for use against a wartime partner, the Viet Minh resorted to prising up huge tracts of line and disappearing with it into the jungle under the cover of darkness. It didn't take long for the French to give up on Vietnam. Not to worry, not long after they left the Americans decided to get a piece of Vietnamese railway action and repaired a stretch from Saigon to Hue. During the Vietnam War both sides took it in turns to blow up the track. Then infamously, the Americans left, and North and South Vietnam finally came back together. The new unifying government decided the re-opening of the track between Hanoi and Saigon would be the perfect symbol of national reunification. Even so, it wasn't until 1976 that the first Thong Nhat Reunification Express train pulled out of Hanoi on its forty hour journey to Saigon. To be fair to the Vietnamese Government, before this could happen, they had to repair one thousand three hundred and thirty four bridges, twenty seven tunnels and one hundred and fifty eight stations.

It still takes just as long to get there today, mainly because it is a single line track. If a train comes the other way you have to pull over in a suitable passing place. It's a bit like two trains meeting each other down a narrow country road in Devon.

I settle my bill on the way out. Because I'd prepaid for the room I only have to pay for some laundry and bottles of water from my mini bar. £2.50. Hanoi may be somewhat lacking in many things but you can't argue with the prices.

'Do you know how much my laundry was in China?' I say to the young man at reception, whom I discover is actually the manager.

'Oh, China always cheating, maybe you pay two times more.'

'No, ten times.'

'Ten times! Maybe I too cheap, maybe make price go up.'

'Good idea I say.' Well, I've paid haven't I?

He makes us both a coffee and we sit together by the reception area while I wait for my taxi.

'You go airport now?'

'No, train station.'

He can't work out why I don't fly to Saigon, it only takes forty minutes in contrast to the train's forty hours.

'I came from England by train.'

'By train! Really? How long you take come Hanoi?'

'Eighteen days.'

'Eighteen days? I tell brother.' He shouts out to his brother in the kitchen. His brother shouts something back.

'He say you mad, plane quick, train slow.'

My taxi arrives and he helps me carry my bags and stow them in the boot. He then enters into a stern conversation with the driver.

'I tell him you good customer, no cheating. You get meter price. OK?'

Yes, I've had meter price before but I offer thanks for the sentiment anyway. We shake hands rather formally, he bows a little and I'm off.

The train station is a shabby affair. Not unlike the Reunification Express that is waiting on platform one, which is in need of a good wash. Streaks of red dirt pepper the sides like machine gun fire. The inside is tatty rather than dirty, but at least the cabin of four berths has clean sheets. Each also has a small pillow and a fetching red checked blanket of the Scottish shortbread variety. It will come in handy if I get cold under the efficient air conditioning. Before I get on I purchase some emergency rations of Ritz crackers and a loaf of soft strawberry flavoured bread. I did this on the recommendation of my man at the hotel.

'Food on train shit. Also don't get down at train at stations, leave without you.' Useful advice that I temper with the knowledge that he's never experienced British Rail in the seventies. Just prior to departure my cabin still only houses me. The rest of the carriage is filling up though, and every few minutes the cabin attendant, a well fed Vietnamese man sporting a pilot's uniform, pokes his head around the door and checks my cabin's occupancy levels. I watch him furrow his brow and point to each empty bunk, counting them out under his breath. The answer is always three, but it doesn't stop him popping his head round the door on a regular basis for a re-count. A scratched forehead and a brief nod towards me accompany each counting session. The train pulls away bang on time. The platform shadows are almost non-existent under a high, bright sun. A sharer arrives offering a nod and settles down on the bunk opposite. His only luggage is a small black briefcase from which he pulls a newspaper. He sets about reading it, coughing in unison with each page turn.

I think this train will be different to all the others because in many respects it's a proper commuter train. There are plenty of stops between Hanoi and Saigon and I suspect my new friend will not be with me long. While he's engrossed in his paper I take the opportunity to scrutinise him. He's the colour of weak coffee, which in Asia probably puts him quite high up the social scale, a civil servant maybe. He has a very neat, full head of hair and quite European features. He's wearing smart brown trousers and a dark short sleeved shirt, his mobile phone and train ticket poke out of the breast pocket.

Leaving to the south of Hanoi, I see evidence of Vietnam's new tiger economy in the shape of belching factories and large scale construction projects. The male and female workers on these sites swathe themselves in clothing to fend off the scorching hot sun. The apparel gives the impression that a posse of bandits are stealing the building rather than constructing it. Health and safety has a uniquely Asian slant in that it only extends from the waist up. For example, the man I spot operating a Kango hammer has a hardhat and florescent yellow high visibility vest but is only wearing flip-flops on his feet.

The train's PA system shifts from ear splitting music to a potted history of the country and, in particular, the route. It is a pre-recorded message and is delivered in competent English by a voice that has a heavy cold. I quickly learn that there are forty nine provinces between Hanoi and Saigon and that I will be passing through all of them. The man in need of a decongestant then explains all this is possible because the great Ho Chi Minh who expelled the imperialist French dogs and the gum chewing bastard Yanks. Before he expires of the agues he goes on to extol the greater power of the Vietnamese people, finally spluttering into a wall of static influenza.

Urban Hanoi is soon replaced with rice growing countryside and I reflect on my experiences in the city. No one can judge a place fairly after such a short visit, but it doesn't stop me thinking about it. And to be honest, I'm confused. Take away the lunatic traffic and the politest, but nevertheless most incessant hawkers, and you are left with friendly, genuinely warm people and, in the Old Quarter, a city within a city. I'm happy to be leaving Hanoi but its not because I hated it. It's because I'm replacing it with the train. I mark it down as a place that deserves more of my time some day soon. Also requiring more of my time is the drinks trolley, which is being pulled by a chubby attendant, and owner of an unruly shock of black hair. This general scruffiness spills over into his official co-pilot's uniform. It looks slept in but to be honest I think this man would look scruffy naked. He is sing-songing along in Vietnamese but stops when he gets to my cabin.

'Ah! Hello, where you from?' His eyebrows dance the cha cha cha as he talks.

'England,' I say.

'Ah! England! You want beer?'

Associating Englishmen abroad with booze is, of course, extremely stereotypical, if not racist. Some might find it offensive but I purchase four bottles of Saigon beer simply to reinforce his jaundiced views of my fellow countrymen. He looks over at his fellow countryman and raises an eyebrow. I assume, stereotypically, that they are being inscrutable. He places the beers and two bottles of water on to the table. I assume the water is complimentary because he doesn't charge me for them.

'Ah, ah! I know English, Saigon beer, ah, ah!' He says, reverting back to singy-songy Vietnamese as he backs out of my cabin and works his way further along the carriage.

What happened ten minutes later requires my constructing some form of context. So before I continue I must now impart a commuting story, because what follows some needs perspective. Many years ago I was travelling back from London on my Friday night commuter train. We stopped at Clapham Junction, a station we'd normally speed through like a bullet. Novice commuters carried on reading or looking out of windows but regulars immediately tuned into their inbuilt delay radar. Some began to vocalise their feelings of wariness. You can spend years travelling on the same train as other commuters without so much as a nod towards each other, but delays create immediate solidarity and produce the perfect environment for mutual tutting. A weary sounding guard eventually came on the intercom and told us to vacate the train. Apparently one of the passengers had been taken ill and needed medical attention. General harrumphing gave way to a chorus of "oh dears," "poor chap." The novice commuters genuinely looked concerned. On the platform we learned from another commuter that the poor fellow had actually suffered a heart attack and died.

'Apparently, it was his last day at work after over twenty five years of commuting. Only fifty odd,' the man said. No one questioned the veracity of this story: it is common amongst commuters to accept, without question, another commuter's embellishment of a delay story. However, details of his life may have been questionable but he was undoubtedly dead. General noises of pity came from the assembled crowd as we waited some more. An ambulance turned up and the paramedics attended to the cadaver on the train. We waited some more. The station announcer explained over the platform speakers that the train would be cancelled, the platform put out of commission, and that we were to wait for further announcements. The mood change was almost immediate. Within moments, the now very dead man with a family waiting for him at home, shifted from being an object of pity to a pariah. There were no stages in between.

'Fucking hell, this always happens on a Friday,' said a man behind me.

'I know, and I'm going out tonight,' said another. The dead man wasn't a well loved family man at all. He was, in fact, a malicious bastard who deliberately timed his fatal heart attack to arrive on the Friday commuter train to prevent fellow commuters socialising. And so it went on. If he hadn't been dead already they would have killed him. The only reason I mention this is I want to highlight how sympathy is but a fleeting acquaintance of the hardened commuter. The truth of it is, the loss of a loved one is only ever truly felt by those who love them.

So, back to the Reunification Express. I'm just opening the first of my Saigon beers when I hear, what sounds like, a side of pork being slammed down onto a butchers slab. It is quickly followed by the screeching noise that accompanies a locomotive when it attempts an emergency stop. I am thrown to the floor but quickly jump up and make my way to the corridor window. Pandemonium reigns. Attendants from other carriages hurtle past me: others have already jumped from the train into the smoke billowing from locked brakes and are sprinting along a busy road running parallel to the track. Some stand in the middle of the road and flag down traffic, which quickly stacks up. People come running over from a small parade of shops and cafes on the other side of the road. Initially I think we may have hit a stray water buffalo but the gathering crowd tells me it is more serious than that. Hands are drawn up to gaping mouths. Some quickly turn away. Straining my neck I look further down the outside of my carriage and see the inert shape of a man on the bank, laying on the ground like a crumpled scarecrow. The impact, which must have been a glancing blow, perhaps as he desperately tried to clear the track, has sent him sprawling up the lightly sloping bank. There is no movement from his twisted body and I can see blood dribbling from his mouth and head. My carriage attendant is first to the body. He lays a red checked blanket, the same as the one on my bed, over the body and quickly sets about rolling the inert shape up in it. Another attendant joins him and they lift the makeshift hammock on to the road. The corpse's legs dangling loosely out of one end and I notice one foot has somehow retained a flip flop. It's clear he's dead. Cars and lorries fed up with the traffic jam begin to pass slowly by. Some rather bizarrely throw money out of their windows onto the corpse. A couple of ladies lay another blanket over him to cover him entirely from view. The police quickly arrive on motorbikes and cars and start to disperse the crowd and manage the traffic. The colour drains from the face of a German girl standing next to me and she places a hand over her mouth. A Western man comes through from the carriage in front and looks at me directly.

'He's dead,' he says simply, before moving on down the carriage.

Thank you Sherlock.

I assume this will take some time to sort out and head back to my cabin. My sharer has not moved from the position I left him in and makes no enquiry as to the delay. I pick up my book and lay back. Then I put it down. It seems wrong somehow to read when there is a dead man just outside my window. I go back to the corridor window. The attendants are getting back on the train. A policeman standing by the corpse is talking animatedly into his mobile phone and simultaneously shouting instructions to his subordinates. Suddenly there is a jolt and the train pulls away. Transfixed, I watch the corpse for as long as I am able. I can't believe we are continuing. No police statements. Not even a change of driver. In the UK the journey would have ended, the track would have been closed for a week, and the driver would have had at least a month off to recover from the trauma. I don't know if we put more value on human life than the Vietnamese, or they are more practical. Whichever it is I can't help wondering about the victim's family.

It's some time, and all of my beer, before I can resume my window gazing. The outlook is changing rapidly from rice cultivation. There are more prawn farms, and dramatic limestone escarpments, some quite close to the tracks. These jagged thumbs, edged with hairy crevices are remarkably relaxing to look at, and we are going so slow I get plenty of time to take in their detail. But if I need a fix of rabid activity all I have to do is turn my attention to the carriage. It's busier than an ant colony that's been prodded with a hot poker.

There is a steady stream of octogenarians shuffling past, each one tarrying by my door to stare at me and check I wasn't the one running through the jungle in 69 shouting how I loved the smell of napalm in the morning. The food and drinks attendants are up and down like a fiddler's elbow. One is offering complimentary yogurt, another sells sweets and crisps, from which I buy some pistachio nuts. Then, a very young man walks by with two large red buckets. When I lift the lid he looks bemused. When I see boiled eggs that were probably boiled before he was born I look bemused. I decline his offer of ancient eggs on account of the escarpments being younger. Chubby singy - songy attendant comes back selling more beer. He spies my empties.

'Ah! More beer English! Ha!'

He also sells me a coupon that I can redeem for food when it's ready. I'll know when this is as they deliver. I think it's going to be chicken, but he might have said gizzards. Still, the price is right at a little over seventy five pence including VAT, postage, packaging and insurance.

Three hours after we had the unfortunate accident that I don't want to think about because it makes my eyes sting, we pull into the port city of Vinh. I look but can find nothing interesting to remark upon about the town, but it must have something going for it as my sharer stands up, says goodbye, in passable English, and gets off. A taller, dark skinned man wearing a baseball cap replaces him quite quickly. When he takes his hat off he reveals a totally bald, chocolate coloured head. He offers me a cursory glance, rolls up his trousers to the middle of his shins, and settles onto the same bunk as the man that just left. There are plenty getting on and off here but no one else makes use of our cabin. This, of course doesn't stop the chief attendant sticking his head around the door half a dozen times to count the two empty bunks.

Soon after I ready myself for bed, which, following my usual routine, means taking off my shoes. It strikes me, as I pull the red checked cover over me and reach for the light, that this will be my last night on the train: in fact, my last night on a train for the foreseeable future. This thought saddens me greatly.

Day 19

Although I wake early I am reluctant to muster. Any motion instigated by me simply hastens the end. I figure if I stay in bed the train might also take my slothful approach. It certainly did during the night, stopping frequently in sidings to allow northbound trains to pass. I also experienced something you don't often associate with train travel. It was bumpy. Honest. Maybe the section we passed in the night had speed bumps on it.

When I finally kick myself into gear we're pulling out of Da Nang, famous for the rest and recuperation it offered weary troops from that country that forgot to declare war on Vietnam. The truth is Da Nang, despite its Hollywood reputation, saw very little military action. In Da Nang, GIs had more chance of dying from herpes than a bullet. The Americans were expelled on 29th March 1975 by a couple of trucks of communist women wearing tabards. What, I hear you say, the great American war machine driven out of town by the Vietnamese Women's Institute? Don't laugh. These ladies had spent the last three years in the jungle up to their armpits in damp leaves living off insects. They stank.

But that's not to say Da Nang wasn't touched by tragedy, because it was. Two days before the evacuation, the Americans sent in two 727s to extract refugees. For refugees read South Vietnamese apparatchiks and American elite special forces. There was no room for the real victims. Desperate throngs of real refugees mobbed the airport only to find a queue to get on a plane that they were never going to jump. Not even if they employed Chinese queuing techniques. As the aircraft taxied down the runway for take off people climbed up into the landing-gear wells. The TV crews in the following plane captured their inevitable descent to earth. It made prime time on American television, shamed a nation and embarrassed a world. Only three Vietnamese civilian refugees actually made it on board and survived. One of them was a baby thrown on by a desperate mother who was left in tears on the tarmac.

My co-sharer is awake and reading the paper, studiously avoiding eye contact. He is using a long fingernail on the little finger of his left hand to gently scratch his caramel pate. The cultivation of a long fingernail is peculiarly Asian. I don't know whether it is to accommodate a guitar-playing fetish or to make picking their noses easier. I pull the curtains back, get bathed in light and find myself travelling through a cemetery. And not any old cemetery, this one is vast and at least a mile wide. Some of the headstones are remarkably ornate or pagoda shaped structures with bright red cornicing. But the oddest thing of all is that the cemetery seems to be in the middle of the jungle. My eye is drawn to a couple of cranes executing an ungainly take off. This inelegance is quickly replaced with the subtlety of a ballerina as they ride a thermal and soar into the sky, wheeling off towards the higher foliage. Impressively horned water buffalo snout around in the wet undergrowth. My sharer heads off to the toilet hoiking up a good grolly on the way. He adds to the growing cacophony of mucous ejectors who fill the carriage with their unusual dawn chorus every morning. It's like listening to emphysema suffers who have just attempted a 100 metre sprint. I blew my nose into a tissue on one of the platforms yesterday and the kids waiting nearby burst into laughter. 'Urgghh,' one of them said as I put it in my pocket.

Most of yesterday I had to endure the traditional twangy music tumbling out of the intercom. It was like listening to a piano falling down a very long flight of stairs. This morning it's been replaced with a piano being manhandled up stairs. Checking my watch, I'm surprised to find it's only just after 7 am. By 8 am breakfast is a distant memory and I start to consider lunch. Not because I want to, but because singy songy scruff bag wants my order. I don't know what I've purchased, but what I do know is, it's the right price. He drops off two beers despite my not asking for them. I don't complain, especially as he refuses my offer to pay for them.

We pull away from the coastal route and travel through a wide plain framed with craggy hills on either side. The train announcer, a live one this time, who also doubles up as the DJ responsible for the irritating music, keeps us informed of our progress by announcing each station prior to arrival, in both English and Vietnamese. He starts the English section confidently enough.

'This is the SE5 train to Saigon.' He then disappears into a forest of static in which only the station name is audible. I think he may be responsible for the static. He pulls it back at the end with a very coherent and jaunty, 'we hope you have a nice journey.' He follows this rather bland statement with a coughing fit that fades out with a hoike. The coughing, hoiking and general DJ badinage is interspersed with songs from his collection. His play list alternates between a Vietnamese Shirley Bassey and the Vietnamese Pet Shop Boys. Each song is played backwards on keyboards made from bamboo.

Pulling into Dieu Tri I get the chance to stretch my legs because we stop for fifteen minutes. I don't think it's a scheduled stop. I think it has rather more to do with the long line of market stalls that run along the track. Before the train comes to a complete stop the majority of the crew have abandoned their carriages and are busy negotiating with the shopkeepers. There are about twenty stalls, all manned by women (or perhaps I should say, womened by women). Each stall is an exact replica of the others, so if I describe one, it will be sufficient. I'll pick the lady with the bamboo hat on, from which hangs a multicoloured headscarf. She's in her early thirties and to protect her further from the sun she has another scarf wrapped around her neck and lower face. In another environment I might be thinking ninja mugger. Her bright red, long sleeved cotton shirt buttons up the middle and is fastened with small ivory coloured toggles. Her cream trousers are three quarter length. She's shouting out the equivalent of 'fifty pence yaaa bananas, come an get 'em, fifty pence a parnd.'

The stall behind her comprises about ten shelves, one slightly higher than the one before it, like steps. She has dried fish hanging from hooks, and flattened calamari that look like they were squashed flat while having a good yawn. Fresh fruit of every colour makes the shelving work hard. Her stocks of oranges are particularly impressive with some partly peeled to reveal succulent flesh within. Standing by the lowest shelf is a stainless steel cauldron on three legs that reflects sharp sunlight back at the train. I can see a ladle sticking out from the lid and instinctively lower my nose for a whiff. She lifts the lid and the smell makes friends with my nostrils immediately. It's a luxurious brown broth, flecked with dangerous bullets of red chilli. This is the national dish of pho – a thick broth with noodles and mainstay of my train's culinary offering. She mimes chopsticks and then opens a carton full of milky white noodles. She then mimes spooning the pho on top. I'm sorely tempted but I've already made an order for lunch with singy songy scruff bag and I don't want to be unfaithful. In a last ditch attempt to get me to part with my Dong she waves a Saigon beer at me before putting it back in the middle of a who's who of the soft drinks industry, including iced tea in lime green plastic bottles. I reach over and touch the beer bottle.

'Too hot,' I say pointing to the sun.

She scurries off behind her shelves and appears with two bottles. I can see the condensation dribbling down them as she touches my arm with one: it's freezing. I buy both. As she hands them to me, she points to a beach ball, 'good price,' she says, handing me millions of Dong in change. Beach ball? Why on earth would I want to buy a beach ball? Undeterred by this rebuff she takes a cover off a basket full of Vietnamese baguettes, they're like French ones that have been flattened with a spade, and the sample she breaks off for me is delicious. I can smell their freshness and buy two, including the one my sample came from.

I stand at the corridor window as we pull away. My friendly stallholder offers a quick wave and then immediately starts to pull a canvas shutter down the front of her stall. It's like watching an eye slowly closing. Her nineteen replicas shut in unison.

When you start your day at five in the morning it should be no surprise that dinner is served at half past ten. Singy songy looks suspiciously at my Saigon beer, he can't remember if he gave them to me. Lunch is noodles with pork in a spicy broth. It's another variation on pho and delicious. My sharer has the same. I know this because he keeps his mouth open throughout his eating of it. The sound he produces is like a horse trotting over cobbled streets. The clippity-clop of chopsticks on carton is broken with the occasional snort, which I realise is the only method of breathing left open to him.

Dinner over I set to work on my navigation. According to my reckoning Nha Thrang will be the next station. I should catch another glimpse of the sea here. In preparation I decide on forty winks. As it turns out I wake to find us travelling through a range of hills just after Yu Hoa, not far from Nha Thrang. It's an odd vista, like a deep green shag pile carpet stretching out to the horizon with sharp grey and black molehill escarpments puncturing it. It's impossible to tell whether the greenery enveloped them or they burst through one day in a fit of volcanic pique.

We disappear into a series of tunnels. As we emerge from each one I am rewarded with a view more beautiful than the preceding one. I see spectacular sweeping bays filled with jutting escarpments. The clear green sea gently pushes small waves up buttercup yellow beaches before ebbing back in a white frothy retreat. Fishing boats are the only sign of life: their blue prows bobbing up and down like nodding dogs. I see smaller vessels further out with occupants hauling up lobster and crab pots. The view is unfeasibly idyllic. It's the sort of place James Bond gets invited to so he can meet the man who is planning to destroy the world before being killed.

On the way into Nha Thrang we pass through fields of dragon fruit. They look like they've attached themselves to cactus. I'd always wondered how they grew. Weird. There are plenty of coconut trees and fat banana fronds that hang down so close to the train I could reach out of the window and grab them. I don't bother. I mean what am I going to do with a handful of banana frond? Beyond the banana plants is the bay of Nha Thrang, which is chock-a-block with blue trawlers and junks.

Nearly everybody leaves at Nha Thrang, including my sharer. He rises, rolls his trousers back down, dons his hat, offers me a small bow, and leaves. Its only six hours and four stops from here to Saigon, and my Reunification Express has become a real commuter train. A new crop of commuters pile in and I get an older lady with her granddaughter. She's about sixty with a jutting chin, dyed brown hair, which unusually, is cut into a short bob. Her granddaughter is about twelve with traditional long black hair and is very coy looking. She's wearing a checked shirt, three-quarter length trousers and flip flops that have a tiny crocodile motif. The designer label across the toe bars is a South East Asian designer label in which they specialise: LaCosta, nearly the real thing but not quite. She takes the upper bunk and her granny spends a happy ten minutes passing her up two huge bags of shopping, four boxes, two carrier bags and a rucksack. I catch the little girl looking at me frequently. As soon as she realises that I have spotted her she looks away quickly. I suspect she has never been in such close proximity to a Westerner before. The head attendant pops his head around the door, does another count up of the available beds (one) and once again looks at me like I've only just got on.

Thap Cham, the next station, arrives quickly and a young girl of about sixteen becomes the proud owner of the remaining upper bunk. Before I have a chance to get a look at her, she's kicked off her shoes and clambered up. Within seconds she's shrouded in her red checked blanket and all I can see when I get up, is her black hair poking out one end and a foot out of the other.

In true Vietnamese style, minus the hoiking, I reconnoitre our carriage. It is jam packed and I'm the only Westerner in it. I'm now measuring the remains of my epic train journey in hours. The four hours that are left are nothing more than a short hop. I've never thought of London to Leeds like that before. But it's fitting to end my journey on the Reunification Express: a perfect circle. I've come a long way. After a few days exploring Saigon I'll become a small cog in the machinery of an airport. I'll be reduced to a ticket number to be processed, a passport to be scrutinised and a seat to be fed. Part of me would prefer to simply turn back and return the way I came. In fact its more than a part, its at least both legs and all of my heart.

Thankfully the view from the train stops me dwelling on air passenger processing. We pick up the coastline again and for the first time I notice obvious tourism, beachside restaurants and modern beach huts are more common. I see a few nice looking low-rise hotels and a wonderfully named restaurant called "Dong Hung." I wonder how long before this is all spoiled with International hotel chains and uncaring developers? I fear it won't be long before Dong Hung becomes McDong-Hung-King.

At about five in the afternoon the young lady and her granny decide its time for tea. They spend twenty minutes unwrapping banana leaf parcels and looking pleasantly surprised by the contents. They finish the meal with a few juicy oranges. Soon after a couple of ladies from next door pop in. They are obviously friends. Each perch on granny's bunk, so the young one climbs back up on her bunk for more space. Once again I catch her looking at me. Once again she quickly looks away.

The visitor doing most of the talking is really quite ugly and reminds me of Ronald Reagan in his Alzheimer years. Granny's phone goes off and she starts a loud conversation, I imagine along the lines of 'I'm on the train.' Then another two friends pop in and the others squeeze up so they can sit down. Another comes in and unashamedly invades my space by sitting at the end of my bunk. The chatty one keeps up her conversation, upping the volume above the hubbub of the multiple conversations going on around her. I take in the scene. We now have nine people in a cabin designed for four including one person speaking at the top of their voice on a loud phone conversation. As we pull into Saigon station my brain latches on to what I'm encountering and hauls up a memory I'd tried to misfile so I would never have to recall it. I've experienced this before. Where? When? Let me think. Ah yes, every day of my commuting life.

Lightning Source UK Ltd.
Milton Keynes UK
UKOW040823120712

195860UK00005B/8/P